The Biblical Seminar
38

A LION WITH WINGS

A LION WITH WINGS

A NARRATIVE-CRITICAL APPROACH TO MARK'S GOSPEL

Stephen H. Smith

Sheffield Academic Press

To the memory of my mother,
Mary Smith
(1920–94)

'There was a lion in Judah
Which whelped, and was Mark.

But winged.
A lion with wings.'

(D.H. Lawrence, *St Mark*)

Copyright © 1996 Sheffield Academic Press

Published by Sheffield Academic Press Ltd
Mansion House
19 Kingfield Road
Sheffield, S11 9AS
England

Printed on acid-free paper in Great Britain
by The Cromwell Press
Melksham, Wiltshire

British Library Cataloguing in Publication Data

A catalogue record for this book is available
from the British Library

ISBN 1-85075-784-4

CONTENTS

PREFACE

A Lion with Wings. Why should that serve as an appropriate title to
a narrative-critical study of Mark's Gospel? There is the superficial
response that the Evangelist is simply represented in traditional Christian
art and symbolism as a winged lion, just as Matthew appears as a man,
Luke as an ox and John as an eagle. But there is more to it than that.
Further insight may be provided by extending the Lawrence super-
scription a little:

> Why should he have wings?
> Is he a bird also?
> Or a spirit?
> Or a winged thought?
> Or a soaring consciousness?
>
> Evidently he is all that,
> The lion of the spirit.[1]

Our lion, then, has a message to proclaim, and his wings are words,
words of the Spirit (rather than mere spirit). The text carries its message
down the centuries, upbraiding, uplifting and inspiring; and its voice is
the voice of a lion—clear and resonant and unmistakable—a voice that
cannot be ignored any more than can the lion's roar. Such is the Gospel
of Mark, whose ageless text continues to recreate itself as it interacts with
each successive generation, drawing outsiders to faith and confirming
insiders in what they already know.

Although narrative-criticism of the Bible is still a relatively adolescent
discipline in comparison with the older-established critical methods,
namely source-, form- and redaction-criticism, the amount of literature
which has already been devoted to it is truly voluminous, and many a
well-known exponent of it has turned his attention to Mark. The problem

---

1. D.H. Lawrence, 'The Evangelistic Beasts: St Mark', *The Collected Poems of
D.H. Lawrence* (ed. V. de Sola Pinto and F. Warren Roberts; Harmondsworth:
Penguin, 1977), p. 323.

for me, therefore, was to find a niche sufficiently unoccupied to justify the writing of this book. In the end, I decided upon the review approach. Rhoads and Michie[2] and Kingsbury[3] have tended to corner the market in popularizing the subject, while more technical works on particular aspects of Markan narrative-criticism continue to flow from the pens of those better placed (geographically-speaking, at least) than I to rise to the challenge. In the five slow years during which my own work has been stuttering its way to completion, major contributions[4] have pipped it at the post, so to speak, and I can only apologize in advance if I have omitted to mention works which have appeared in the latter stages of preparing my book for publication. In any case, it is impossible in a work of limited proportions to take account of every tiny development in the field. As Ernest Best remarked in the preface to his *Following Jesus*, 'there comes a time... when a line has to be drawn and nothing more can be read nor more time be spent assessing what others have written'.[5]

If there is one book which can be said to serve as a model for the present work, it is Culpepper's *Anatomy of the Fourth Gospel*[6] which treats the various facets of narrative-criticism systematically. I can only express surprise that, given the wealth of narrative-critical studies which have appeared since then, this model has not been fully applied to other Gospels until now. Taking its cue from Culpepper, then, *A Lion with Wings* takes each of the chief aspects of narrative-criticism and devotes a

2.   D. Rhoads and D. Michie, *Mark as Story: An Introduction to the Narrative of a Gospel* (Philadelphia: Fortress Press, 1982).

3.   J.D. Kingsbury, *Conflict in Mark: Jesus, Authorities, Disciples* (Minneapolis: Fortress Press, 1989).

4.   On reader-response, R.M. Fowler, *Let the Reader Understand: Reader-Response Criticism and the Gospel of Mark* (Minneapolis: Fortress Press, 1991); on characterization, J.F. Williams, *Other Followers of Jesus: Minor Characters as Major Figures in Mark's Gospel* (JSNTSup, 102; Sheffield: JSOT Press, 1994); on plot, P.L. Donove, *The End of Mark's Story: A Methodological Study* (Leiden: Brill, 1993); on irony, J. Camery-Hoggatt, *Irony in Mark's Gospel: Text and Subtext* (SNTSMS 72; Cambridge: Cambridge University Press, 1992); see also G. van Oyen, 'Intercalation and Irony in the Gospel of Mark', in F. van Segbroeck *et al.* (eds.), *The Four Gospels 1992* (Festschrift Frans Neirynck; BETL; Leuven: Leuven University Press, 1992), pp. 949-74.

5.   E. Best, *Following Jesus: Discipleship in the Gospel of Mark* (JSNTSup, 4; Sheffield: JSOT Press, 1981), p. 7.

6.   R.A. Culpepper, *Anatomy of the Fourth Gospel* (Philadelphia: Fortress Press, 1983).

chapter to each. Chapter 1 deals with reader-response criticism, of which narrative-criticism is sometimes seen to be a particular manifestation. It is true enough that the one does emerge from or arise out of the other, and that both, in the final analysis, show an intimate concern for audience/reader-response; but narrative-criticism can be studied in its own right in just the same way as, say, differential calculus can be considered in its own right as a particular branch of mathematics. Certainly, a comparison of the approach taken by Iser and Booth[7] on the one hand, with that of Chatman[8] on the other, indicates that this distinction is clearly made in the field of English literature in which biblical narrative-criticism has its origin.

The remaining chapters deal with the specifically narrative features of Mark's story—characterization, plot, time and space, point of view, and irony. In each case the literary or narrative theory is examined first, and the relevant principles are then applied to Mark's Gospel. Obviously, it is not possible to treat the text systematically here—that would require a narrative-critical commentary. My method is to select passages which serve to illustrate the points under discussion; there is no attempt to be exhaustive. Chapter summaries attempt to capture the essence of each chapter, and the overall conclusion offers some remarks on the relationship between narrative and history.

It is hoped that this book will not only provide a convenient survey of recent work on Markan narrative-criticism, but will also serve to fill the lacuna between those popularizing works whose market demands a rather superficial approach, and the weighty technical contributions which tend to deter all but the intrepid specialist.

---

7. W. Iser, *The Implied Reader* (Baltimore: The Johns Hopkins University Press, 1974); W.C. Booth, *The Rhetoric of Fiction* (Chicago: University of Chicago Press, 1961).

8. S. Chatman, *Story and Discourse: Narrative Structure in Fiction and Film* (Ithaca, NY: Cornell University Press, 1978).

ACKNOWLEDGMENTS

Many authors have recourse to a long list of individuals who have somehow contributed to ensuring that their work sees the light of day. I am afraid I am not in that category. I wrote the manuscript, and its shortcomings can be blamed on no one else. I also word-processed it, proof-read it, and in general prepared it for its dispatch to the publisher. My debts of gratitude, therefore, tend to be less specific and more long-standing than is usually the case.

My first debt of thanks must go to my family who supported and encouraged my choice of career, and enabled me not only to keep body and soul together, but also to succeed in my student days. Next, I must acknowledge the contribution of the staff of the Biblical Studies Department at the University of Sheffield during my sojourn there during the period 1979–86. Although they are not directly associated with the making of this book, they were responsible for providing me with a solid grounding in the critical methods on which it is based. My thanks go especially to Professor Bruce Chilton, now of Bard College, who awakened my interest in St Mark's Gospel and guided my first faltering steps in the (mine)field of Markan research.

Much of the work on the book itself was carried out at the Tyndale House Library of Biblical Research in Cambridge, and I am most grateful to the Warden, Dr Bruce Winter, and to his library staff for making these much-needed facilities available to me during a four-year period between 1987–91, and subsequently.

Last, but not least, I should like to thank Dr John Jarick, Senior Academic Editor of Sheffield Academic Press, and the other staff of the Press, for their clear advice on technical matters, and for their unstinting efforts in bringing the manuscript to publication.

If there are others who feel they should have received a mention here, I can only apologize for my negligence. It would, however, be impracticable to list the scores of fellow Bible students with whom I have engaged informally in conversation down the years. No doubt they have contributed to the development of my thinking in all kinds of unrecorded ways. To them I am grateful for their encouragement, and for any suggestions they made which have found their way surreptitiously into the pages of this book.

ABBREVIATIONS

BETL	Bibliotheca ephemeridum theologicarum lovaniensium
BR	*Biblical Research*
CBQ	*Catholic Biblical Quarterly*
CogPs	*Cognitive Psychology*
ETR	*Etudes théologiques et religieuses*
EvQ	*Evangelical Quarterly*
ExpTim	*Expository Times*
HSCP	*Harvard Studies in Classical Philology*
Int	*Interpretation*
JAAR	*Journal of the American Academy of Religion*
JBL	*Journal of Biblical Literature*
JEdPs	*Journal of Educational Psychology*
JVLVB	*Journal of Verbal Language and Verbal Behaviour*
JR	*Journal of Religion*
JSNT	*Journal for the Study of the New Testament*
JSNTSup	*Journal for the Study of the New Testament*, Supplement Series
JTS	*Journal of Theological Studies*
LCL	Loeb Classical Library
NLH	*New Literary History*
NovT	*Novum Testamentum*
NovTSup	*Novum Testamentum*, Supplement
NTS	*New Testament Studies*
PMLA	*Proceedings of the Modern Languages Association*
QJEP	*Quarterly Journal of Educational Psychology*
RB	*Revue biblique*
RevQ	*Revue de Qumran*
RSR	*Recherches de science religieuse*
SBL	Society of Biblical Literature
SBLDS	Society of Biblical Literature Dissertation Series
SBS	Stuttgarter Bibelstudien
SBT	Studies in Biblical Theology
SNTSMS	Society of New Testament Studies Monograph Series
SUNT	Studien zur Umwelt des Neuen Testaments
TAPA	*Transactions of the American Philological Association*
WBC	Word Biblical Commentary
ZNW	*Zeitschrift für die neutestamentliche Wissenschaft*
ZTK	*Zeitschrift für Theologie und Kirche*

Chapter 1

MARK'S GOSPEL: AUTHOR, READER, TEXT

1. *The Question of Critical Method*

a. *The Development of Literary Criticism*
There is a sense in which literary criticism as applied to the Bible is as
old as biblical criticism itself, for prior to the advent of modern literary
criticism, the label was attached to that holy trinity of critical methods—
source-, form- and redaction-criticism. Now that new methods have been
introduced, however, it is necessary to make clearer terminological distinctions than hitherto, for there are radical differences between the old
and new criticisms. Accounts of all these methods are by now manifold,[1]
so it will not be necessary to review them in detail; there are, however,
broad distinctions between the older types of literary criticism (better,
historical criticism) and the newer varieties which need to be elucidated.

Let us, first of all, examine the ends to which each category of
criticism is working. It is clear that the older methods are all attempting
to say something about the evolution of the text in history, if not about
the historicity of the stories it contains. Source-criticism, as its name
suggests, is interested in recovering the sources behind the finished
product. Although this method is now over 200 years old, and has
perhaps suffered something of an eclipse in more recent years, it would
be far from the truth to say that it is dead. The fact that the Gospels

---

1. For a detailed introduction to the historical-critical methods, see R.F. Collins,
Introduction to the New Testament (London: SCM Press, 1983). Convenient studies
of the more recent varieties of literary criticism include: T. Longman III, *Literary
Approaches to Biblical Interpretation* (Leicester: Apollos, 1987); J.C. Capel and
S.D. Moore (eds.), *Mark and Method: New Approaches in Biblical Studies*
(Augsburg: Fortress Press, 1992); M.A. Powell, *What Is Narrative Criticism? A
New Approach to the Bible* (London: SPCK, 1993). A work which takes account of
both these categories is E.P. Sanders and M. Davies, *Studying the Synoptic Gospels*
(Philadelphia: Trinity International Press, 1989).

must have been drawn from sources of some kind makes this a live issue still. True, we do not now have quite the confidence that Streeter had in postulating his widely-accepted hypothesis in 1924; the source problem is somewhat more intractable than was generally felt to be the case then. But recent studies on orality in ancient literature and its relationship to the written word[2] have refuelled the debate to some extent.

It is precisely this oral period, before the traditions became crystallized in writing, in which the form-critic is interested. Form-criticism is a more recent development, beginning in 1919 with the pioneering works of Schmidt and Dibelius,[3] and then, in 1921, of Bultmann.[4] The aim was to classify the Gospel material into its various forms (myths, legends, parables, sayings, paradigms and so on) with a view to discovering something about the ecclesiastical communities which spawned them. The more radical critics like Bultmann decided that little of the historical Jesus could be recovered, but that much could be learned about the Church's faith from the gloss it imposed upon the original traditions.

Of course, many people were unhappy about the eclipse of the historical Jesus, and sought ways to recover him. Traditio-historical critics, for

2.   Notable among these are A.B. Lord, *The Singer of Tales* (HSCL, 24 Cambridge, MA: Harvard University Press, 1960); *idem*, 'Homer as Oral Poet', *HSCP* 72 (1967), pp. 1-46; *idem*, 'The Gospels as Oral Traditional Literature', in W.O. Walker (ed.), *The Relationships among the Gospels: An Interdisciplinary Dialogue* (San Antonio, TX: Trinity University Press, 1978), pp. 33-91; W.H. Kelber, 'Mark and the Oral Tradition', *Semeia* 16 (1979), pp. 7-55; *idem, The Oral and the Written Gospel: The Hermeneutics of Speaking and Writing in the Synoptic Tradition, Mark, Paul, and Q* (Philadelphia: Fortress Press, 1983); J. Dewey, 'Oral Methods of Structuring Narrative in Mark', *Int* 43 (1989), pp. 32-44; W.J. Ong, *Orality and Literacy: The Technologizing of the Word* (London: Methuen, 1982); *idem*, 'Text as Interpretation: Mark and After', *Semeia* 39 (1987), pp. 7-26; C.H. Lohr, 'Oral Techniques in the Gospel of Matthew', *CBQ* 23 (1961), pp. 403-35. Most studies of orality in biblical literature tend to acknowledge the ground-breaking work of M. Parry on Homeric literature—'Studies in the Epic Technique of Oral Verse-Making', *HSCP* 41 (1930), pp. 73-147 and 43 (1932), pp. 1-50. A very full bibliography on orality can be found in B.W. Henaut, *Oral Tradition and the Gospels: The Problem of Mark 4* (JSNTSup, 82; Sheffield: JSOT Press, 1993), pp. 311-24.

3.   K.L. Schmidt, *Der Rahmen der Geschichte Jesu* (Berlin: Trowitzsch & Sohn, 1919); M. Dibelius, *From Tradition to Gospel* (trans. B. Lee Woolf; Cambridge: James Clarke, 1935).

4.   R. Bultmann, *The History of the Synoptic Tradition* (trans. J. Marsh; Oxford: Basil Blackwell, 1963).

instance, developed a set of authenticating criteria in an attempt to distinguish the genuine sayings of Jesus from those which, according to some form-critics, had been devised by the community and retrojected back onto Jesus' lips.[5] Even pro-Bultmannians like Norman Perrin had to concede to this methodology.[6]

The third major critical development was the rise of redaction criticism in the 1950s.[7] In a way, this was a logical progression from form-criticism. The earlier method had treated the evangelists, rather disparagingly, as threaders of pearls. The pearls were, of course, the nuggets of tradition which each evangelist had threaded in a more or less rational order. The redaction-critic now sought to examine the string on which the pearls were threaded, and discovered that the Gospel-writers were much more than mere compilers; they were genuine authors in their own right, each with a distinctive theological message to communicate. This interest in the evangelist as author was bound to lead, eventually, to an emphasis on the Gospels as literary wholes created by bona fide authors for pre-conceived theological purposes. Hence, modern literary criticism came to be applied to the field of Gospel study.

Taken as a whole, the historical-critical methods complement one another to show how the text evolved into its present state. Traditio-historical criticism endeavours to recover what can be known of the original historical sayings and events; form-criticism traces the development of the tradition through the oral period of the early Church; source-criticism seeks to find evidence for the earliest written sources behind the Gospels; and redaction-criticism shows how the evangelists arranged and edited these sources to form full Gospels. All these methods, therefore, are exclusively text-based. The text is used in the search for clues about its own historical evolution.

This consideration of the text's historical development, it should be said, is not totally foreign to literary-criticism. Prior to the rise of the New Criticism in the 1940s, when it was argued that the meaning of a

---

5.   See R. Latourelle, *Finding Jesus through the Gospels: History and Hermeneutics* (trans. A. Owen; Staten Island, NY: Alba House, 1979).

6.   See N. Perrin, *Rediscovering the Teaching of Jesus* (London: SCM Press, 1967), pp. 39-43.

7.   For example, H. Conzelmann, *The Theology of St Luke* (trans. G. Buswell; London: Faber, 1960); W. Marxsen, *Mark the Evangelist* (trans. R.A. Harrisville; Nashville: Abingdon Press, 1969); G. Bornkamm, H.J. Held and G. Barth, *Tradition and Interpretation in Matthew* (trans. P. Scott; London: SCM Press, 1963).

work resided in the text alone without recourse to any external factors, it was common enough to take the author's social and historical circumstances into account when interpreting his writings. Thus, biblical scholars were only asking the same kind of questions when they enquired into a text's background—the socio-cultural origin of the author, the kind of community for which he was writing, and so on. Nevertheless, the New Criticism, though it was too radical to survive for long as a movement in its own right, did alter the general perception about meaning, and the author, text and reader came to be seen as a trinity facilitating the act of communication. From this point on it was not the personalities and backgrounds of the real author and real reader which were felt to be significant so much as their mirror-images within the text—the implied author/reader. The text was no longer an end in itself, but a means to an end—a fertile acre where implied author and implied reader could interact in order to arrive at meaning. Powell has made this point concisely and clearly.[8]

To reiterate: whereas the historical-critical methods see the text as the final element in an evolutionary chain, from which we can discern something of its historical circumstances (the historicity of its content, the circumstances of the community implied by it, or the author who edited it, and so on), modern literary-criticism regards it rather as the medium through which the author communicates with the reader. Precisely how this communication takes place is a much debated question, and has led to a veritable bomb-burst of movements under the aegis of literary-criticism.

Stephen Moore makes a similar point to the above when he draws attention to the spatio-temporal dichotomy between historical- and certain brands of literary-criticism.[9] The former, he argues, is based on the spatial aspect of enquiry, where the scholar studies the arrangement of words and sentences on the printed page. But according to the communication model on which much of the literary-critical approach is based, the reader does not apprehend the text spatially, but temporally. Whether the text is read or heard, it is consumed word by word, line by line, over a period of time, and the full meaning does not emerge until the end has been reached. The relationship between orality and textuality,

8.   Powell, *What is Narrative Criticism?*, pp. 8-9.
9.   See S.D. Moore, *Literary Criticism and the Gospels: The Theoretical Challenge* (New Haven: Yale University Press, 1989), pp. 71-107.

in fact, is a close one on the temporal basis, whereas it does not exist at all on the spatial one.

Perhaps the most widely recognized difference between historical- and literary-criticism is that while the former usually takes account only of specific sections of text at any one moment, the latter views it holistically. Form-criticism, for instance, may examine, let us say, the miracle stories in Mk 4.35–5.43 to determine whether they may have circulated as an independent miracle catena in the pre-Markan church, and if so, what function it might have served in the community.[10] Literary-criticism, on the other hand, is said to be interested only in the Gospel as a whole, in its overall literary effect as a finished product.

While this observation is true generally, it does require qualification. The pioneers of redaction-criticism, for example, certainly did not regard it as a method which involved lifting individual pericopae out of context. Subsequent studies, it is true, have often done that, but Conzelmann, Marxsen and Bornkamm all submitted studies which examined broad themes within each Gospel as a whole. Conversely, it is possible to apply literary-critical canons to the study of specific pericopae, and Mark Powell has set out a possible programme for doing so.[11]

This leads us on to the question of how compatible are the historical-critical methods with the literary-critical ones. Must we forego the older, well-established methods in order to embrace the new ones, rather as new wine is unsuitable for old skins? Some literary-critics have tended to be rather disparaging of historical criticism. R.M. Frye, for instance, dismissed redaction-criticism as a 'disintegrating methodology' which was incapable of providing a holistic view of the text.[12] It could be argued, no doubt, that Frye's rather jaundiced view may be the result of a misunderstanding of redaction criticism. After all, he is a secular literary critic, and redaction-criticism is a peculiarly biblical methodology. But S.D. Moore, too, appears to be rather cool towards it,[13] and other

---

10. See P.J. Achtemeier, 'Toward the Isolation of Pre-Markan Miracle Catenae', *JBL* 89 (1970), pp. 265-91; *idem*, 'The Origin and Function of the Pre-Markan Miracle Catenae', *JBL* 91 (1972), pp. 198-221.

11. Powell, *What is Narrative Criticism?*, pp. 103-105.

12. R.M. Frye, 'A Literary Perspective for the Criticism of the Gospels', in D.G. Miller and D.Y. Hadidian (eds.), *Jesus and Man's Hope* (Pittsburgh: Pittsburgh Theological Seminary, 1971), pp. 192-221.

13. Moore, *Literary Criticism and the Gospels*, pp. 56-58.

biblical critics, like C.C. Black, have questioned the extent of its claims.[14]

In view of these objections, it should be reiterated that redaction-criticism was not initially conceived as a 'disintegrating methodology' at all, so at the very least it does have the capacity to take a holistic view of a work. Moreover, the current view of redaction-criticism is that the evidence of the redactor's hand should be sought not only in the seams, summaries and characteristic vocabulary, but also in his selection and arrangement of the material at his disposal, and even in what he appears to omit. In that case, nothing is really exempt from the possibility of redactional handling, which brings redaction-criticism in its current form very much into line with the general principles of literary-criticism.

On the other hand, there is no intrinsic reason why specific pericopae should not be taken out of context for the purposes of detailed study. Indeed, it would frequently be a logistic impossibility to study pericopae in sufficient depth were it not valid for scholars to examine them as independent units.

As Norman Perrin recognized more than twenty years ago,[15] there is nothing inherently problematic in acknowledging the value of both historical- *and* literary-criticism. The two categories have different, but complementary aims, and if we are to gain full insight from our reading of the gospels, we need to draw upon all the critical methods at our disposal. This is not to say that these methods are all interdependent. As Powell reminds us,[16] the literary critic is perfectly at liberty to go about his business without recourse to historical considerations, but this is not to invalidate historical enquiry or the tools used therein. It is a fact, nevertheless, that many such critics proceed on the presupposition that the material with which they are dealing has little historical basis. On consideration, however, it is surely better for the literary critic to leave that issue out of account, and to allow it to be decided on the basis of those historical-critical methods which have been developed for the purpose.

b. *What is Narrative Criticism?*
Narrative criticism has been regarded in some circles as a specialized form of reader-response criticism, but while many reader-response theories are

---

14. C.C. Black, *The Disciples according to Mark: Markan Redaction in Current Debate* (JSNTSup, 27; Sheffield: JSOT Press, 1989).

15. N. Perrin, 'The Evangelist as Author: Reflections on Method in the Study and Interpretation of the Synoptic Gospels and Acts', *BR* 17 (1972), pp. 5-18.

16. Powell, *What is Narrative Criticism?*, p. 8.

heavily oriented towards the reader, narrative criticism is very much text-centred. Powell puts the matter very clearly:

> Despite similarities, structuralism and narrative criticism differ from the reader-response approaches in that the former focus on ways in which the text determines the reader's response rather than on ways in which the reader determines meaning. They are therefore said to view the reader as being *in the text*, that is, encoded within it (structuralism) or presupposed by it (narrative criticism).[17]

Classically, narrative criticism has been seen to address the 'what' and 'how' of a story. Chatman's *Story and Discourse*, for instance, expends most of its pages in spelling out this distinction. The story has to do with the content of the narrative—the events, plot, characters and settings (notably of time and place). Discourse, on the other hand, deals with how the story is told—the nature of the rhetoric and its effects on the implied reader. This includes particular rhetorical strategies such as point of view, text-arrangement and irony.

In the current work, I shall be dealing with most of these issues. In the present chapter, I need to make a brief statement about the relationship between the various components which make up what we call the Markan text (real/implied author, real/implied reader, narrator/ narratee, characters), and about Mark's rhetorical technique. The next three chapters will deal with the literary content of the Gospel by way of an examination of plot, characterization and setting (time and space), while the final two chapters will look at the Gospel as discourse, paying particular attention to point of view and irony, respectively.

c. *What is Reader-Response Criticism?*

Reader-response criticism is now widely recognized as a useful tool for engaging the biblical text, although it should be noted at once that, since it was devised by literary critics for use in studying modern secular literature, its application to biblical and other ancient texts should not be pressed too far. Excellent surveys of reader-response have been made by Mailloux, McKnight, Suleiman and Tompkins,[18] and a full-scale

---

17. Powell, *What is Narrative Criticism?*, p. 18.

18. S. Mailloux, 'Reader-Response Criticism?', *Genre* 10 (1977), pp. 413-31; E.V. McKnight, *The Bible and the Reader: An Introduction to Literary Criticism* (Philadelphia: Fortress Press, 1985), pp. 75-111; S.R. Suleiman and I. Crosman (eds.), *The Reader in the Text: Essays on Audience and Interpretation* (Princeton, NJ: Princeton University Press, 1980), pp. 3-45; J. Tompkins (ed.), *Reader-*

application of the method to Mark's Gospel has recently been produced by R.M. Fowler,[19] so there is no need to tread an already well-worn track. This, in any case, is not primarily a study of reader-response, but of narrative criticism. My purpose in alluding to it here is twofold: first, we need to be clear about the relationship between the two methods, a matter to be dealt with in the next section; and secondly, the chapter on point of view necessarily entails that we have a grounding in reader-response terminology, and the manner in which the various terms are related. Readers interested in pursuing the reader-response question in depth are referred to the works already cited. It is enough to point out at this juncture that we do not have to deal with one clear-cut method, but with a whole galaxy of theories[20] which have but one common denominator—

Response Criticism: From Formalism to Post-Structuralism (Baltimore: The Johns Hopkins University Press, 1980), pp. ix-xxvi.

19. Fowler, *Let The Reader Understand*. Shorter studies on reader-response in the gospels include R.M. Fowler, *Loaves and Fishes: The Function of the Feeding Stories in the Gospel of Mark* (SBLDS, 54; Chico, CA: Scholars Press, 1981), pp. 149-79; *idem*, 'Reader-Response Criticism: Figuring Mark's Reader', in Capel and Moore (eds.), *Mark and Method*, pp. 50-83; J.L. Resseguie, 'Reader-Response Criticism and the Synoptic Gospels', *JAAR* 52 (1984), pp. 307-24; Moore, *Literary Criticism and the Gospels*, pp. 71-107; Sanders and Davies, *Studying the Synoptic Gospels*, pp. 240-51; N.R. Petersen, 'The Reader in the Gospel', *Neotestamentica* 18 (1984), pp. 38-51.

20. These reader-response theories can be classified, along with their chief proponents, as follows:

i) Rhetorical—W.C. Booth, *Rhetoric of Fiction*.

ii) Semiotic/structuralist—J. Culler, *Structuralist Poetics: Structuralism, Linguistics and the Study of Literature* (Ithaca, NY: Cornell University Press, 1975).

iii) Phenomenological—W. Iser, 'The Reading Process: A Phenomenological Approach', *NLH* 3 (1972), pp. 279-99; G. Poulet, 'Phenomenology of Reading', *NLH* 1 (1969), pp. 53-68.

iv) Subjectivist/psychoanalytic—N. Holland, *5 Readers Reading* (New Haven: Yale University Press, 1975); *idem*, 'The New Paradigm: Subjective or Transactive?', *NLH* 7 (1976), pp. 335-46; *idem*, 'Unity, Identity, Text, Self', *PMLA* 90 (1975), pp. 813-22; D. Bleich, *Readings and Feelings: An Introduction to Subjective Criticism* (Urbana, IL: National Council of Teachers of English, 1975); *idem*, *Subjective Criticism* (Baltimore: The Johns Hopkins University Press, 1978).

v) Sociological/historical—H.R. Jauss, 'Literary History as a Challenge to Literary Theory', *NLH* 2 (1970), pp. 7-37.

vi) Hermeneutic—E.D. Hirsch, *Validity in Interpretation* (New Haven: Yale University Press, 1967); G. Hartman, 'Literary Criticism and Its Discontents' *Critical Inquiry* 3 (1976), pp. 203-20.

namely, their emphasis on the reader's response to the text. At the centre of such enquiry is the communication model—the perception that meaning requires three elements: an author, a text and a reader.

The complexity of this theoretical web is compounded by the fact that the various hypotheses can be classified in more than one way, and the different classifications cut across one another. Suleiman and Mailloux, for instance, opt for a grouping along linguistic and scientific lines, while Tompkins draws up an author-reader axis along which the theories are ranged according to whether they regard the author, the text or the reader as the most significant factor in the making of meaning. Thus, while both Poulet and Iser are regarded as taking the phenomenological approach to reader-response, Poulet thinks that the meaning lies primarily in the text and that the reader is a somewhat passive figure, while Iser argues that the reader plays a vital rôle in the production of meaning.[21]

It would be tempting at this stage to review the various kinds of reader-response theory, and to consider which of them, if any, might be appropriate for an understanding of the reading of Mark's Gospel, but we must resist that urge, and consider instead the question of how this method generally might be related to narrative criticism.

d. *Are Narrative- and Reader-Response Criticisms Compatible?*

It has sometimes been argued that narrative- and reader-response criticisms are two different methodologies which cannot be happily married within a single literary-critical account of a text.[22] The one is text-centred, while the other is reader-centred. So how can they be compatible? The solution would seem to lie in the observation that reader-response theories take up their positions along an axis which extends from 'author' at one end to 'reader' at the other, with 'text' in between; and by no means all such theories lie at the 'reader' end of the axis. The axial view indicates that all reader-response theories acknowledge the necessary presence of all three elements: the debate is simply about which of them is the most significant. Given this, there is no reason at all why the insights of a theory at one end of the spectrum cannot be compatible with those of a theory at the other end. Moore would appear to be in agreement with this judgment when he comments:

21. See Tompkins, *Reader-Response Criticism*, pp. xiv-xv.

22. Longman (*Literary Approaches*, pp. 25-27, 38-41), for instance, seems to distinguish rather sharply between text-centred theories, based on the New Criticism of the 1940s, and reader-centred theories.

A preoccupation with the unfolding plot of a gospel marks a substantial overlap between reader-response and narrative criticism in the New Testament context. Narrative criticism frequently shades over into reader-response criticism. Indeed, reader-oriented gospel studies generally seem specialized extensions of narrative criticism.[23]

Actually, not only are these two complementary, but they should be used as mutually interpretive methods if the full scope of a text's meaning is to be revealed. Using them simultaneously will enable the critic to meet himself at the textual centre, because questions can be asked at opposite ends of the critical spectrum in order to better disclose the meaning that lies within. From the narrative-critical end we can ask *what* the text contains, and *how* it means what it means. We can presuppose an author who has determined to write the text in a particular fashion in order to exert the maximum possible persuasive force on the intended audience. From the reader-oriented end, we can seek to establish just what it is that the reader must bring to the text in order to discover meaning—not so much the purely subjective meaning supplied solely by the reader's personality, imagination or whatever, but the objective meaning that emerges out of the text when the implied reader interacts with the implied author. These matters will be touched upon when we examine point of view in Mark, but for the most part we shall be occupied with the *what* and the *how* of the text.

2. Who's Who in the Making of the Text?

a. *The Chatman Legacy*
While Seymour Chatman[24] cannot be said to have originated the distinction between real author/reader on the one hand, and implied author/reader on the other,[25] it is nevertheless his diagrammatic representation which has become the most convenient starting point for a large number of subsequent narrative critics.[26] Chatman's original diagram is as follows:

23. Moore, *Literary Criticism and the Gospels*, p. 73.

24. Chatman, *Story and Discourse*.

25. The term 'implied author' had earlier been coined by Wayne Booth (*Rhetoric of Fiction*). The expression 'implied reader' was taken up by Chatman (*Story and Discourse*, p. 150 n. 7) from Booth's 'postulated reader'.

26. Cf. B.C. Lategan, 'Coming to Grips with the Reader', *Semeia* 48 (1989), pp. 3-17 (10); W.S. Vorster, 'The Reader in the Text: Narrative Material', *Semeia* 48 (1989), pp. 21-39 (30); N.R. Petersen, 'Reader', p. 39; J.L. Staley, *The Print's First*

Narrative Text

Real→	Implied→	(Narrator)→	(Narratee)→	Implied→	Real
Author	Author			Reader	Reader

In this form, it suggests that the making of a text involves three pairs of figures or concepts: real author–real reader; implied author–implied reader; and narrator–narratee. The first of these pairs lies outside the purview of the text: real author and real reader both have a life of their own which proceeds quite unaffected by the text which they create. The remaining pairs are 'immanent to the narrative', that is they are a construct of the text and cannot exist outside or beyond it.

'Narrator' and 'narratee' have been bracketed because their respective functions can vary enormously from one text to another. The presence of the narrator, for instance, depends on the extent to which the reader feels he or she is being 'told' the story: the greater the sense of telling (or *diegesis*) rather than of showing (*mimesis*), the greater the sense of a narrator. A pure showing, as in Hemingway's *The Killers* would suggest the total absence of a narrator although, as Chatman observes, in the last analysis this is always an illusion.[27]

Subsequent scholars have modified Chatman's diagram in various ways. Lategan, for instance, regards the narrator as being essentially identical with the implied author, and the narratee with the implied reader.[28] Thus, in accordance with Occam's razor, there is no need to multiply entities. He also points out that there is no direct contact between real author and real reader. In his words:

> The real author, when writing, is reaching out for the implied reader (as no other reader is present at this moment). The real reader, when reading, is reaching out for the implied author (as no other author is present). Thus, instead of real author → implied author (narrator) → implied reader (narratee) → real reader, the process is more like:

Kiss: A Rhetorical Investigation of the Implied Reader in the Fourth Gospel (SBLDS, 82; Atlanta: Scholars Press, 1986), p. 22; E.S. Malbon, 'Narrative Criticism: How Does the Story Mean?', in Capel and Moore (eds.), *Mark and Method*, pp. 23-49 (27); Fowler, *Let the Reader Understand*, pp. 31-34.

27. Chatman, *Story and Discourse*, p. 147.

28. Lategan, 'Coming to Grips', pp. 3-17. But against Lategan, cf. G. Prince ('Introduction to the Study of the Narratee', in Tompkins [ed.], *Reader-Response Criticism*, pp. 7-25). As it so happens, however, there is essentially no difference between implied author and narrator in the Gospel of Mark, and there is thus no problem in treating them as one.

Real authors can address only what they imagine or intend their readers to
be; real readers can reach the real authors only via the implied authors, that
is, they have to figure out what the real authors are getting at by concen-
trating on the clues and signals given by the encoded [implied] authors.[29]

Chatman's diagram has also come under fire for its mono-directional
linearity. The fact that the arrows point exclusively in one direction,
Fowler observes,[30] indicates that Chatman subscribes to the common
but erroneous view that communication is a one-way process: there is a
sender to dispatch the message and a receiver to receive it. But, if
Wolfgang Iser is to be believed,[31] the reader is far more active than that:
the reader is instrumental in the construction and interpretation of the
text because, while he or she does not write it, it is he or she rather than
the author who creates the implied reader (contra Booth). In that case,
the arrows should be pointing towards the centre of Chatman's diagram,
and in Petersen's version of it, that is what happens. Staley, too, reshapes
the diagram to take this factor into account, and also adds the term
'characters' to denote that it is often here where the bulk of the interaction between author and reader takes place.[32] It is what the characters
in the story-world do and say that determines the nature of the implied
author/reader, regardless of whether or not there is a visible narrator.

Having examined how these various terms may relate to one another,
let us now explore each one as an entity in its own right.

b. *The Real Author*
The real author is, quite simply, the finite, flesh-and-blood person
responsible for the work in question. It is his or her mind and hand
which produces the text, but he or she cannot share the omniscience and
the omnipresence of the implied author who emerges from it. While the
latter must always be a single entity, there can be a multiplicity of real
authors. It is certain, for instance, that Homer's *Iliad* and *Odyssey* are

29. Lategan, 'Coming to Grips', p. 10.
30. Fowler, *Let the Reader Understand*, p. 34 n. 31.
31. Iser, 'Reading Process', pp. 279-99.
32. Staley, *The Print's First Kiss*, p. 22.

the work of many tale-tellers over a substantial period of time. Similarly, Mark's Gospel is not the work of a single person (regardless of whether or not he is the man of Paul's acquaintance). Most scholars now accept that the name 'Mark' should be applied to the final redactor who makes liberal use of earlier material—certainly oral, and probably in written form, too—in the fashioning of his own Gospel.

c. *The Implied Author*

W.S. Vorster conveniently sums up the rôle of the implied author in the following way:

> ...the implied author is the governing and organizing principle in, or implied by, the narrative text, the source of the judgments and values embodied in the text. It chooses what we read and how we read, and exerts power over our reading process. It is the implied author that chooses the detail and quality that is found in the work or implied by the work. Its function is to instruct the implied reader how to read by the signs of its presence in the text... An implied author may embody totally different views and values in a narrative than the real author who created the implied author. That is why implied authors in different works of the same author need not be and often are not the same.[33]

One or two interesting points emerge from this description. First, we may notice that Vorster assiduously avoids the use of gender-specific language because he recognizes, as we all must, that the implied author is not a person at all, but simply a literary construct or concept within the text. Some, indeed, have gone so far as to reject the notion altogether because, they say, it does not even exist in the text, but only in the critic's mind for the purpose of controlling interpretation.[34] Perhaps, however, this is to go too far. With Staley, it is better to acknowledge that while the implied author cannot be the singular preserve of any one character or voice, it does exist as a feature of the characters and voices of a text in general.

It is noteworthy that, according to Chatman,[35] the implied author can only become functional within the text as long as there is a reader to reconstruct him/her/it. Although this may seem obvious, it is not always stressed sufficiently that the precise nature of the author's 'second self'

---

33. Vorster, 'Reader', pp. 22-23; also Booth, *Rhetoric of Fiction*, p. 151.
34. So S. Rimmon-Kenan, *Narrative Fiction: Contemporary Poetics* (London: Methuen, 1983), pp. 86-89.
35. Chatman, *Story and Discourse*, p. 148.

may well be apprehended differently from one reader to another, so that the so-called 'ideal reader' may well be just that—an ideal, rather than a reality.

Another point worth stressing is that although the implied author need not share the views and values of the real author, the sophistication of such incongruity is a feature to be found only in comparatively modern literature. In ancient texts the correspondence between implied and real author is rather more direct.

d. *The Real Reader*

The 'real reader' is a somewhat more elusive entity than the 'real author', for whereas the latter is generally (though not always) identifiable as a single person, the 'real reader' is an expression for an indeterminate number of people—possibly a huge galaxy of personalities from different ages and cultures. Petersen, indeed, in constructing his diagram to show the various factors involved in the reading process, distinguishes between the authorial reader for whom a work is originally intended, and subsequent readers who may bring to the text values and expectations not envisaged by the original author, and for whom the interpretative experience may be radically different from that of the authorial reader.[36] The impact of the text on the reader, and the reader's impact on it, may vary enormously from one individual to another. Not only that, but even the individual reader's interaction with the text may differ from one reading to another. Staley points up the problem in the following manner:

> Real readers can change from one reading to the next, and, depending upon their backgrounds, may bring to the text a different set of socially-constructed reading competencies than those implied in the text. If we take into account psychological change as well as sociological/historical change, we must conclude that the real reader of a text always changes, since even upon a second reading, the reader brings different feelings and attitudes to the text than he or she did to the first reading.[37]

e. *The Implied Reader*

The 'implied reader' corresponds to the 'implied author' in that, unlike the real reader, he/she/it exists only within the text. As Vorster puts it:

---

36. Petersen, 'Reader', p. 39.
37. Staley, *The Print's First Kiss*, p. 24.

The reader in the text is a literary construct, an image of a reader which is selected by the text. It is implied by the text, and in this sense it is encoded in the text by way of linguistic, literary, cultural, and other codes. It is not identical to any outside flesh-and-blood reader. It is an image that is created by the author which has to be constructed by the real reader through the reading process in order to attribute meaning to the text, that is to actualize the text.[38]

Further, the implied (or 'ideal' or 'postulated') reader is meant to endorse the values and beliefs in the narrative as mediated through its reliable characters or narrator, and to reject the views of an unreliable character or narrator. Indeed, it is the ability to distinguish between reliable and unreliable values and beliefs which is instrumental to our definition of 'implied reader'.[39]

We have seen that there is some dispute over how, exactly, the implied reader is created. Booth inclines to the view that the author is primarily responsible, whereas Iser stresses the rôle of the reader who creates the implied reader on the basis of the values and expectations brought to the text. Vorster, however, is surely correct in avoiding this dichotomy by recognizing the complementary rôles of the two. The author may create the implied reader as a 'second self', as Booth says, but it can only remain potential until energized by the presence of the reader and his or her values. It is only once the reading process begins that the implied reader can spring into life.

f. *The Narrator*

Like implied authors, narrators are not flesh-and-blood figures. They are not bound by time and place, and they can be omniscient, having the ability to perceive the inner thoughts and feelings of the characters in a way that no human could. This omniscience, of course, is not essential. An author may choose to have his narrator as one of the characters on the ground, someone whose knowledge of the action is limited. Or, there may be several narrators, or none at all. They may be fully reliable, sharing values and beliefs with the implied author, or totally unreliable. The flexibility is almost endless. As Staley puts it, 'the possibilities are as manifold as those of personality itself'.[40]

In speaking of the narrator, it is important not to confuse him or her

38. Vorster, 'Reader', p. 27.
39. See Booth, *Rhetoric of Fiction*, p. 138.
40. Staley, *The Print's First Kiss*, p. 38.

with the implied author. According to Chatman, the latter is the principle
that invents the narrator. The narrator, if there is one, may be used as
the vehicle through which the implied author communicates its attitudes,
beliefs and values, for the implied author has no voice of its own; it
cannot tell us anything in the manner of a narrator. Again, narrators are
not indispensable: they need not outlive the story or, as we have noted,
even be present in it. But, of course, the absolutely mimetic narrative is
ultimately illusory. Even in stories where no narrator seems to be
present, there must always be an ultimate tale-teller—namely, the author
himself.

g. *The Narratee*

The narratee is the exact counterpart of the narrator in that he or she
belongs exclusively to the text, and may take up a position ranging from
prominence to absence. Fundamentally, the narratee is simply that entity
with which the narrator communicates, but there can be various
manifestations. The most obvious is that in which the narratee appears in
the guise of one of the characters in the story world and is fed information by one of the other characters. There are, however, many instances
in which the narratee's presence is implicit, and is hidden behind the
narrative.

Of course, wherever the narratee happens to lie along this spectrum,
ultimately every story implies a reader or listener. Yet we must not
confuse the narratee with the real reader or listener. Chatman makes the
point succinctly:

> The 'you' or 'dear reader' who is addressed by the narrator of *Tom Jones*
> is no more Seymour Chatman than is the narrator Henry Fielding. When
> I enter the fictional contract I add another self: I become an implied reader.
> And just as the narrator may or may not ally himself with the implied
> author, the implied reader furnished by the real reader may or may not
> ally himself with a narratee.[41]

Despite this clear espousal of the distinction between implied reader
and narratee, there are certain more recent scholars, such as Lategan,
who would oppose this view and argue instead for the identity of these
two concepts. While it is certainly true that their rôles overlap they
cannot, in the last analysis, be identical because the narratee is much less

41. Chatman, *Story and Discourse*, p. 150.

stable than the implied reader. The former can appear in various guises or, ostensibly, not at all, whereas the latter must always exist as the ideal recipient of the preconceived authorial viewpoint or set of values. The narratee need not always share the moral or ideological stance of the ideal reader, particularly if he or she is shown in the text to believe what he is told by an unreliable narrator. On the other hand, ancient texts are not as subtle as this, and the narratee and implied reader there can generally be taken to be virtually identical.

h. *Characters*

If, with Vorster and Staley, we modify Chatman's initial schema of agents involved in the reading process into the form of an inverted pyramid, the characters will appear at the lowest level, for they are confined by the temporal and spatial constraints of the story-world, and even if, on occasion, they serve as narrators, they are inevitably limited in what they can say. Indeed, they may frequently appear as 'second order' narrators who tell a story within a story, but do not enjoy the omniscience or omnipresence of a first-order narrator. They are always subservient to the implied author, yet, despite their comparatively lowly position, they are essential to the hierarchy of agents involved in the reading process: they are the keystone without which the whole edifice collapses. The characters lie at the heart of so much that goes on that without them there can be no viable narrative at all.

Having outlined the various agents involved in the narrative reading process, we can now depict their relationship in the following diagram:

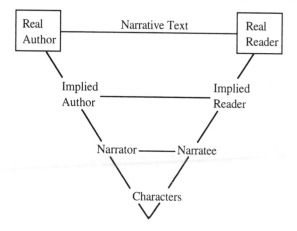

3. *Real Readers or Real Hearers? The Orality-Literacy Question*

'But what if the readers were listening?' That is one of the sub-headings in Moore's discussion of reader-response[42]—and a very pertinent question it is, too. For despite Mark's 'aside' in 13.14, where he exorts the *reader* to understand (ὁ ἀναγινώσκων νοείτω),[43] it is extremely likely that he began with a genuine audience rather than a readership. The cumulative evidence for this is rather compelling.

First, there is the logistical problem. Writing was an expensive business, and copying, quite apart from the expense, was a laborious, time-consuming process. Yet we are led to believe that the first Christians were poor, on the whole. We do hear of property-owners, it is true (Acts 4.36-37), but we also hear of the sorry plight of the Jerusalem church, and of the need to send aid (Acts 11.29-30; Rom. 15.26; 1 Cor. 16.1-4). One wonders if the situation at Rome (assuming that Mark was writing for that community) was very much different. Certainly a large proportion of the members there seem to have been slaves, if their names are anything to go by (Rom. 16), whose wealth would have been minimal. And even if such people could have afforded to make sufficient copies of Mark to be widely circulated, there must have been a time when only the original manuscript existed, and the only way that its content could have been broadcast immediately would have been by means of public reading.

Secondly, if public recitation sounds an unlikely event, it should be remembered that for a Roman audience, such performances would not have been uncommon. Indeed, it has been suggested with some conviction that at least some of the tragedies of Seneca, which were contemporaneous with Mark's Gospel, and in all probability written in the same city

---

42. Moore, *Literary Criticism and the Gospels*, p. 84.

43. Various attempts have been made to overcome the difficulty of Mark addressing his *audience* as 'the reader'. Some have argued that the reader in question is not the general body of recipients, but the person who was to read aloud to the gathered throng: perhaps it was the author's direction as to how the 'abomination of desolation' passage should be read (cf. Fowler, *Let the Reader Understand*, p. 84). An alternative proposal is that of Joanna Dewey ('Oral Methods', pp. 35-36) who suggests that by 'reader' the author is referring to the reader of Daniel from which the term 'abomination of desolation' is derived. In other words, he is saying that the key to understanding this curious phrase lies in Dan. 9.27. Fowler (*Let the Reader Understand*, pp. 82-87) has a full discussion of Mk 13.14.

(Rome), were composed not to be acted, but for dramatic recitation.[44]

Finally, and perhaps most important of all, it is becoming increasingly apparent that the essential dynamics of this gospel are oral rather than textual. Mark's paratactic and episodic technique, it is claimed, is none other than a device for assisting memorization of the *spoken* word; and the same may be said of many other literary devices, including duality, chiasm, inclusio, intercalation, echoing and foreshadowing.[45] Indeed, when we compare Mark with Homer, whose works we know to have had a long oral germination period, we find all these devices there also.[46]

My justification for the claim that Mark's first readers were, in fact, listeners, has necessarily had to be brief, but, in any case, it is fully worked out in the literature cited. Settling this issue, however, only serves to raise further questions which we can do no more than pose here. For instance, given that Mark's Gospel was based on an oral dynamic, in what sense would its new form as a written text have affected the recipients? This is the question which W.H. Kelber addresses in *The Oral and the Written Gospel*. The most obvious change, of course, was that once the tradition had been committed to paper, its temporal power gave way to a new, spatial understanding. The prospect of textual disintegration arose because the recipient was no longer committed to a linear, temporal experience, but was free to move to and fro through the text in space rather than time.[47] To put it succinctly, the

44. So R.J. Tarrant, *Seneca's Thyestes* (Atlanta: Scholars Press, 1985), pp. 13-15; E.F. Watling's translation of Seneca's *Four Tragedies and Octavia* (Harmondsworth: Penguin, 1966), p. 19. Lack of theatrical direction is one of the reasons given for this conclusion. Moreover, according to the ancient sources, the practice ascribed to Seneca appears to have been rather widespread (cf. Ovid, *Tristia* 5.7.27; Pliny, *Epist.* 7.17; Tacitus, *Dial.* 2.1-3.3). But F. Ahl (in his translation of Seneca's *Three Tragedies* [Ithaca, NY: Cornell University Press, 1986], p. 26) feels that performance—private rather than public—was possible. He finds evidence for his view in Suetonius, 'Domitian' 7, where the emperor forbids actors to use the public stage, but allows them to perform in private houses.

45. See Dewey, 'Oral Methods', pp. 32-44; *idem*, 'Mark as Interwoven Tapestry: Forecasts and Echoes for a Listening Audience', *CBQ* 53 (1991), pp. 221-36.

46. See particularly, J.A. Notopoulos, 'Parataxis in Homer: A New Approach to Homeric Literary Criticism', *TAPA* 80 (1949), pp. 1-23; *idem*, 'Continuity and Interconnexion in Homeric Oral Composition', *TAPA* 82 (1951), pp. 81-101. It would take two or three pages to make a comprehensive list of the books and articles dealing with Homeric oral techniques.

47. Obviously, this is not to say that reading (as opposed to hearing) is not a

text became an object rather than an event.

A second question to arise—and one which seems not to have been much explored—concerns what might have been remembered from an oral performance of the Gospel compared with what is recalled after a personal reading. Studies in the field of cognitive science tend to suggest that, under laboratory conditions at least, when a subject is asked to recall words from a simple series, the primacy-recency factor tends to apply. In other words, items from the beginning and end of the list are recalled more readily than those in the middle. Of course, different variables may have an effect on the results. The amount of material which a subject is asked to retain (for example, paragraphs instead of single words), and the length of time which is allowed to lapse before recollection, are obviously important determining factors, as is the degree of conscious structuring. A structured folktale, for instance, may not be remembered in quite the same way as a simple word series. Could cognitive science shed light on the way in which Mark's original hearers might have recalled the Gospel story, and how, indeed, that recollection might differ from what a modern, print-conscious reader commits to memory?[48]

Finally—and this is an observation rather than a question—it is certain that the orality-literacy issue exposes the sharp distinctions between ancient hearer and modern reader.[49] It might be helpful, in fact, to understand these factors as the opposite poles of an axis along which they interact more or less intimately. The pre-Markan church was perhaps purely a listening community; certainly there would have been no notion of a written Gospel, even if there were certain formal or thematic

temporal as well as a spatial experience. As Moore (*Literary Criticism and the Gospels*, pp. 87-88) has indicated, reader-response criticism is sensitive to temporality, and hence to the original orality behind the text, in a way that the historico-critical methods are not. See also Petersen, 'Reader', pp. 42-43.

48. Relevant material might include B.F. Meyer, 'What Is Remembered from Prose: A Function of Passage Structure', in R.O. Freedle (ed.), *Discourse Production and Comprehension* (Norwood, NJ: Ablex, 1977), pp. 307-36; *idem*, 'What Is Recalled after Hearing a Passage?', *JEdPs* 65 (1973), pp. 109-17; G.H. Bower, 'Experiments on Story Understanding and Recall', *QJEP* 28 (1976), pp. 511-34; P.W. Thorndyke, 'Cognitive Structures in Comprehension and Memory of Narrative Discourse', *CogPs* 9 (1977), pp. 77-110; R.E. Johnson, 'Recall of Prose as a Function of the Structural Importance of the Linguistic Units', *JVLVB* 9 (1970), pp. 12-20; J.M. Mandler and N.S Johnson, 'Remembrance of Things Parsed: Story Structure and Recall', *CogPs* 9 (1977), pp. 111-51.

49. See Dewey, 'Mark as Interwoven Tapestry', p. 236.

collections of miracles or sayings. At the other end of the spectrum, the contemporary church in Britain and elsewhere is almost totally reliant on the printed text. The tightly-woven mnemonic structures of Mark are easily lost on the modern reader for whom remembering the story is largely unnecessary. In between these extremes, orality and literacy go hand in hand. The writing of the Gospel did not immediately affect the oral consciousness of the first readers: it is likely that they would have read it rather as they had first heard it—aloud, and with an eye to temporality and linearity. Only at a later stage did reflection on and contemplation of the written word emerge. Even well into medieval times, however, when literacy was well-established, orality was still a force to be reckoned with.[50]

All this raises the question as to the purpose of narrative criticism. Does the narrative critic take account of the Gospel's original orality, and is there any reason why he or she should? The answer to both these questions would appear to be in the negative. Narrative criticism dwells on the final, written form of the text, and on the various factors which make it what it is. By examining the plot, characters, rhetorical devices, points of view, settings and so on, it seeks to discover what the text can tell us rather than what it meant to its original hearers. Even reader-response criticism which, as we have seen, shares with studies in orality a concern for the temporality and linearity of the text, does not seek to recover its meaning for the original recipients. The upshot of this is that, while it is legitimate to approach Mark's Gospel from a narrative-critical angle, we need to remember that the conclusions drawn will be those of a contemporary, print-conscious readership, and not those of a first-century oral-conscious community hearing the text for the first time.

4. *Literary Theory and the Gospel of Mark*

a. *Who Was/Is the Author of Mark?*
i) *The Real Author.* Discovering the identity and interests of the flesh-and-blood author of Mark's Gospel is the province of historical criticism. Redaction criticism claims the ability to isolate the evangelist's theological concerns by examining those passages which clearly bear his stamp, though it is now generally recognized that this quest is a good deal more complex than it was once assumed to be. The identity of the author

---

50. See Ong, *Orality and Literacy.*

himself is far less certain than the nature of his theology. Early church tradition tends to make him the companion of both Peter (1 Pet. 5.13) and Paul (Acts 12.25; 13.5; Col. 4.10),[51] and he is presumably the John Mark who resided with his mother Mary in Jerusalem (Acts 12.12); but while his name appears to have been attached to the Second Gospel at a fairly early date, the fact remains that the actual text is anonymous, and its authorship can be little more than a matter of speculation.

Happily for both the reader-response and the narrative critic, it is not necessary to know who the actual author was. For the former it is the implied author within the text that is of chief significance, while for the latter it is the text itself. Indeed, it is of no consequence to the literary critic whether just one or several real authors were responsible for the making of the text. In the case of the Second Gospel, it is certain that the material must have passed through several hands, and the name of Mark is generally given only to the final redactor.

ii) *The Implied Author.* We have seen that, regardless of who was responsible for the text, the implied author is the one constant factor within it, which only the destruction of the text can eradicate. Just how the message of the text is communicated to the reader, and with what degree of success, rather depends on the theory we adopt. If we take it that the author creates not only an 'implied' self, but is instrumental in creating an implied reader also, we must conclude that the actual reader has only a minimal contribution to make. But if we decide, like Iser, that the reader creates meaning, the success of the author's intention would seem to be less certain. On balance, it is preferable to conclude that the author does exert a fair degree of control over the text, and that he or she devises certain means of conveying intention to readers. Booth refers to this as 'reliable commentary',[52] and Fowler has done a good deal of work to show how this applies to Mark.[53]

Given Fowler's admirably thorough treatment of reliable commentary

---

51. The view that Mark was Peter's disciple and interpreter is widely reported by the post-apostolic church (Papias [*apud* Eusebius, *HE* 3.39.15]; Irenaeus, *Adv.Haer.* 3.1.1; Clement of Alexandria [*apud* Eusebius, *HE* 2.15.22; 6.14.6-7]; Origen [*apud* Eusebius, *HE* 6.25.5]; Tertullian, *Adv.Marc.* 4.5; Eusebius, *Ev.Dem.* 3.5; Epiphanius, *Panarion*; Jerome, *de Vir. Ill.*

52. Booth, *Rhetoric of Fiction*, pp. 169-209.

53. Fowler, *Loaves and Fishes*, pp. 157-79; *idem, Let the Reader Understand*, pp. 81-154.

in Mark, it is hardly necessary to discuss the issue in detail here. Suffice it to say that the means by which the author seeks to establish his 'second self' are many and varied. In *Loaves and Fishes*, Fowler suggests the following list:[54]

1. Direct comments to the reader (e.g. Mk 13.5, 9, 14, 23, 29, 37)
   a. Title (1.1) and epigraph (1.2-3)
2. Linking statements (e.g. 6.52; 8.19-21)
3. Parenthetical constructions:
   a. Explanations of foreign customs and concepts (3.22; 7.2, 3-4; 9.43; 12.18, 42; 14.12; 15.16, 32, 42)
   b. Translations of foreign words (3.17; 5.9, 41; 7.11, 34; 10.46; 14.36; 15.22, 34)
   c. Winks at the reader (2.10, 28; 3.30; 7.19b; 8.32a; 9.41; 11.32; 14.49b, 62)
   d. Explanatory γάρ clauses (1.16, 22; 2.15; 3.10, 21; 5.8, 28, 42; 6.14, 17, 18, 20, 31, 48, 50, 52; 7.3; 9.6, 31, 34; 10;22, 45; 11.13, 18, 32; 12.12; 14.2, 40, 56; 15.10; 16.4, 8)
   e. Markan insertions (2.6//8b; 2.9b//11a; 3.7//8; 3.14//16; 4.31//32; 5.10//23; 5.29//34; 6.14//16; 6.31b//32b; 6.35//35; 7.1-2//5; 7.20//23; 8.1//2; 8.17//21; 8.29//9.5; 9.12//13b; 10.23b//24b; 11.11//15; 13.5a//9//23//33; 13.33b//35b; 13.35//37; 14.18//22; 14.56//59; 15.2//4; 15.24//25, etc.)
   f. Intercalations (3.20-21/22-30/31-35; 5.21-24/24-35/35-43; 6.7-13/14-29/30-31; 11.12-14/15-19/20-25; 14.1-2/3-9/10-11 14.53-54/55-65/66-72; 15.6-15/16-20/21-32)
   g. Doublets (6.35-44/8.1-10; 7.31-37/8.22-26, etc.)
4. Inside views (1.22, 27, 34, 41; 2.5, 6-7, 8, 12; 3.2, 5; 4.40, 41; 5.15, 20, 28, 29, 30, 33, 42; 6.2, 3, 6, 19, 20, 26, 33, 34, 48, 49, 50, 51-52 54; 7.24, 37; 8.2, 11, 16-21, 33; 9.6, 15, 30, 32, 34; 10.2, 14, 21, 22, 24, 26, 32, 38, 41; 11.18, 21, 31-32a, 32; 12.12, 13, 15, 17, 24, 34; 14.1, 4, 10, 11, 18, 19, 27, 30, 33, 40, 56, 57, 72; 15.5, 10, 15, 43, 44; 16.5, 8)
5. Unanswered questions (1.24, 27. 4.41; 6.2, 37; 8.4, 17-21; 9.19; 11.28)
6. Reliable characters:
   a. Jesus
   b. The voice from heaven (1.11; 9.7)
   c. Demons (1.24, 34; 3.11-12; 5.7)
   d. Centurion (15.39)
   e. Young man (14.51-52; 16.5-7)

54. Fowler, *Loaves and Fishes*, pp. 157-75.

7. Prospective passages—that is, passages which prove to be reliable
    with the benefit of hindsight, and which can thus be read as a reliable
    backdrop against which certain other passages can be read. The central
    thesis of Fowler's *Loaves and Fishes*, indeed, is that Mark himself
    composed the story of the feeding of the five thousand (6.35-44),
    basing it on the traditional feeding of the four thousand (8.1-10) in
    order to direct the reader as to how the latter ought to be read.

There is a wealth of 'reliable commentary' here, and not all of it is
related to the chief themes which run throughout the Gospel. We might
obtain a flavour of how it works, however, if we take one aspect of the
fundamental assertion of the text—that Jesus is Son of God. Mark
announces this fact in the title verse (1.a in Fowler's list), and the
remainder of the Gospel is, in short, a demonstration of this conviction.
But there are many ways in which the implied author can drive home
the point. He can tell us directly by means of statements made by wholly
reliable characters (1.24; 3.11; 5.7; 15.39); he can select stories about
miraculous feats in which Jesus is seen to be acting like God (4.35-5.43;
6.35-56, etc.); and he can emphasize Jesus' identity by setting it in sharp
contrast to the infidelity and misunderstanding of unreliable characters
like the disciples. Let us take this last situation as an example of how the
Markan implied author shapes the reading experience of the readers.

We might begin with Mk 6.52 which not only summarizes the
disciples' failure to understand Jesus' identity, but has been seen by one
scholar as the key to interpreting the entire Gospel.[55] How do we know
that this is a piece of reliable commentary? First of all, it is what Fowler
calls a 'linking statement'; that is to say, it serves to link two separate
pericopae—in this case, the walking on the water (6.45-51) with the
feeding of the five thousand (6.35-44), to which it refers back. Secondly,
it opens with an explanatory γάρ clause; the author appears to be offering,
direct to his readers, two reasons why the disciples were so astounded at
Jesus' walking on the water: it was because they did not understand
about the loaves; and also because their hearts were hardened. It should
be added that not only is this verse an authorial explanation, but it also
embodies an 'inside view'—information about the inner thoughts and
feeling of the characters which the author shares with his readers, and to
which none of the other characters are privy.

55. Q. Quesnell, *The Mind of Mark: Interpretation and Method through the Exegesis of Mark 6:52* (Analecta Biblica, 38; Rome: Pontifical Biblical Institute, 1969).

A third point is that the information given here corresponds very closely to that found on the lips of Jesus himself in 8.17-21. Not only does this latter passage itself stand as reliable commentary on at least four counts (2, 3.e, 4, 5 in Fowler's list), but the fact that Jesus is presented by Mark as a totally reliable character confirms the truth of the information found in 8.17-21, and, by implication, also in 6.52.

What, then, do we learn from the reliable commentary presented in these verses? Most obviously, we discover that the disciples do not understand about the loaves, and we find, too, that Jesus disapproves of their failure (8.17-21). Furthermore, it is clear that one important reason for their blindness is their 'hardness of heart'—the very shortcoming which, back in 3.5, is ascribed to the hostile Jewish authorities. This appears to place the disciples closer to the authorities than to Jesus. Could it be that they, too, are 'outsiders'? Jesus' rhetoric in 8.17-21 confirms that, in one sense, that is precisely what they are. In language reminiscent of that used in 4.12, he accuses them of being deaf and blind, just like those outsiders for whom the parables appear to obstruct rather than facilitate entry into the kingdom.

Thus far, the implied author has assured us that the disciples' predicament is wholly undesirable, and that the feeding miracles provide the key to the problem. What should the reader understand about them that the disciples could not? Surely it is that with the eye of faith, the fullness of Jesus' person could be seen in them. In yet another fragment of reliable commentary (4.40-41) we are told that the disciples lacked such faith, and so could only ask, 'Who is this?' The point is that the true believer does not ask, 'How is one able to feed these men here in the desert?' (8.4), for he knows that the feeding miracles are about much more than the multiplication of loaves; they are about the inbreaking of divine activity upon the earth. As God fed the wilderness generation with manna (Exod. 16), so now in *this* wilderness, his presence is again testified—this time through his Son.

Now it might be that Mark could have made this point in other ways, but by using the faithlessness and incomprehension of the disciples as a foil for the power and self-sufficiency of Jesus' activity, he ensures that Jesus' true identity is announced all the more effectively.

As final confirmation that the implied author is at work here, we might ask whether the picture we have presented is consistent, and we have to conclude that it is. We find that all the nature miracles (4.35-41; 6.35-44, 45-51; 8.1-10) are characterized by the theme of the disciples' failure to perceive Jesus' messianic identity—a theme which is later developed (after Peter's confession, 8.27-30) along the lines of their failure to understand the nature of that identity.

b. *Who Was/Is the Reader of Mark?*

When we enquire about the 'reader' of Mark, we must be clear as to which reader we mean. Are we referring to the real reader or to the implied reader? And if the real reader, do we have in view the community for whom Mark was writing, or some later community or individual—the contemporary reader, perhaps? It is important that we do distinguish between them, since different audiences may interact with the text in different ways, depending on the presuppositions they bring to it.

i) *The First Real Readers/Hearers.* As we have already suggested, the initial Markan community probably consisted of listeners rather than readers. They may well have gathered to hear a complete oral performance or recitation of the gospel. We have little more idea about who these people were than we have about the author's identity. Gleaning what we can from the text, it would appear that some of them were Gentiles. Mark feels it necessary to translate his Aramaic phrases into Greek (3.17; 5.41; 7.11, 34; 10.46; 14.36; 15.22, 34), and to explain Jewish customs and ideas (3.22; 7.2, 3-4; 12.18, 42; 14.12; 15.32, 42); and the possibility of women initiating divorce seems to have been in evidence (10.12). On the other hand, much of the Gospel seems to reflect a Jewishness that perhaps goes beyond the bare requirements of the narrative. The controversy stories, especially, often betray evidence of rabbinic-style debate which would have been familiar to a Jewish audience. Perhaps all this points towards a mixed community of Christians, which there certainly would have been in a large metropolis like Rome, the traditional proclivity of the gospel.

ii) *The Modern Real Reader.* The mechanics of reading Mark's Gospel today are very different from the methods employed by the first readers/ hearers. Reading as done by the contemporary, print-conscious community is an altogether more reflective business than it was in Mark's church. Speaking specifically of the reader's creation of meaning in a text, Iser comments,

> We look forward, we look back, we decide, we change our decisions, we
> form expectations, we are shocked by their non-fulfillment, we question,
> we muse, we accept, we reject: this is the dynamic process of recreation.[56]

While the first-time listener could certainly have engaged in some of
these activities, the reflectiveness inherent in others ('musing', for
instance) is a quality or luxury which only the print-conscious reader can
afford. Listening is a much more immediate activity than reading, and
one can only reflect on what is retained by the memory—hence the
various mnemonic devices such as chiasm, intercalation, parataxis, duality,
and so on, which tend to characterize oral literature. The printed text, on
the other hand, invites a wholly reflective approach. We do not have to
proceed from beginning to end in one breath, as it were. We can pause
for reflection; we can jump ahead to the end, then read the intervening
material in the light of that; or we can turn back to earlier passages to
see what bearing they may have on the current material, and, indeed,
what bearing the current material may have on them. We are perhaps
more aware than the ancient oral communities of the extent to which
the various passages within a text impinge upon and interpret each
other, although the means for such mutual interpretation are inherent in
oral literature, too. Interpretation of any kind, of course, is dependent
upon the intercourse between implied author and implied reader, so we
need now to consider the latter of these as applied particularly to Mark's
Gospel.

iii) *The Implied Reader.* Before we attempt to discover how the implied
reader operates, we need to address a few preliminaries involving the
terminology used, and the dynamics of the reading process.

We noted earlier that most literary critics—though not all—find it
helpful to distinguish between the implied reader (the ideal reader
envisioned in the text) and the narratee (the intratextual entity to which
the narrator addresses his story). In Mark's Gospel narrator and narratee
are, for all practical purposes, identical with the implied author and
implied reader respectively, and need not be considered separately from
them. There is one overt reference to the narratee ('the reader' in 13.14),
but otherwise the narratee is covert throughout. The same applies to the
narratee's counterpart, the first-order narrator, although there are, of
course, second-order narrators within the story, notably Jesus himself.

---

56. Iser, 'Reading Process', p. 293.

Having established this terminological point, it should next be ascertained what it is that the reader actually does when he or she reads. According to Fowler, the reader participates in a dynamic, temporal event:

> If our concern is no longer with the text *per se*, but the experience of reading the text, and if the reading experience is not static but dynamic and not spatial but temporal, then meaning can no longer be described in terms of content. We must speak not in terms of the meaning of the text *per se*, but of the meaning of the reading experience, and in dynamic, temporal terms.[57]

The implication of this statement is that there is no objective meaning arising from the text; readers must make their own meaning out of their personal experience of reading it, though the text is still the controlling factor:

> We could say that the Gospel is not so much designed to construct its own world as it is designed to construct its own reader; it is not designed so much to say something about its implied world as it is to do something to its implied reader; the narrative does not strive to convey meaning as referential content as much as it strives to achieve communion with its audience by means of a forceful event that takes place through time.[58]

Petersen, too, acknowledges the temporality of the reading process, and speaks of the interaction between reader and text as an experience in which a new world is created:

> While the works we create from texts are subjective in the sense of being mental phenomena, and are therefore *in us*, it is also and more importantly true that while reading *we are in the world of our works*. In order to appreciate this seeming paradox, it is necessary to remember the temporal, processual nature of the reading experience. Precisely because reading is processual, moving from the beginning of the text to its end, we not only gradually build up a narrative world from the text we are processing, but we also progressively create that world from within it. While reading, we build up a world around us. For this reason, a text's narrative world has its primary reality as an imaginatively visual phenomenon experienced during the process of reading...Reader-response criticism must therefore take into account not only the relationship between readers and texts, but also the relationship between readers and the worlds they create from texts.[59]

---

57. Fowler, *Let the Reader Understand*, p. 47.
58. Fowler, *Let the Reader Understand*, p. 57.
59. Petersen, 'Reader', pp. 42-43.

The reader, then, is urged to enter the narrative world of the text and become part of it. This, it is suspected, is what the first recipients did. Theirs was a dynamic aural experience which no doubt made a deep impression on them. The impact would hardly have been the less for their having known the story-line as kerygma, for Mark's presentation would have been startlingly new to them—not simply a presentation of the bare facts, but theology through story. Perhaps this is an example which the modern reader should be exhorted to follow. After all, Mark himself is acutely time-conscious. Using his favourite term, εὐθύς, he propels the story along with great gusto in the early chapters, later reduces speed so that events begin to happen in 'days', and then in 'hours', until finally, with the cry of dereliction (15.34), time seems, momentarily, to stand still. The point about this is that the author clearly wants his readers to keep time with the story. Much is lost when, as in the contemporary church, we dismantle the text in order to facilitate lectionary reading, Sunday by Sunday. Perhaps, as Alex McKeown seems to have been aware,[60] Mark's Gospel, while having the potential to surprise, outrage, inspire, and incite to action, will be unable to do so effectively until the practice of holistic reading is rehabilitated.

Another issue which cannot be taken lightly is the distinction between what Moore calls 'virginal' and 'experienced' readers.[61] A virginal reader/hearer is one who comes to the story for the first time. There must always be a first time, but whereas for the original audience this first time probably comprised a complete recitation, as surely intended by the author, for the modern, print-conscious reader, the experience is normally diffused over months, or even years. Be that as it may, the experience of a virginal reader is different from that of the experienced reader, that is, one who is engaging the text for a second or subsequent time. Once the narrative is known, readers' expectations begin to change; they know how the story ends, and are able to read it a second time in the light of that knowledge.

To see how this phenomenon works out in practice, let us take Mk 8.22-26, the healing of the blind man at Bethsaida, as an example. What might a virginal reader make of this text? Might he or she not be mystified at Jesus' failure to heal the blind man instantly? Perhaps the

---

60. On McKeown's one-man 'performance' of the Gospel according to Mark, see A. Stock, *Call to Discipleship: A Literary Study of Mark's Gospel* (Wilmington, DE: Michael Glazier, 1982), p. 1.

61. Moore, *Literary Criticism and the Gospels*, pp. 78-81.

suppliant does not have the requisite faith? But as the reader reads on, things may begin to fall into place. The next pericope (8.27-33), in which Peter, like the blind man, gains partial 'sight', may suggest that 8.22-26 is intended as a paradigm for that story. Or perhaps, on reaching the healing of blind Bartimaeus (10.46-52), the reader recalls the earlier healing, and is thereby encouraged to contrast the intervening material (8.27-10.45) with it. Thus, the first-time reading is an adventure of discovery, and will have a different kind of impact from that of a subsequent reading.

A second reading of Mark will undoubtedly be transformed by a knowledge of the Passion and empty tomb scenes, and will be in a state of perpetual anticipation. References from the early chapters, such as 2.20 and 3.6, will be perceived for what they are—foreshadowings of Jesus' final days in Jerusalem; and a second-time reader of 8.22-26 can hardly fail to notice, in this new light, its metaphorical power. The half-seeing blind man anticipates the half-seeing Peter, so surely his restoration to full sight suggests that Peter, too, will see clearly—some day.

Now we come to the question of how the implied reader operates within the text. We saw earlier that the implied author is evident in various ways—in direct authorial comments or asides, in seam and summary passages, in explanatory clauses, and in various rhetorical devices like chiasm, intercalation, repetition and so forth. But equally, the implied reader, too, must be active in the creation of meaning. How is this activity set in motion? Vorster argues that if the real reader is to create a 'second self' in the text, he or she must take full account of its many narrative components:

> All the narrative features such as plot, characterization, point of view, narrative commentary, order of narration, and time and space give clues to the actual reader in his or her construction of an image of the implied reader.[62]

Sound advice, perhaps—but does it go far enough? Is not the reader left wondering just what it is about these features that are supposed to be noticed? And does not Vorster neglect—temporarily, at least—the author's rôle in creating the implied reader? In any event, Fowler seems to me to have seized upon the implications of Vorster's insight and drawn some promising conclusions.[63] By taking full account of the various

62. Vorster, 'Reader', p. 32.
63. Fowler, 'Reader-Response Criticism', pp. 50-83.

metaphors used by reader-response critics of the reading process, we can gain some insight into what readers actually do when they participate in creating a reader in the text. Five metaphors are examined in detail:

1.   *'Looking forward'/'looking back'*. As we proceed through the text, we are continually reviewing and anticipating—in a phrase, we are treading the hermeneutic circle; for our reading at any given moment is always conditioned by that part of the text which has preceded it, and we often have to adjust our opinions and expectations in the light of what we have already read. Equally, however, passages which we encounter later on in the work may cause us to revise our interpretation or under-standing of earlier sections. 'We re-view and pre-view con-stantly to make as much sense of our experience as possible at each individual moment.'[64] Our expectations, therefore, are dynamic, moving apace with the reading process which carries us from beginning to end of a text.

This oscillating process is readily apparent in Mark's Gospel. 'Immediately' (εὐθύς) is the stock word for carrying the action forward, and it is not without significance that it occurs most intensively in the first chapter of the gospel (11 times) where Mark has the task of getting his story off the ground, and the bulk of the plot lies ahead.

The counterpart of εὐθύς is 'again' (πάλιν). It was once felt that Mark used this word in a rather arbitrary fashion, rather as many people nowadays intersperse their speech with 'you know'. More recently, however, it has been established on the basis of work done by Peabody[65] and others that each instance of πάλιν tends to have a specific referent which encourages the reader to connect the content or ideas of two pericopae, which are often at some distance from each other in the text. Let us briefly consider two examples:

Mark 3.1 begins, 'And again he entered a synagogue' (καὶ εἰσῆλθεν πάλιν εἰς συναγωγήν). This urges the question, When did Jesus enter a synagogue previously? There are two possible candidates: 1.21, where Jesus enters the synagogue at

---

64. Fowler, *Let the Reader Understand*, p. 45.
65. D. Peabody, *Mark as Composer* (Macon, GA: Mercer University Press, 1987).

Capernaum; and 1.39, where he undertakes a tour of the synagogues throughout Galilee. Once we have established the
referent of 3.1a, we will be tempted to ask what happened there,
and in the present case, it does not matter which of the two
alternatives is the intended referent, because the answer is the
same: Jesus taught and exorcised demons. Now, having 'looked
back', the reader is able to 'look forward' with some relish,
knowing that when Jesus enters a synagogue things start to
happen. And, in engaging with the text of 3.1-6, the reader is
not disappointed. The reader gets that same 'teaching with
authority' that is found in 1.21-28, and bears witness to another
healing.

Another point at which πάλιν is of considerable importance is 8.1: 'In those days again when there was a large
crowd, and they had nothing to eat...' (ἐν ἐκείναις ταῖς
ἡμέραις πάλιν πολλοῦ ὄντος καὶ ἐχόντων τί φάγεσιν...).
At once, the πάλιν leads us to recall a previous situation similar
to this one, and our minds rest on the feeding of the five
thousand. We remember what happened then, and how Jesus
fed people rather as God fed the wilderness generation, so that
even before Jesus has done anything in 8.1-10, we are expectant;
and the disciples' question in 8.4, 'How can one feed these
men with bread here in the desert?' seems little short of
incredible—which, of course, is precisely the response which
Mark wants to draw from his readers.

2.   *'Filling gaps'.* One of the reader's most important activities is
to apply imagination to filling in the gaps left by the author. In
this way he or she fully participates in the making of the text.
Mark leaves many gaps in his story, and in many cases
Matthew and Luke show how, as the first interpreters of Mark,
they dealt with this challenge. Fowler discusses several examples
of this phenomenon in Mark;[66] it will suffice for us to take just
one. In 3.6 the Pharisees and Herodians conspire to destroy
Jesus; then, in 3.7, he withdraws to the Sea of Galilee. The
reader is left to speculate why. Matthew's interpretation of this
event makes the necessary inference: Jesus became aware of
the plot, and decided to make himself scarce (Mt. 12.15).

66. Fowler, 'Reader-Response Criticism', pp. 61-65.

3. *'Reconstruction'*. As I shall be dealing with this factor in my chapter on irony, I need mention it only briefly at this point. Fowler bases his discussion on Booth's hypothesis[67] that the reader arrives at an understanding of the author's stable ironic meaning via a four-step progression. The reader rejects the surface meaning, enquires into possible alternative interpretations, makes a judgment about what the author really believes, and finally on this basis reconstructs the ironic meaning so that he or she can stand with the author on a stable platform of meaning. Thus, when the chief priests and scribes address Jesus on the cross as 'the Christ, the King of Israel' (15.32), we reject their surface meaning because their previous behaviour in the narrative has suggested that they are bitter opponents of Jesus. Surely, then, they cannot mean what they say. We then consider what the author believes, and we know from the reliable commentary in the Gospel not only that he believes that Jesus really *is* the Christ, but also that the chief priests and scribes are enemies of Jesus. From this information we can be confident of the ironic meaning: the opponents are blissfully unaware that in using the terms 'Christ' and 'King of Israel' to mock Jesus ('Of course he is not the Christ!') they are actually acclaiming his true identity—an identity which author and reader are together agreed upon.

4. *'The self-consuming artifact'*. This metaphor is taken from a book of that title by Stanley Fish.[68] Its chief thesis is that the intercourse between text and reader comprises a knitting together and subsequent unravelling of the textual fabric. The raw material is without meaning until touched by the reader, but once the reader has passed by, it begins to self-destruct so that the meaning afforded by that particular interaction can never be reconstructed. Fowler, in his commentary on this concept, uses the illustration of a railway crew who tear up the track which the train has passed over, and re-lay it in front of the train so that the journey can continue. He adds:

67. Booth, *Rhetoric of Irony*, pp. 10-14.
68. S. Fish, *Self-Consuming Artifacts: The Experience of Seventeenth-Century Literature* (Berkeley: University of California Press, 1972).

>...once the present moment is past we may never be in this
>particular place...ever again. Indeed, subsequent reading
>experience may give us such insight and understanding that
>we may never be able to retrace our steps in exactly the same
>way again, even if we should happen to re-read the text.[69]

Fowler applies this principle to Mk 4.11-13. In 4.11 the
secret of the kingdom of God is given to the disciples as
opposed to the outsiders for whom everything is in parables.
The reader, since he or she is not one of the Twelve, must
therefore consider him or herself to be an outsider. But then, in
4.13, there is a reversal: here, it is clear that the disciples do *not*
understand, and the reader now feels him or herself to be at an
advantage over the disciples; in fact, the reader finds that he or
she has taken their place as a privileged insider. Thus, we can see
how the track is laid (the disciples are insiders) only to be dis-
mantled and relaid, thereby realigning the reader's understanding (since now, the rôles of the reader and the disciples
have been reversed; those on the outside are now on the inside,
and vice versa).

5. *'The resisting reader'*. The final metaphor which Fowler dis-
    cusses is drawn from a book by Judith Fetterley.[70] In her view,
    American literature is traditionally written for men, and the
    female characters in it are victimized. The reader, including the
    female reader, is expected to accept this state of affairs as the
    status quo. Fetterley, therefore, pleads for a principle of
    'resisting reading' which rejects what she calls the 'sexism and
    misogyny' found in such works, and appeals for a new kind of
    reading—one which takes place through feminist eyes.

    In applying this metaphor to the Bible, Fowler broadens its
    appeal by suggesting that it might be applied not only to
    feminism, but to numerous other issues as well, including war,
    racism, economic justice, religious bigotry and the environment.
    He sees Matthew as the resisting reader of Mark, and discusses
    his interpretation of Mk 16.1-8 (cf. Mt. 27.62-28.20) as an
    example.[71] There is no space here to consider this fully, and in

69. Fowler, *Let the Reader Understand*, p. 46.
70. J. Fetterley, *The Resisting Reader: A Feminist Approach to American
Fiction* (Bloomington: Indiana University Press, 1978).
71. Fowler, 'Reader-Response Criticism', pp. 75-81.

any case, Fowler has already done it most adequately; but perhaps we can allow ourselves a brief comment on one nugget of the story as an instance of how resisting reading operates.

In Mk 16.8 the Gospel ends (assuming that Mark intended it to end here) with the observation that the women fled from the tomb in terror. The last words are, 'And they said nothing to anyone, for they were afraid.' And the cause of their fear? They had seen a 'young man' (νεανίσκος) who had told them that Jesus was not in the tomb, and to tell his disciples that he would be going before them into Galilee. Rather embarrassingly for the church, these women, who were supposed to have been close to Jesus, disobeyed the young man's command so that, as far as the text is concerned, the disciples never receive the message to go to Galilee. Matthew, however, sees the awkwardness of this, and so resists the original reading. He turns the young man into an angel who reminds the women that Jesus predicted his own resurrection, and they, though still afraid, proclaim with joy what they have heard, thereby fulfilling the angel's command. Thus, what for Mark is an event surrounded by fear and mystery is resisted by Matthew, and turned instead into one in which the theme-words are joy and proclamation (Mt. 28.1-8).

c. *What Is the Text of Mark?*

Several times to date, I have mentioned 'the text' as the catalyst through which author and reader make meaning. We should not, however, think of the text as a static object. In the case of Mark (and all ancient texts) it is an entity which has been composed out of thousands of variant readings. Textual critics, of course, must eventually arrive at some consensus about which readings are most likely to have been the original, and must develop a working text from that, but a cursory glance at the apparatus in any Greek Testament will indicate the wealth of alternatives which exist. It certainly cannot be said that there is one definitive edition of the Greek text of Mark. We need to bear this in mind in our reading of this Gospel since certain textual variants might well affect our perception of meaning. It is a matter of some importance, for instance, as to whether the opening words of Mark are, 'The beginning of the gospel of Jesus Christ' (with manuscripts ℵ*Θ 28 pc armPtgeoPtIr Or Bas Vict HierPt) or, 'The beginning of the gospel of Jesus Christ, *Son of*

God' (with manuscripts ABDW pc f¹f¹³565 700 pm latt co). This
constant fluidity in the text is something that all scholars—historical- and
literary-critics alike—must learn to live with.

d. *What Is the Rhetoric of Mark?*

In any full discussion of narrative criticism, rhetorical criticism will
inevitably be included, for these methods have certain factors in
common. In particular, they are both designed to examine how the
author gets the message across. By considering the plot, setting, characterization, points of view and irony in a work, the narrative-critic seeks
to determine how these factors make an impact on the 'reader'. The
final two, in fact, are particularly rhetorical in character since they are
concerned not with the objective content of the story, but with its
discourse—how the story is told. Irony, for instance, is one way of
telling. It is generally recognized that its use tends to drive home the
author's point more effectively than a simple disclosure, so it has long
been of interest to discover and understand the underlying mechanics of
the device.

About rhetorical criticism, certain distinctions in meaning should be
noted. The rhetorical instruction manuals composed by classical authors
like Aristotle, Cicero, Quintilian and others dealt with the rhetoric of
persuasion which was used primarily in the law-courts, and dealt with
the various stages and modes of delivery necessary for the making of an
effective speech.[72] The classicist, George Kennedy pioneered the attempt
to apply these principles to the New Testament.[73] Since then, many
biblical scholars have followed suit, focusing attention largely on the
Pauline and other epistles, since they accord more closely with rhetorical
speech-making techniques than does the narrative material in the Gospels.

Narrative rhetoric, however, is rather different from the traditional
form. It tends to focus on the pattern and structure of the narrative, and
seeks to examine the possible reasons for arranging it in one particular
way rather than another. It also takes account of the strategic importance
of key-words and phrases, repetition and so on. Joanna Dewey, whose

---

72. Aristotle, *Ars Rhetorica*; Cicero, *de Oratore*; Quintilian, *Institutio Oratoria*.
Another important source, the *Rhetorica ad Herennium*, once thought to be the work
of Cicero, is now generally no longer attributed to him. All these works can be found
in translation in the Loeb Classical Library series.

73. G.A. Kennedy, *New Testament Interpretation through Rhetorical Criticism*
(Chapel Hill: University of North Carolina Press, 1984).

seminal work on narrative rhetoric (or literary rhetoric, as she terms it) in Mark appeared in 1980,[74] lists several literary techniques which Mark uses to help deliver his theological message, including inclusio (the repetition of a word or phrase at the beginning and end of a pericope or unit), hook words (words which are repeated in two adjoining pericopae), key words (which are used repeatedly as a kind of *leitmotiv*), foreshadowing/retrospection, repetition and various kinds of inversion, including chiasm and intercalation.[75] It will be noticed that some of these devices are precisely what readers are looking for as clues to interpreting the text. The foreshadowing/retrospection element, for instance, assists the reader in the act of 'looking forward'/'looking back', which phenomenologists like Iser claim is so important to an adequate creation of the text in/by the reader.

It is impossible in the space available here to demonstrate how Mark uses these various devices. Suffice it to say that in 2.1–3.6 (which Dewey chooses for study) alone, they are all to be found more or less frequently, and many other narrative rhetorical studies have been produced during the past decade which have collectively dealt with virtually every section of the Gospel.

Whatever distinctions we may make between narrative- and rhetorical-criticism, there is a considerable degree of overlap too. Both come firmly under the aegis of literary criticism, and both seek to analyse the text with a view to discovering the principles and techniques at work behind its rhetorical power. So what about the differences? One obvious distinction is that rhetorical criticism is more limited in its scope than narrative criticism. Whereas the first seems to be restricted to a concern for narrative structure, pattern and arrangement, the latter takes account of all narrative components. Further, narrative criticism is very much a text-centred theory. As Powell has observed, the only reader with whom the method is much concerned is the *implied* reader.[76] Rhetorical criticism, on the other hand, tends to take greater account of the flesh-and-blood audience on whom the rhetoric is intended to have an impact. Even though this point may be particularly applicable to traditional classical rhetoric, it is still relevant to narrative rhetoric to some extent.

I conclude that, while I am not engaged in the kind of detailed

74. J. Dewey, *Markan Public Debate: Literary Technique, Concentric Structure and Theology in Mark 2:1-3:6* (SBLDS, 48; Chico, CA: Scholars Press, 1980).

75. Dewey, *Markan Public Debate*, pp. 31-34.

76. Powell, *What is Narrative Criticism?*, p. 15.

rhetorical inquiry initiated by Dewey, rhetorical criticism cannot be divorced from narrative-critical study, and due attention will be paid to it as occasion arises, though not in any formal sense.

5. *Summary*

The present chapter has been concerned to lay the foundation for my discussion as a whole by tracing the historical development of narrative-criticism, defining literary-critical method, and clarifying terminology. Four chief issues were examined:

1. A broad distinction was made between the older-established forms of literary-criticism (namely, source-, form- and redaction-criticism) and the newer varieties (chiefly rhetorical-, reader-response- and narrative criticism). I also discussed the relationship between reader-response and narrative-criticism, particularly the question as to whether the latter is merely a specialized form of the other.

2. The next part of the chapter was devoted to defining the terminology used by reader-response critics. Taking Seymour Chatman's seminal work as the starting-point, I was able to distinguish between real authors and readers on the one hand, and implied authors and readers on the other. I also defined the terms 'narrator' and 'narratee', noticing that, like the implied author, these are not flesh-and-blood figures, but operate entirely within the text.

3. I next touched upon the orality-literacy question, and marshalled evidence in favour of the possibility that Mark's first 'readers' were listeners. This is an important question, since the transition from orality to literacy almost certainly affected the way in which people understood and interpreted the Gospel. However, the concern of the narrative-critic is with the text as it stands in its final written form rather than with its oral development. The orality-literacy issue is a complex one, and has been ably treated by W.H. Kelber (*The Oral and the Written Gospel*), and others.

4. In the final part of the chapter, I applied the results of my theoretical study to the text of Mark. It would be interesting, if not particularly instructive, to know who the flesh-and-blood author of the Gospel was,[77] but for the literary-critic it is far more important to identify the activity of the *implied* author, and, using R.M. Fowler's *Loaves and*

---

77. On this issue see now C.C. Black, *Mark: Images of an Apostolic Interpreter* (Columbia: University of South Carolina Press, 1994).

Fishes, I discovered that there is an abundance of such evidence in Mark. Mark's reliable commentary represents a reaching out to the reader, and provides the reader with a key to the interpretation of the narrative. The reader invites much the same remarks we have made above: it would be of interest to know who Mark's real readers were, but as far as the literary-critic is concerned, it is a more vital task to determine the nature and activity of the *implied* reader; it is the experience of reading the text rather than who reads it which is all-important.

Chapter 2

MARK'S GOSPEL: THE CHARACTERS

1. *Markan Characterization*

Mark's Gospel is a Gospel of action. Primarily, our author is interested in what God is *doing* through Jesus Christ, and the characters are there to serve that aim. On the other hand, what would a narrative be without characters? Certainly, those who occupy the Markan stage are sharply drawn and contrasted with one another, and we shall need to consider them—Jesus, the disciples, the opponents, the minors—as characters in their own right. Before doing that, however, I must pause to take account of some important theoretical and methodological points about characterization in general.

First, what is a 'character'?[1] Is he or she a flesh-and-blood individual, or a mere figment of the text? In a work of fiction, no character can be *identical* with an actual person, even if based on one. It is well-known that the Miriam Leivers of D.H. Lawrence's *Sons and Lovers* is modelled on the real Jessie Chambers who recognized herself in the novel, much to her chagrin, without difficulty. But Miriam Leivers is not thereby Jessie Chambers, even though she is perhaps an imitation of her—an imitation of reality, that is. With regard to fiction, then, this

---

1. On characterization in literature generally, see Chatman, *Story and Discourse*, pp. 107-38; R. Scholes and R. Kellogg, *The Nature of Narrative* (London: Oxford University Press, 1966), pp. 106-206; E.M. Forster, *Aspects of the Novel* (Harmondsworth: Penguin, 1962 [1927]), pp. 54-84; Rimmon-Kenan, *Narrative Fiction*, pp. 29-42, 59-70. On characterization in Mark's Gospel, see Rhoads and Michie, *Mark as Story*, pp. 101-36, 154-58; Kingsbury, *Conflict in Mark*; idem, 'The Religious Authorities in the Gospel of Mark', *NTS* 36 (1990), pp. 42-65; R. Tannehill, 'The Gospel of Mark as Narrative Christology', *Semeia* 16 (1979), pp. 57-92; idem, 'The Disciples in Mark: The Function of a Narrative Role', *JR* 57 (1977), pp. 386-405; E.S. Malbon, 'The Jewish Leaders in the Gospel of Mark: A Literary Study of Marcan Characterization', *JBL* 108 (1989), pp. 259-81.

much is clear, although precisely how a character functions in a narrative—mimetically (as a representation of reality) or semiotically (as symbols of meaning in the text)—has long been a matter for debate. But, of course, Mark's Gospel is *not* fictitious—not, at least, in the manner of a novel. All the characters, we assume, are historically authentic. Few people seriously doubt that Jesus lived. Are we, then, to take it that the Jesus of Mark's Gospel is the Jesus of history? Although we might be tempted to answer in the affirmative, I think we must make a similar distinction in this case as we have just made between Miriam Leivers and Jessie Chambers. Undoubtedly, the Jesus of history serves as a model for Mark's characterization. Many, if not all, the incidents reported will, in essentials, have been real events in which the real Jesus participated; but the Markan Jesus is nevertheless a character who serves the interests of the plot; he is, for example, taken out of real time and relocated in plotted time[2]—the time-sequence of the narrative—and his actions not only conform to the structure of the plot, but disclose certain traits of his narrative character. In that sense, then, Jesus is a victim of the story and not, in Mark's hands, the flesh-and-blood individual of whom we know less than perhaps we would like to think.

The presence of characters implies the presence of character traits. Every action involves some kind of behaviour; every statement, a preceding thought. And these disclose something about the character of the actor or speaker. But, to deal with the issue systematically, what means of revealing character traits does an author have at his disposal?

1. There is the 'direct disclosure' alternative in which a reliable narrator or character expresses the trait directly. Thus, in Mk 1.41,[3] and again in 10.14, we are told by the omniscient author that Jesus was angry or indignant.

2. There is the 'indirect presentation' option in which character traits are revealed indirectly by means of some action or statement of one of the characters. This may occur in one of several ways.

First, a particular action may be revealing. When Jesus drives the traders out of the Temple and overturns their furniture (11.15), he is

2. On plotted time in Mark, see N.R. Petersen, 'Story Time and Plotted Time in Mark's Narrative', in his *Literary Criticism for New Testament Critics* (Philadelphia: Fortress Press, 1978), pp. 49-80.

3. Jesus' emotional state in Mk 1.41 depends on the particular reading we accept. According to certain Western manuscripts he was 'moved with anger' (ὀργισθείς), but the majority reading is 'moved with pity' (σπλαγχνισθείς).

disclosing a good deal about himself—his sense of justice and religious sincerity, for instance, as well as something earlier expressed directly by the reliable narrator, his anger. We understand, therefore, that this particular trait, like many others, is disclosed by Mark in two principal ways—telling and showing.[4]

Secondly, a character's speech, whether self-referential or not, may betray certain traits. A celebrated example among the many that could be taken from Mark is the request of James and John to have positions of priority in the kingdom of God (10.37) by which they show their lack of understanding—a significant trait in the disciples as a whole.

Thirdly, the description of a person's physical appearance may reflect a facet of character. On the Mount of Transfiguration, Jesus' appearance is dramatically transformed (9.3), revealing something of his divine glory: to use an Homeric epithet, we are led to suppose that Jesus is 'god-like'.

Fourthly, environment, too, may be a useful indicator of character. Rooms, houses, streets, towns, landscapes—all these may be revealing in this way.[5] Perhaps this is less evident in Mark's Gospel than in the modern novel; nevertheless, setting is all-important there. 'In the house', for instance, is a phrase used by Mark when he wants to portray Jesus as an intimate teacher (7.17; 9.33; 10.10), while synagogue and Temple are frequently the places where the opponents display their negative characteristics.

3. According to Rimmon-Kenan,[6] once a character trait has been established by the various methods described above, it is possible to reinforce it by analogy; an analogous feature simply confirms what has already been affirmed by other means. One such kind of reinforcement, it is claimed, may be the naming of the characters. A name may be suggestive of a character trait in a number of ways—visually, acoustically, morphologically and so on. The novels of Dickens are rich in such examples, as are allegories like Bunyan's *Pilgrim's Progress*. The principle can certainly be applied to Mark, though perhaps not quite in line with Rimmon-Kenan's expectations. James and John receive the name Boanerges, 'sons of thunder' (3.17), which aptly reflects their

4.   On 'telling' and 'showing' in narrative, see W.C. Booth, *The Rhetoric of Fiction* (Harmondsworth: Penguin, 2nd edn, 1983), pp. 3-16.

5.   In Brontë's *Wuthering Heights*, for example, the traits of the main characters, Cathy and Heathcliffe, are emphasised by the wild, moorland setting of the novel.

6.   Rimmon-Kenan, *Narrative Fiction*, pp. 67-70.

impetuous nature (9.38-41; 10.35-41), and because it is Jesus, the one totally reliable character in the gospel, who bestows the name, we are expected to accept that it serves as an accurate indicator of a character trait of the bearers. Simon's nickname, Peter, is tinged with irony. Petros, 'Rocky', conjures up visions of resolution and reliability, the very qualities which are found to be lacking when they are most required (14.37-42, 50, 66-72).[7]

Where Mark departs from the principle as laid down by Rimmon-Kenan is in his use of names not so much to reinforce character traits as to anticipate them. The traits suggested by the conferring of nicknames on the leading disciples are not evident before these names have been given, so 'Peter' and 'Boanerges' serve to foreshadow the development of those traits in the second half of the Gospel.

Having now described the various methods of revealing character traits, it will be as well at this point to insert an important caveat: the mere disclosure of some act or thought or reaction is not of itself sufficient evidence for a character *trait*. To return for a moment to the incident involving James and John, the one moment of impetuosity in 10.37 would not alone be enough to testify to an acknowledged *characteristic* of the brothers; it is what we learn throughout the narrative as a whole, by a combination of the means under discussion here, that persuades us to accept their behaviour as evidence of a trait.

To proceed now to another matter, it may be said that the number and diversity of character traits may differ enormously from one character to another. Those bearing few and predictable traits have been labelled 'flat' characters, while those with a large number of contrasting ones are said to be 'round'.[8] Who are the flat characters in Mark? We might nominate the minor actors, but most of them make such fleeting appearances that they hardly qualify for assessment at all. Rhoads[9] has attempted to group them as one corporate character, arguing that they share similar traits—a childlike faith, capacity for sacrifice, and a disregard for personal status and power. In that case flatness would be

7.   Indeed, in Mk 14.37, when Peter falls asleep in Gethsemane, despite his charge to keep watch, Jesus reverts to using his original name, Simon, as if his refusal to use the nickname Peter is a comment on the bearer's failure to live up to what the name implies.

8.   See Forster, *Aspects of the Novel*, pp. 73-81.

9.   D. Rhoads, 'Narrative Criticism and the Gospel of Mark', *JAAR* 50 (1982), pp. 411-34 (419).

an appropriate attribute. Nevertheless, it is doubtful that even these traits can legitimately be ascribed to every minor character. Simon of Cyrene (15.21), for instance, who is compelled to carry Jesus' cross, shows no sign of faith or willingness for sacrifice, and we know nothing of his attitude towards status and power. The same may be said of the young man who flees naked from the scene of the arrest (14.51-52). The purpose of the minor characters, in fact, is not to possess traits of their own so much as to serve as foils or vehicles of action for the more significant characters. Thus, the handicapped exist to make possible Jesus' divinely appointed healing ministry. Healing is a significant sign of the in-breaking of the Kingdom which would not be possible if there were no people to be healed. Then there are people like the poor widow (12.41-44) whose religious sincerity exposes the religious hypocrisy of the scribes (12.38-40).

Among the more significant characters who can legitimately be described as 'flat' are the opponents. Although, in reality, these are composed of various independent groups—the scribes, Pharisees, Herodians, Sadducees and so on—they clearly play a concerted rôle in the narrative, and the scribes seem to serve as a cohesive force, sometimes appearing independently, sometimes in association with other groups. It is true that, like the more rounded characters, the opponents possess several traits—malice, hypocrisy, cunning, desire for prestige, and fear, to mention just a few—but the significant point is that they are all negative and therefore predictable reactions to the protagonist. Apart from the one scribe in 12.28-34 whose view of Jesus is more favourable, there are no surprises, and so the opponents remain essentially flat characters throughout.

Who, then, are the 'round' figures? We are tempted to think at once of Jesus, yet Rhoads would demur here: 'Jesus is not a round character in the sense of having conflicting or changing traits...'[10] Nevertheless, his many attributes, while not contradictory, are widely divergent: compassion and anger, for instance, are not easily married. Moreover, according to Forster, the litmus test of a round character is 'whether it is capable of surprising in a convincing way. If it never surprises, it is flat.'[11] Yet Jesus does surprise because, as Rhoads himself declares, he thinks the things of God rather than of men.[12] Surely, given the general

10. Rhoads, 'Narrative Criticism', p. 418.
11. Forster, *Aspects of the Novel*, p. 81.
12. Rhoads, 'Narrative Criticism', p. 416; also Kingsbury, *Conflict in Mark*, p. 2, *passim*.

impression that the parables are intended to reveal divine truths, it is utterly astounding to be told in 4.11-12 that their purpose is to conceal. And how frequently does the Markan Jesus astonish his fellow characters by word and deed! But, these are the 'things of God', not the 'things of humans'. On Forster's criterion of surprise, then, Jesus is surely a much rounder character than Rhoads would allow.

More rounded still, however, are the disciples. Apart from exhibiting a large number of character traits, their behaviour is inconsistent and unpredictable. Nowhere is this more clearly reflected than in the pattern of their loyalty to Jesus. For the most part, they do adhere to their Master, and even towards the end there are vehement protestations of loyalty (14.31). Immediately thereafter, however, we find evidence for the exact opposite trait: in Gethsemane the disciples cannot so much as stay awake to keep watch with Jesus (14.32-42); they all forsake him when he is arrested (14.50); and Peter denies him (14.66-72).

Thus it is that by allowing free interaction between the 'flat' and the 'round' characters, Mark makes them live in the mind of his readers.

Another important feature of characterization is the concept of 'distance'[13] (which I shall treat more thoroughly in the chapter on 'point of view'). If the author or narrator leads a reader to identify or sympathize with a particular character, we can say that there is little distance between the two. If, on the other hand, a character is presented as repellent in one way or another, then of course the reader's distance from that figure is much greater. Sympathy can be aroused and distance created by all manner of literary techniques—by means of an authorial comment or 'aside', for instance; by contrasting characters of varying reliability; or by means of an 'inside view' by which the character reveals his innermost (and thereby, most genuine) attitude to a person or situation. Let us see how this principle works in Mark.

From the very first, the author of the Gospel nails his colours to the mast: Jesus Christ is none other than the Son of God, and this is his gospel (which could mean either the gospel concerning him, or the gospel he is proclaiming). Everything the omniscient author states about him is favourable; consequently, everything that Jesus says or does is to be accepted as reliable information. The reader is invited to accept Jesus

13. On 'distance' in narrative, see Booth, *Rhetoric of Fiction*, pp. 155-59, 243-66. The issue is really quite complex, because distance may feature not simply between reader and characters, but may also involve implied author and narrator as well.

because the author accepts him; the reader is urged to cross the cultural and temporal divide in order to get close to him. So it is that the distance between reader and character is in one sense significantly reduced. Yet despite the fact that the reader can sympathize with Jesus, and is encouraged to do so, he or she can never fully identify with him: Jesus is too 'other' for that; he is divine as well as human, and as such is capable of feats far beyond the limitations of the mere mortal. The Markan Jesus is more human than any of the other Gospel portraits, and so arouses the reader's sympathy, but he can be only imperfectly imitated, and his unimpeachable ethical conduct naturally sets him well above the reader's moral frailties.

The group with which the reader most readily identifies is that of the disciples. Like the reader, they are thoroughly human, having both faults and virtues.[14] They are bearers of both reliable and unreliable information; and, most significantly, the author regulates their distance from the reader. He does this by presenting them in both a good and a bad light, but—what is more to the point—not in any arbitrary fashion. The disciples are so presented that the reader, who willingly identifies with them at the outset, is progressively distanced from them as the story proceeds; for, generally speaking, they slide from loyalty to apostasy, and the reader is thereby alienated. We shall refer in more detail to this process later; for now, we might simply mention that its purpose is to underscore the consistency and reliability of Jesus and his teaching. The righteous resolution of Jesus is emphasized all the more by the disciples' contrasting failure, and the effect of distancing them is to lead the reader from their side to that of Jesus. The disciples are introduced as loyal and obedient followers; the reader, too, imagines him or herself to occupy this position. But soon the disciples begin to lack understanding; they become detached from Jesus' mission and purpose; and at last they even lose their loyalty. In all this, a gulf emerges between character and reader. Thanks to the omniscient author, the latter does know who Jesus is, and so the need for unwavering loyalty is understood.

The relationship between reader and opponents is less ambiguous. The

14. Pertinent here is E.S. Malbon, 'Disciples/Crowds/Whoever: Markan Characters and Readers', *NovT* 28 (1986), pp. 104-30. According to this author, readers are drawn to identify with both disciples and crowds because both are characterised by both human fallibility and virtues which should be imitated. See also her 'Fallible Followers: Women and Men in the Gospel of Mark', *Semeia* 28 (1983), pp. 29-48.

opponents are virtually always set at a distance because they are nearly always in conflict with the reliable information and positive character traits offered by Jesus (12.28-34 being the one notable exception). Jesus is the protagonist; the opponents are the antagonists. As we have seen, the reader, who begins by taking the side of the disciples, is invited to respond, like them, positively to the person of Jesus, and to maintain that response, even when the disciples as narrative characters begin to fall away; so they are naturally led into the opposite camp from the religious leaders who are characterized by negativity.

One further factor to be considered is the relationship between characters and plot: which is the more dominant? In some novels the plot is relatively weak, so that the main interest rests largely with the development of the characters; in others, where the plot is much stronger, the characters tend to serve its interests. Mark, as a Gospel of action, has a very distinctive plot—one which would already be familiar to the first readers/hearers, as we shall see. Consequently, the characters are subservient to it. The disciples, for instance, are by turns loyal, obedient, obtuse, insightful, errant, disloyal. But these traits are not arranged arbitrarily: they are designed to serve the plot, so they must afford evidence of proper development, and this they do, as we have noted above.

A similar subservience to the plot can be seen in the behaviour of other characters, too. The opponents, for example, become progressively more hostile to Jesus as the action develops. Disputes over legal matters give way to tirades against Jesus' own person, and finally to a conspiracy to kill him.

We end this introductory section with a word of caution. A number of scholars have tended to credit Mark with the most astounding literary-critical awareness—a trend that has been in evidence at least since the time of M.S. Enslin.[15] Yet it should be stressed that although modern literary-critical techniques may provide us with new insights into the Gospel as narrative, they are applied to the text by the critic, and do not necessarily imply that Mark himself was conscious of them. The literary conventions of Mark's age and culture were quite independent of our own, and any suggestion of similarity, where not mediated through Aristotle, is likely to be purely coincidental.

15. M.S. Enslin, 'The Artistry of Mark', *JBL* 66 (1947), pp. 385-99.

2. *Jesus*

Jesus is, of course, the protagonist, the central character in the Gospel. As such, Mark uses him, as well as the implied author, to convey reliable commentary. In other words, we can be sure that Jesus always provides essential truths, whereas all the other main characters exhibit faults and are thus unreliable—or at least not totally reliable. The disciples, for instance, although sometimes correct (as, for instance, at 8.27-30) are frequently wrong-headed; so we can never totally rely on what they tell us. Some of the minor characters, on the other hand, *are* totally reliable in that they consistently say and do the right thing. We might mention Bartimaeus, who has faith in Jesus, correctly addresses him as Son of David and becomes a genuine follower 'on the way' (10.46-52). But figures like him play such a minor rôle that they are simply not on stage long enough to be inconsistent. Only Jesus, among the chief actors, is consistently reliable.

How, then, does Mark present his character? As we saw earlier, several avenues are open to him in this respect. In the main he chooses the following three:

1. In the guise of omniscient author, Mark himself furnishes us with information about Jesus by means of direct comments or 'asides' which are imparted to the reader but not to the characters. Frequently, this information may involve some direct assertion about who Mark thinks Jesus is (1.1; 2.10, 28) an insight into Jesus' emotional state (1.41; 3.5; 6.6, 34; 8.12) or an 'inside view' into his relationship with God (14.35-36).

2. Jesus, by his words and actions, reveals much about his own character. It would be pointless to list examples here because, essentially, his entire narrative life is the supreme example. The manner in which he comports himself, all that he does and says, testifies to his character as Mark wishes to present it. In Mark's Gospel, the words and deeds of Jesus are under the tight control of the author.

3. A third method of depicting Jesus' character is by focusing on what others say about him, or how they react to him. Perhaps this is truer of some characters than others. We tend, for instance, to recognize Jesus' charismatic qualities by observing how, time after time, people flock to him (1.37, 45; 2.2; 3.7-10, 20; 4.1; 6.31-34, 54-55; 8.1; 9.15, and so on), and by observing the hostile reaction of those who would themselves court popularity (11.18; 12.12; 14.1-2). We gather that Jesus is the Son of God by listening to what various characters say about him: certainly,

the demons (1.24; 3.11; 5.7) and the centurion (15.39) are agreed on this issue; but what makes their commentary so reliable is not only that it agrees with the author's initial statement (1.1), but that it conforms to God's own judgment (1.11; 9.7). Thus, the reader, unlike the characters, is left in no doubt as to who Jesus is.

Having determined how Jesus' character is revealed, we now proceed to consider what the main traits are. In a brief sketch such as this I cannot enter into any great detail; nevertheless, the following traits may be noted:

First, Jesus is *authoritative*. This is disclosed to us in several ways: (i) The implied author tells us so: Jesus has authority to forgive sins (2.10), and he is Lord of the Sabbath (2.28). Even if these words are taken to be Jesus' own, as traditionally they have been, their reliability would, of course, remain assured, because Jesus is never an unreliable character.[16] (ii) We are informed by certain other figures: the onlookers at Capernaum, for instance, sharply contrast the potency of Jesus' authority with that of the scribes (1.27), echoing, as they do so, what the omniscient narrator has already asserted (1.22). (iii) We can deduce this authority from Jesus' action: he has control of the wind and the waves (4.35-41; 6.45-52), and he can invest authority in the disciples (3.15; 6.7). (iv) Most intriguingly of all it is present even in what Jesus omits to tell us. Thus, when the opponents question his authority (11.27-33), he is deliberately evasive, and simply demands to know the source of John the Baptist's authority. In effect, this becomes a rhetorical question which the opponents dare not answer, but which for the reader demands an implicitly affirmative response: of course, John's authority was from God! But implicitly too, Jesus has already drawn a parallel between John and himself—simply by raising the question; so if we are to affirm that John's authority is divine, we find ourselves obliged to affirm the same of Jesus' authority.

Secondly, Jesus is *wise* and *shrewd*. The touchstone of his wisdom is God's word. By means of it he successfully argues against his opponents (2.25-26; 7.6-13; 11.17; 12.26, 36), and declares it to be the word of eternal life (10.17-19). The Scriptures, in fact, are at the centre of his dealings with others. Though he uses them to refute his opponents, he also uses them to command and confirm. Thus it is that a scribe who takes Jesus' reliable view (12.28-34) finds that he is accepted through a

---

16. On Mk 2.10, 28 as authorial comments or 'asides', see W.L. Lane, *The Gospel of Mark* (Grand Rapids: Eerdmans, 1974), pp. 98, 120; R.M. Fowler, *Loaves and Fishes*, p. 162.

compliance with God's word, not rejected because of the manner of man that he is. The wisdom of Jesus consists not in social and cultural considerations, but in his pointing beyond himself to God, and to the necessity of a human's relationship to him. Jesus, like God, looks on the heart. Similarly, although some of his pronouncements seem outrageous to the human characters of the narrative (e.g. 10.23-27), the reader is exhorted to remember that Jesus is not here concerned with the human mind, but with the mind of God.

In dealing with the deviousness of his opponents, Jesus again exhibits a kind of wisdom, though in this case it might better be described as shrewdness. We see it at work in such passages as 8.11-12; 10.2-9; 11.27-33; 12.13-17, 18-27 where the opponents, intent on catching him out, are rebuffed by Jesus' superior intellect, one that is imbued with divine perception.

Again, Jesus is *resolute*; he will not allow anyone to deflect him from his course. When Peter tries to do so (8.31-33) he is soundly rebuked; when James and John begin to conceive of positions of power in God's kingdom (10.35-37) they are corrected. Throughout the narrative, Jesus never loses sight of his Passion (2.20; 8.31; 9.12, 31; 10.33-34, 45), even in the midst of his popularity. Consequently, when the scene of the betrayal arrives, there is not a hint of surprise for Jesus, nor for the reader, as Jesus states: '…the hour has come; the Son of man is betrayed into the hands of sinners' (14.41). Because the implied author has invited the reader to walk side by side with Jesus through the narrative, there has been an awareness all along of what is to happen.

The Gospel bristles with descriptions of Jesus' *humanity*. He is angry (1.41; 10.14), compassionate (6.34; 8.2), sorrowful (14.34), exasperated (8.17-21), austere (1.25; 3.12; 4.39; 8.30, 33; 9.25) and long-suffering (8.12; 9.19). He suffers mental anguish (14.33-37) and physical tiredness (4.38). On the other hand, he is the Son of God; thumb-prints of the divine abound, not least in his exorcisms, healings and nature miracles— and perhaps most of all in the empty tomb. It would be possible to greatly expand on my comments on this human-divine axis, but given its self-evident standing in the text, and constrained as I am by considerations of space, it is not necessary to do so here.

Despite this wide range of character traits, Jesus remains totally consistent throughout the narrative. He is the great luminary around which all the other characters revolve, and against whom they must be judged by the reader. The implied author invites his readers, by means of various literary devices, to walk hand in hand with his protagonist because, given that he represents God's point of view, he can never be wrong. By interacting with the various characters in the story, the less reliable as well as the more reliable, the reader is led at last to the conclusion that Jesus alone is the one who should be imitated.

3. *John the Baptist*

From the viewpoint of the 'stage time' he occupies, John the Baptist has only a minor rôle to play, although he does serve an important function. He is a reliable character because he is clearly on the side of Jesus, and he says or does nothing which is contrary to the thrust of the Gospel as a whole; indeed, he reinforces it.

His character traits, not surprisingly, are similar to those of Jesus, but not as numerous. He is, above all, charismatic, drawing people to him by the power of his person and preaching (1.4-8) in order to point them to the protagonist; and he is morally resolute, as can be seen from the episode in which he condemns Antipas's adultery with Herodias (6.17-18).

Most significantly, however, Mark is keen to present John as Jesus' forerunner. Essentially, he manages this in two ways. First, unlike the other evangelists who either implicitly or explicitly integrate John's ministry with that of Jesus (Mt. 11.2-19; Lk. 7.18-35 [but cp. 16.16]; John 1.19-42; 3.22-36), Mark testifies that it was only after John's arrest that Jesus' ministry began (Mk 1.14). Although John's ministry is later referred to (6.14-29; 9.11-13; 11.27-33), it is always as an event of the past.

Secondly, John is presented as a new Elijah—implicitly in 1.6 where his clothing recalls that of the Old Testament prophet (2 Kgs 1.8); and explicitly in 9.11-13 where Elijah's rôle as messianic forerunner is mentioned directly. By casting John in this rôle Mark is implying that he has assumed the function of messianic herald, and that the one he is proclaiming—Jesus—must be none other than the long-expected messiah.

4. *Disciples*

Before we can proceed to consider the disciples as a character group we should be aware that, since they appear in various guises, there is a problem of definition. We need first, then, to distinguish the various groupings one from another. These groups are: (i) the main unit of disciples as chosen by Jesus and referred to variously as 'the disciples' (2.15, 16, 18, 23; 3.7, 9; 4.34; 5.31; 6.1, 35, 41, 45; 7.2, 5, 17; 8.4, 6, 10, 27, 33, 34; 9.14, 18, 28, 31; 10.13, 23, 24, 46; 11.1, 14; 12.43; 13.1; 14.12, 13, 14, 16, 32; 16.7), 'the Twelve' (4.10; 6.7; 9.35; 10.32; 11.11; 14.10, 17, 20, 43), or 'the apostles' (6.30);[17] (ii) a smaller group of three or four which seems to be set apart for special privilege (1.16-20, 29; 5.37; 9.2; 13.3; 14.33); (iii) individual disciples like Peter (1.30; 8.29, 32, 33; 9.5; 10.28; 11.21; 14.29, 37, 54, 66-72) (who seems often to represent the others), James and John (9.38; 10.35, 41), Judas Iscariot (14.10, 43), and other individuals not belonging to the Twelve, such as Levi (2.13-14)—if not identical with Matthew (3.18)—and Bartimaeus (10.46-52); (iv) a rather ambiguously defined larger group of followers beyond the circle of the Twelve (1.36; 3.21; 4.10).

These distinctions are important because they tend to affect our handling of certain literary concerns. The question of whether we regard the disciples as round or flat characters, for instance, depends on whether we have in mind the corporate body—the Twelve—or only particular individuals. As a whole, the disciples do indeed form a rounded character. By turns they are loyal, disloyal, perceptive, obtuse and so forth. In a word, their requisite inconsistency is exemplary; they could never be mistaken for stock characters. Yet certain individuals from within the group are portrayed as relatively flat. Of the list in 3.16-19, the four disciples who receive some kind of epithet (Simon, 'Peter'; James and John, 'Boanerges'; Judas, 'the betrayer') are also those who play some kind of independent rôle later on. James and John, 'the sons of thunder', always live up to their billing (9.38-41; 10.35-41), as does Judas (14.10-11, 43-45); so, independently of the rest, they operate as flat, even stock, characters. Only Peter, who in any case seems to represent the roundedness of the corporate group, remains rounded as an individual.

Many of the disciples' character traits tend to gravitate around two important axes: non-understanding/misunderstanding, and loyalty/ apostasy. In the first act of the Gospel (1.1–8.26), they consistently fail to perceive Jesus' true identity. After the storm on the lake, for instance, they can only look on in awe and gasp, 'Who then is this, that even the wind and sea obey him?' (4.41) Later, despite being given authority to

---

17. The term 'apostle' is related in this one instance to their activity at that time: they had just returned from being 'sent out' (ἀποστέλλειν) on their mission (6.7-13). Some manuscripts, notably BΘf[13]28 syr[h mg] sa bo[pl.] read ἀπόστολος at Mark 3.14 too.

heal and exorcise (6.7-13), they cannot make sense of the feeding miracles (6.35-44; 8.1-10): they feel that the multitudes cannot be fed except by natural means (6.37; 8.4). For the disciples to ask, on the second occasion, 'How can one feed these men with bread here in the desert?' when they have witnessed the first feeding, seems to betray in them an incredible degree of stupidity. But, of course, the reader is favoured with omniscience: along with the implied author, the reader already knows what the characters can only grope for. Consistently, from this point, the disciples fail to understand 'about the bread' (6.52; 8.14-21). Mark 6.52, in fact, is particularly interesting in this regard. Its reference to the disciples' non-understanding about the bread might lead us to suspect that it would have been better placed directly after the first feeding episode rather than after the walking on the water (6.45-51); after all, it seems strange to state, as a response to Jesus' astounding water exploits, '…they did not understand about the *loaves*'. Possibly Mark intends to assert that if the disciples could not grasp Jesus' identity through the miracle of the loaves, neither would they be able to do so through his walking on the water.

At the heart of the Gospel comes Peter's confession (8.27-30). Now, at last, light dawns on the situation: Jesus is none other than the messiah. This recognition makes possible some in-depth teaching; now that the disciples have grasped who Jesus is, he is able to proceed with revealing the *nature* of that identity. And so, in 8.31, '…he began to teach them that the Son of man must suffer many things…' The word 'began', regarded as a superfluous semitism in some contexts, is no doubt genuinely meant here: Jesus is just beginning the long process of instruction about the nature of messiahship. That this process is to be long and difficult is suggested by Peter's negative response to the first Passion prediction (8.31-33): surely Jesus could not mean to suffer and die! To change the disciples from 'thinking the things of men' to 'thinking the things of God'—to lead them from non-understanding, through misunderstanding, to complete understanding—that was the momentous task in which Jesus was engaged. And so, in 8.31–10.45, we encounter a recurring pattern in which misunderstanding by the disciples (8.32-33; 9.33-34, 38; 10.13, 35-37) is followed by corrective teaching by Jesus (8.34-38; 9.35-37, 39-41; 10.14-16, 42-45). And over all this looms the shadow of the cross (8.31; 9.12, 31; 10.33-34, 45)—the ultimate corrective to the disciples' notion of messianic glory.

The other main axis around which the corporate character of the

disciples is developed is that of loyalty/apostasy. That there is a steady
progression from one pole to the other has been noted by Kingsbury,[18]
though this pattern should not be accepted too rigidly: acts of loyalty,
such as Peter's following Jesus to the High Priest's house (14.54) occur
even after the disciples have apostasized. Nevertheless, it does seem at
first blush that the disciples are in complete harmony with Jesus' purposes. They readily leave their nets (meaning, no doubt, their livelihoods)
and follow when Jesus calls (1.16-20); they sit firmly in his camp during
his disputes with the Jewish authorities (2.15-17, 18-20, 23-28; 7.1-5);
they are obedient to the letter when he sends them on their mission (6.7-
13, 30); and in response, Jesus takes them into his confidence, providing
special in-house teaching when necessary (7.17; 9.28, 33; 10.10): as a
reliable character he never forsakes them, even when they begin to
falter. It is around the time of the feeding miracles that events begin to
take a turn for the worse. The 'before' and 'after' effect is emphasized
by the 'insider'/'outsider' motif. When reference is made to it in 4.11-12
the assumption is that the disciples are 'insiders'—to them has been
given the secret of the kingdom; but after the feeding miracles they are
clearly numbered with the 'outsiders' whose hearts are hardened (6.52;
8.17), who have eyes but do not see, and ears but do not hear (8.18; cf.
4.12). As they struggle to make sense of Jesus' identity they begin to
waver in their support for him. Although, even at the last, there are
moments of loyalty and obedience (11.1-10; 14.12-16), the predominant
trait, when the crisis comes, is one of apostasy. Judas makes arrange-
ments to betray Jesus (14.10-11), while in Gethsemane the three future
'pillars' of the Church cannot even stay awake to keep watch with their
Master (14.37). Then, when the betrayal comes (14.43-45), a feeble
attempt is made to resist by violence (14.47)—still the true nature of
messiahship had not been understood—before the mass desertion
(14.50). Finally Peter, who had previously protested his loyalty to Jesus
(14.31), now denies ever having known him (14.66-72). There is not
even the suggestion, within the confines of the narrative, that the disciples
are forgiven their apostasy and restored to their former position, for the
message of Jesus' resurrection which the young man at the tomb
entrusts to the women (16.7) seems not to reach Peter and the others.
The reader, however, knows that one way or another that restoration
did take place, so the story-world must be viewed against the real world

18. Kingsbury, *Conflict in Mark*, pp. 8-14, 89-117.

experienced by the Markan community.

The diversity of sub-groups and character traits within the 'disciple' character group as a whole indicates a diversity of functions as well. We can say that the Twelve, in particular, serve at least four functions:

1. Through their misunderstandings and errors they demonstrate to Mark's community the kind of behaviour that should be avoided. The quest for power and wealth, especially, is discouraged (10.13-45).

2. The reverse side of the coin is that if the disciples are shown to be in error, they provide Jesus with an opportunity for corrective teaching that indicates the type of behaviour to be imitated and encouraged.[19] Thus, the logical antidote to the quest for power is humility (9.35-37; 10.14-16, 31, 42-45).

3. The disciples occasionally step aside from the main flow of the action in order to comment upon it in a rather more detached way—the kind of function often given to the chorus in Greek tragedy. In Mark's Gospel this technique is normally used to provide insight into Jesus' person. There is, in fact, no little irony here. In the very act of expressing their bewilderment by means of the rhetorical question, 'Who then is this...?' (4.41), the disciples are actually confirming for the reader exactly 'who this is'.

4. Lastly, they provide continuity between 'then' and 'now'. The members of Mark's community know that they are the heirs of the first disciples, and that they must carry on the work of evangelism which they received as a legacy. The implied author leads his readers to identify with the disciples as long as they remain loyal and obedient to Jesus, but tends to draw them away from their influence once those qualities begin to wane. In doing this he shows that while it is easy to step into the shoes of the Twelve because they and the reader alike are subject to human failings, their behaviour is to be imitated only in as far as it accords with that of the totally reliable protagonist, Jesus.

5. *Jesus' Family*

Mark's portrait of Jesus' family is less ambiguous than his presentation of the disciples. Everywhere the darkness of tone is evident. The relatives have no belief in Jesus—in fact they think he is mad (3.20-21). At Nazareth, those who knew him as a boy are first astonished, then take

---

19. E. Best, 'The Role of the Disciples in Mark', *NTS* 23 (1976–77), pp. 377-401.

offence at him (6.1-6): they certainly do not accept him as the local boy made good. Jesus' response is to adopt a new family—the family of God; for it is those who do the will of God who are members of Jesus' genuine family (3.31-35). A similar message seems to be registered by 10.29-31: those who leave their biological family will be sure to receive new relatives almost without number in the future. Given the ecclesiastical background of Mark's Gospel, this must be taken to mean that those who were separated from their families because of their adherence to the Christian faith would find new brothers and sisters in the Church of Christ.

It is significant, too, that despite the presence of women at the cruci-fixion and burial of Jesus (15.40-41, 47), two of whom are called Mary, Jesus' own mother is conspicuous by her absence—a fact that is even more striking when it is recognized that from a relatively early date a tradition about her presence at the cross did exist (Jn 20.25-27).[20]

Mark's attitude to Jesus' family, then, is—to say the least—rather cool—some, indeed, have said hostile. Certain scholars[21] have attempted to explain this historically. Dominic Crossan, for instance, thinks that control of the church in Jerusalem had been seized by James the brother of Jesus and other relatives who were wielding power as a family dynasty, and that Mark's coolness towards Jesus' relatives as depicted in the narrative was a reaction to this situation. However, a literary explanation may be preferable: Mark endeavoured to play down the prominence or influence of Jesus' earthly family in order to highlight, by contrast, the importance of the Church—the extended family of believers.

---

20. It has sometimes been asserted that the James and Joses of 15.40 are the brothers of Jesus (cf. 6.3), and that their mother Mary is consequently Jesus' mother. But, as has often been pointed out, had Mark intended to imply this, he would have done so far more directly than is the case here. Certainly, he has no reservations about doing so elsewhere (3.31-35; 6.3).

21. J.D. Crossan, 'Mark and the Relatives of Jesus', *NovT* 15 (1973), pp. 110-13; *idem*, 'Empty Tomb and Absent Lord', in Kelber (ed.), *The Passion in Mark*, pp. 135-52 (p. 149); T.J. Weeden, *Mark: Traditions in Conflict* (Philadelphia: Fortress Press, 1971), p. 22 n. 9; E. Trocmé, *The Formation of the Gospel according to Mark* (trans. P. Gaughan; London: SPCK, 1975), pp. 130-37. See also the well-considered comments of J. Lambrecht, 'The Relatives of Jesus in Mark', *NovT* 16 (1974), pp. 241-58—Mark's primary purpose was to teach his community the meaning of true kinship.

6. *Opponents*

The most unreliable of all Mark's characters are the opponents of Jesus, the Jewish leaders. Apart from the one righteous scribe (12.28-34), they are implacably hostile. They oppose all Jesus' claims to be acting on God's authority, and claim that authority for themselves. Consequently, they deny that Jesus is messiah, the Son of God (whereas the reader, having been fed reliable information by the implied author and the reliable characters, knows that this is, in fact, the case). They believe, too, in a rigid legal observance of Torah as opposed to obedience to the spirit of the law as espoused by Jesus.

Although collectively the Jewish leaders are rather flat in terms of character, much can be gleaned from an analysis of the various sub-categories; for while the opponents do, indeed, function as a corporate identity at one level, the sub-groups are made to function independently too.

1. The scribes are Mark's stereotypical group *par excellence*. They are the only group to appear, either individually (1.22; 2.6, 16; 3.22; 9.11, 14; 12.28, 32, 35, 38) or in partnership with other opponents (7.1, 5; 8.31; 10.33; 11.18, 27; 14.1, 43, 53; 15.1, 31), throughout the Gospel. They tend to act as a unifying force in the story of opposition to Jesus. Thus, in Galilee, they collude with the Pharisees in their legal disputes with Jesus, while in Judea they conspire with the chief priests and elders to condemn the man himself. Their aims, therefore, tend to be directed by those of the particular group with whom they are in collusion.

Geographically, the scribes serve to link the story of opposition in Galilee with that of opposition in Judea. On two occasions (3.22; 7.1), hostility to Jesus in Galilee comes from scribes who have come from Jerusalem. The effect of this is to show that scribal disputes over law and authority, which tend to dominate in the Galilean phase of opposition, will lead ultimately to the fatal conspiracy against Jesus in Jerusalem in which the scribes are implicated along with the chief priests and elders.

The upshot of all this is that, in the absence of the scribes, with their peculiar binding rôle, the story of opposition would disintegrate; only disparate fragments would remain. It is only the function of the versatile yet stereotyped scribes which enables the parts to hang together as a whole.

2. Left to their own devices, the Pharisees are interested mainly in points of legal procedure. Their disciples observe the appropriate fasts

(2.18), while they themselves are keen to uphold Sabbath law (2.23-28). It is true that, later on, they are said to 'test' Jesus, both in the matter of messianic identity (8.11-12) and in that of divorce (10.2), but it is still to be maintained that, both as an independent force and in partnership with the scribes (7.1, 5), they are absorbed with issues of legality; only when they team up with the Herodians (3.6; 12.13) do these concerns become subservient to the overriding aim of destroying Jesus himself.

3. A good deal of ink has been expended on the question of the Herodians' identity,[22] but given their strategic appearances in Mark (3.6; 12.13) and the fact that they are to be found only once elsewhere—and then in a passage which is dependent on Mark (Mt. 22.16)—they may be better understood as a literary device. We notice that they emerge at the end of the first controversy cycle (Mk 2.1–3.6) in league with the Pharisees, and again at the beginning of the second (12.13-40). Their intention to destroy Jesus in 3.6 foreshadows later passages where the same word (ἀπόλλυμι) is used (11.18; 12.12), and their efforts in the second instance to 'entrap' (ἀγρεύω) Jesus in his words (12.13) recalls the earlier attempts of the Pharisees to 'test' (πειράζω) him (8.11; 10.2). The result of this literary interdependency is to provide the element of conflict in the narrative with a sense of flow and continuity. Mark 12.13 picks up where 3.6 leaves off, suggesting that hostile encounters in Jerusalem are a direct consequence of the earlier Galilean legal debates.[23] The Herodians, therefore, serve as a catalyst by which

22. B.W. Bacon, 'Pharisees and Herodians in Mark', *JBL* 39 (1920), pp. 102-12; E. Bickerman, 'Les Hérodiens', *RB* 47 (1938), pp. 184-97; P. Joüon, 'Les "Hérodiens" de l'évangile', *RSR* 28 (1938), pp. 585-88; H.H. Rowley, 'The Herodians in the Gospels', *JTS* 41 (1940), pp. 14-27; H.W. Hoehner, *Herod Antipas* (SNTSMS, 17; Cambridge: Cambridge University Press, 1972), pp. 331-42; C. Daniel, 'Les "Hérodiens" du Nouveau Testament sont-ils des Esséniens?', *RevQ* 6 (1966), pp. 31-53. Doubts about the historicity of this group are raised by M.J. Cook, *Mark's Treatment of the Jewish Leaders* (NovTSup, 51; Leiden: Brill, 1978), pp. 16-17; and W.J. Bennett, 'The Herodians of Mark's Gospel', *NovT* 17 (1975), pp. 9-14. But, of course, historicity need not be a consideration for the literary critic.

23. M. Albertz (*Die synoptischen Streitgespräche* [Berlin: Trowitzsch & Sohn, 1921], p. 6) and W.L. Knox (*The Sources of the Synoptic Gospels*. I. *Mark* [Cambridge: Cambridge University Press, 1953], p. 8) both suggest that in the Markan context the controversies in Mk 2.1–3.6 are intended to show why Jesus was put to death.

the various controversy elements are fused into a literary whole.[24]

4. The Sadducees make only one appearance (12.18-27), on which occasion the nature of the case requires their presence. Their cynical rejection of the resurrection belief serves as a foil for Jesus' acceptance of it. The fact that, in contrast to Matthew, Mark introduces the Sadducees only when strictly required may suggest that he tends not to present characters simply for their own sake, but only in as far as they contribute to the essentials of the narrative.

5. The chief priests and elders represent the cultic and political heart of Judaism. They never appear outside Jerusalem, and they alone seek to get things moving as far as the arrest of Jesus is concerned, though in the end they need the help of an inside agent—Judas. Joined by the legalistic scribes, they become a triad[25] representing the entire spectrum of the Jewish establishment—legal, cultic and political, so Jesus' struggle is with the entire institutional edifice, not simply with one facet of it. When Mark twice refers to scribes 'from Jerusalem' he may, in effect, be testifying to a distinction of rôles. The Galilean scribes, like the Pharisees, are concerned only to dispute with Jesus on points of *halakhah*,[26] whereas the scribes 'from Jerusalem', though they, too, may fill this rôle (7.1-5), are chiefly embroiled in the conspiracy to do away with Jesus.

While all these groups can and do operate individually, there is also a significant and purposeful degree of interlinking. Pharisees appear as an

---

24. It is feasible that, apart from the two passages mentioned (3.6; 12.13), there is a third reference to Herodians in Mark. At 8.15, 'Beware of the leaven of the Pharisees, and the leaven of Herod', there is an alternative reading, 'Herodians', which is supported by the comparatively early P[45] (also WΘf[1]f[13]sa). Whether this was, in fact, the original is impossible to say for certain. On reflection, it may be a scribal attempt to assimilate the passage to the two other references to Herodians.

25. Neither the triadic grouping of the chief priests–scribes–elders, nor its order is sacrosanct, as the following list shows:

chief priests–scribes–elders—11.27; 14.43
chief priests–elders–scribes—14.53; 15.1
elders–chief priests–scribes—8.31
chief priests–scribes—10.33; 11.18; 14.1; 15.31
chief priests—14.10; 15.3, 10, 11.

Cf. A.F.J Klijn, 'Scribes, Pharisees, Highpriests and Elders in the New Testament', *NovT* 3 (1959), pp. 259-67.

26. In post-biblical Judaism the term *halakhah* was applied to the legal traditions passed down by the scribes and rabbis for the purpose of interpreting and clarifying the written law of Moses.

independent group in both Galilee (2.23-28; 8.11-12) and Judea (10.2-9),
yet they are also allied with the Herodians, again in both provinces (3.6;
12.13), and with some of the scribes 'from Jerusalem' (7.1). These
particular scribes appear in Galilee early in Jesus' ministry; later they
conspire with the chief priests and elders (11.18, 27; 14.1, 43, 53; 15.1,
31)—a fact which is foreshadowed repeatedly on Jesus' journey from
Caesarea Philippi to Jerusalem (8.31; 10.33). In 3.6 the Pharisees and
Herodians seem to be working independently of any other opposition
groups, while in 12.13 they appear to be subject to the direction of the
chief priests and scribes even though, in one curious passage (2.16) the
position of scribe seems somehow subservient to the chief religious
parties. All things considered, this interlinking shows that Mark offsets
the diversity of his various opposition groups with a kind of homogeneity
whereby they are presented as a single character group which (with the
celebrated exception of one scribe) is implacably opposed to Jesus.

The chief character traits of the religious authorities can be broadly
classified as follows:

1. They are devious and conspiratorial. They mutter their disapproval
under their breath, as it were (2.6; 11.31-32), or else maintain a hostile
silence (3.4); they make demands or frame questions in a manner
intended to catch Jesus out (8.11; 10.2; 11.27-33; 12.13-17), and they
conspire to put him to death (3.6; 12.12; 14.1-2).

2. They are frivolous and hypocritical. The Sadducees' question in
12.18-23 has no purpose other than to ridicule Jesus' own position.
Similarly, the scribes and Pharisees argue interminably over trivial
matters of *halakhah* while neglecting the weightier matters of the law
(see especially 3.1-5; 7.1-13). The saying about straining at a gnat and
swallowing a camel (Mt. 23.24), though absent from Mark's Gospel, is
certainly applicable here. Again, although the Markan Jesus' only once
refers directly to his opponents as 'hypocrites' (Mark 7.6)—and Mark
himself once describes their activity as 'hypocrisy' (12.15)—it is evident
throughout that their behaviour is hypocritical. Mark 7.9-13 is a good
example. The religious leaders had no qualms about piously using
halakhah concerning korban to nullify the much more vital fifth
Commandment: 'Honour your father and your mother' (Exod. 20.12;
Deut. 5.16). So too, we are told in Mk 12.38-40 that the scribes wanted
their piety to be seen by all. This is exemplified in a list of the various
ways in which they 'put on appearances'. But, tellingly, amid all the
ostentation, Mark inserts an item of covert behaviour—the scribes

devour the houses of widows (12.40).[27] Such hypocrisy can lead only to condemnation. By contrast, in the following story (12.41-44) a poor widow, of the kind exploited by the scribes, demonstrates what true religion is all about, by quietly and unceremoniously giving her whole living to God. In this light, the hypocrisy of the scribes is exposed all the more.

The main bone of contention in the controversy stories, which can be seen as a thread running throughout the narrative, is the question of authority.[28] Who is it who, in the last analysis, enjoys divine authority—the religious leaders or Jesus? Quite clearly, our implied author is in no doubt as to where he stands on the issue. He sets up the contest as early as the first chapter: in a nugget of authorial commentary he declares that Jesus taught 'as one who had authority (ἐξουσία) and not as the scribes' (1.22). The following exorcism (1.23-27) is described by the onlookers as a 'teaching' (1.28), which suggests that Jesus' authority consists not only in words, but in powerful, wonder-working action—something that, for all their verbosity, the scribes cannot match. This sets the pattern for what follows. In 2.5b-10a, for instance, the scribes question Jesus' authority to forgive sins, but his wonder-working response leaves them dumbstruck. This divine authority is reaffirmed in a snatch of authorial commentary in 2.28;[29] Jesus' lordship overrides *halakhah*. The question of lordship is resumed in 12.35-37. In one sense, the scribal view that Messiah was to be a son of David was quite right, if by that expression was meant a descendant of David. Jesus himself

27. It seems that the scribes were not allowed an official salary for their duties, and counted on financial support from the people, including widows who could ill-afford it. The Talmud refers in at least one instance to the resentment felt by some women towards this practice. It may be this kind of situation to which the phrase 'devouring widows' houses' refers.

28. Kingsbury, *Conflict in Mark*, pp. 14-15.

29. Why should we accept that 2.28 *is* authorial commentary? The term 'so that' is a conjunction of consequence suggesting that the saying in v.28, '...the Son of man is Lord even of the Sabbath', should somehow be a conclusion drawn from the proverbial saying which precedes, 'The Sabbath was made for man, and not man for the Sabbath.' But the last statement does not logically follow from the first. It looks as though the cornfield incident in 2.23-28 once took the form of a pronouncement story which ended with the single punch-line in v. 27, as pronouncement stories are wont to do. A redactor (Mark?) then added v. 28 more as a christological comment on Jesus' authority over Sabbath as expressed in vv. 23-26 than as an attempt to explain or interpret the proverbial statement in v. 27.

seems happy enough to accept the designation in 10.47-48. But in this later passage he is intent on stressing the *lordship* of the son, and quotes from Ps. 110.1 to make his point. It is not that the scribes (who are absent here) would have disputed his argument: the crux of the matter was the identity of Messiah—was Jesus the man or not? This issue is earlier taken up in 8.11-12 where the Pharisees demand that Jesus produce his messianic credentials: they want to see signs! There is more than a touch of irony here, for the preceding three chapters have been replete with signs and wonders, including two exorcisms (5.1-20; 7.24-30), three healings (5.21-43; 7.31-37)—one of them a resuscitation miracle, no less—two feeding miracles (6.35-44; 8.1-10) and walking on the water (6.45-52), as well as a general summary of healings (6.53-56). But, of course, it may be surmised that the Pharisees wanted a demonstration on their own terms. At certain points in the rabbinic literature which, admittedly, is of much later vintage than the Gospels, certain signs are specified which any claimant to messianic status would be obliged to perform successfully before being accepted as genuine.[30]

The question of authority comes to a head in 11.27-33 where the chief priests, scribes and elders ask: 'By what authority are you doing these things (ταῦτα), or who gave you this authority to do them?' (11.28). Although Jesus has just cleansed the Temple (11.15-18) the use of the plural, 'these things', suggests that the question goes beyond that incident alone to embrace Jesus' ministry generally. The second question is really a clarification of the first: it is not so much a case of *what* authority, but *whose* authority. Jesus' response is to ask of his opponents whether the baptismal work of John came 'from heaven or from men' (that is, was authorized by God, or was of his own making). Once again, the religious leaders are out-manouevered, as is evident from their deliberations in 11.32-33; but the reader is left in no doubt as to the answer. John's authority, of course, came from God, so it must follow that the authority of the greater one—'he who is mightier than I' (1.7)—must emanate from the same source.

Collectively, then, the passages we have been discussing suggest that Mark uses the corporate character of the religious leaders, at least in

30. These 'signs' were said to include an appearance on the parapet of the Temple; the resurrection of the dead—especially of Moses and the wilderness generation; the grinding of the mountains of Israel to powder; and the restoration of the lost treasures of the Temple—namely the ark, the cruse of oil and the flask of manna.

part, to stress that, in sharp contrast to themselves whose authority is self-proclaimed, Jesus demonstrates through word and deed against them that his own authority is divinely approved.[31]

7. Demons

For Mark, the demons, too, represent a character. They are given human attributes and powers of speech and, unlike the human opponents, they offer reliable commentary because they know who Jesus is (1.24; 3.11; 5.7), and they proclaim it to such an extent that Jesus finds it necessary to silence them. The demonic story actually proceeds along cosmic pluralistic lines. Conflict is enjoined between one who is filled with the Spirit of God (1.10, 12) and the demonic spirits whose ultimate source is Satan (1.13). Exactly how this conflict with demons features in the plot as a whole rather depends on our interpretation of the temptation account: strictly speaking, we are not told of the outcome. Without wishing to forestall alternative interpretations, it appears that if Jesus defeats Satan at the outset, then he somehow takes on the rôle of the stronger one who plunders the strong man's house (3.27), and his victory over demons who, after all, are merely Satan's minions, is perpetually assured (1.23-27, 34, 39; 3.11; 5.1-20; 7.24-30; 9.14-29): he has, in fact, already defeated them at their source.

The one problem with this view is that, if Satan has been bound, the continued prevalence of evil, human as well as demonic, is difficult to explain. In this case, it is worth considering a theory of a two-stage operation. Indeed, to suggest that Satan had been bound once-for-all at the outset would have raised the question as to why, then, the cross was necessary at all. A Satan bound only in an incomplete sense, however, would explain a good deal. It would mean that he no longer had free reign over the world, and could operate only with his power much diminished; but it would also be evident why his evil influence persisted. Further, if the cross could somehow be regarded as a more decisive expunction of his powers its ultimate significance would not be diminished, but enhanced. That is why Danker's view that the cry of

31. Several attempts have been made to work out a narrative approach to the religious leaders in Mark's Gospel: Kingsbury, *Conflict in Mark*, pp. 14-21, 63-88; *idem*, 'The Religious Authorities', pp. 42-65; Malbon, 'The Jewish Leaders', pp. 259-81; Rhoads and Michie, *Mark as Story*, pp. 117-22; S.H. Smith, 'The Role of Jesus' Opponents in the Markan Drama', *NTS* 35 (1989), pp. 161-82.

dereliction (15.34) represents a form of exorcism in which Jesus expels the demonic at the expense of his life proves, in essentials, so attractive.[32]

8. *Minor Characters*

Under the heading 'minor characters' may be included any group or individuals who occupy the stage only for a brief moment, or who come and go intermittently. It is impossible to generalize here, since the minor characters are so diverse both in their attitude to Jesus and in their significance in the narrative. We must not imagine that the latter factor is proportional to the length of time a character spends on stage. The centurion, for instance, makes only a fleeting appearance (15.39), yet his testimony forms the climax to the entire Gospel.

It is because of the above-mentioned diversity that it is so difficult to establish any consistent character traits for the minor figures. We cannot know, for example, what sort of person the deaf mute of 7.31-37 was, other than that, along with most of the people Jesus healed, he seems to have had the requisite faith. Again, because the individuals in the category play such small rôles, it is often impossible to assess their degree of reliability, since they make no comment, nor do they initiate any act: this factor simply does not apply to them.

Because most of the minor individuals seem to emerge out of the ubiquitous crowd—the ὄχλος (2.4, 13; 3.9, 20, 32; 4.1 (× 2), 36; 5.21, 24, 27, 30, 31; 6.34, 35; 7.14, 17, 33; 8.1, 2, 6 (× 2), 34; 9.14, 15, 17, 25; 10.1, 46; 11.18, 32; 12.12, 37, 41; 14.43; 15.8, 11, 15) or, less frequently, the οἱ παρ᾽ αὐτοῦ/πέρι αὐτόν (3.21; 4.10)—we should pause to see how this general body functions in the narrative. Perhaps the most notable characteristic of the crowd is its fickleness. How quickly the 'many' who acclaim Jesus on Palm Sunday (11.8-10) turn to become those implicated in his arrest a few days later (14.43); how easily the chief priests are able to turn the crowd against Jesus during his trial (15.11). Of course, it will be said that the people who acclaim Jesus are not the same ones who cry, 'Crucify him!' a week later. From a literary-critical viewpoint, however, this line of reasoning is invalid. At the narrative level, Mark treats all the crowds as a single character, using its fickleness as a foil for Jesus' steadfastness. The fact that these people go to such great lengths to seek Jesus out (1.37, 45; 3.7-8; 6.33; 8.3) and

32. F.W Danker, 'The Demonic Secret in Mark: A Re-examination of the Cry of Dereliction (15:34)', *ZNW* 61 (1970), pp. 48-69.

are so full of amazement at his words and works (1.22, 27; 2.12; 6.2; 7.37; 9.15)—even the fact that they hear him gladly (12.37)—does not make them any less shallow. After all, they are numbered with the outsiders who are destined not to understand (4.11-12), and one receives the impression all along that they are not resolute in their support of Jesus, but are easily led. Indeed, Mark tells us that Jesus had compassion on them because they were like sheep without a shepherd (6.34), and later Jesus quotes Zechariah 13.7 to show that once the shepherd is removed the sheep will be scattered (Mark 14.27)—which is precisely what does happen.

The crowd also has a dramatic choral function in that it sometimes passes comment on the action which is taking place. In 1.27, for instance, the congregation in the synagogue at Capernaum exclaims, after Jesus' exorcism there, 'What is this? A new teaching! With authority he commands the unclean spirits, and they obey him.' Although the crowd is overcome with amazement, the reader can learn a great deal from what is said—that Jesus teaches by both word and deed, and that it is a new teaching with authority (compared with that of the scribes, which lacks authority, 1.22). We know from the outset, then, that Jesus is a very special character.

In 2.12 Jesus' uniqueness is again attested: 'We never saw anything like this!' And in 7.37, 'He has done all things well; he even makes the deaf hear and the dumb speak.' In affirming what Jesus is doing the crowd is, in effect, providing the reader with some insight into who Jesus is (as if the reader did not know already!); the message, by repetition, is being driven home. As with the disciples, when they play this choral rôle, there is irony in the fact that in the very process of expressing amazement and bewilderment over Jesus' identity, the crowd is actually affirming it for the attentive reader.

As we have said already, most of the minor characters play too much of a cameo rôle to manifest any consistent character traits as individuals. Occasionally, even a single brief act may be enough to give the reader some idea of what kind of character it is intended to depict. In the story of John's death (6.14-29), for instance, Herod comes over as a weak, shallow, easily-manipulated ruler with a superstitious disposition (6.14-16). So, too, the decision of Joseph of Arimathea to take charge of Jesus' body (15.42-46), along with the authorial comment that he was seeking the kingdom of God (the imperfect tense indicating an on-going process) suggests that his favourable disposition to Jesus should be regarded as habitual, even though this one appearance is all we have to rely on. About many of the other minor characters, however, it is impossible to say anything of substance. The appearance of the various children (5.35-43; 7.24-30; 9.14-29, 36-37; 10.13-16) is a case in point. We have no idea what any of them felt about Jesus; even those who are healed are dependent on the faith of their parents.

Yet despite our lack of knowledge about these various individuals as characters, it is possible to compile a list of traits which are common to many of them. For instance, it is evident that faith is an ever-present commodity among those healed (5.34; 10.52) or those who bring others for healing (2.5; 5.36; 9.23-24). Even when not specifically mentioned, it is clearly visible in the actions of those involved—in the parents who earnestly beg Jesus to heal their children (5.22-23; 7.25-26; 9.22-24); in those who believe that even so much as touching the fringe of Jesus' garment will effect a cure (6.56); in the leper who seeks out Jesus, fully confident of being made clean (1.40), and so on.

Another common trait among the minor characters is humility. On two occasions children are introduced purely to serve as models for this kind of attitude: to receive the kingdom, one must become as humble as a child. Those who beseech Jesus to heal their children or friends find that they must throw themselves completely upon his mercy. Jairus is a prominent synagogue official, but he recognizes that in the crisis in which he finds himself his position is of no use at all; all he can do, despite his office, is fall on his knees, begging (παρακαλέω) Jesus for help. Similarly, the Syrophoenician woman has to endure the indignity of being compared to a little dog (7.27) if she hopes to see her daughter healed; she must be prepared even for humiliation if she is to be satisfied.[33] Then, of course, there is the poor widow at the Temple (12.41-44), whose humility contrasts sharply with the proud and arrogant behaviour of the scribes described in the preceding story (12.38-40).

Yet another feature of the minor individuals as a whole is the art of persistence. The four friends of the paralytic are not deterred by the crowd which blocks their way to Jesus; they simply climb onto the roof, break through it, and lower the cripple at Jesus' feet (2.3-4). The woman with the haemorrhage has to fight her way through the crowd in order to touch Jesus and be healed (5.27). The Syrophoenician woman is not put off by Jesus' apparent objection, on racial grounds, to his healing her

---

33. A point noted by Rhoads and Michie, *Mark as Story*, p. 131.

daughter; on the contrary, it inspires her to reply with great wisdom (7.27-28), so that Jesus actually appears to concede to her request as a consequence. The father of the epileptic boy persists with his quest for a cure, even after the disciples have failed him (9.17-18). Bartimaeus perseveres until he has attracted Jesus' attention, despite the efforts of the crowd to hinder him (10.47-48). In these and other instances members of the crowd demonstrate their determination to have Jesus satisfy their needs.

By means of these various traits, the minor characters—or 'little people', as they are known to Rhoads and Michie[34]—serve as a foil for the disciples. The faith so often shown by these people is in marked contrast to the disciples' lack of faith. Hardly has Jesus finished rebuking his disciples for their faithlessness during the storm (4.40) than he is commending the woman with the haemorrhage for having faith (5.34). The same applies in the case of humility: in contrast to the minor characters who are generally humble in their approach to Jesus, the disciples consistently manifest signs of pride or arrogance (9.33-37, 38-41; 10.13-16, 35-45) and have to be taught repeatedly that those who would be first must be last of all (9.35; 10.31, 44). With regard to the trait of persistence, too, we notice a pronounced contrast between the minor characters and the disciples. By and large, the 'little people' do have sticking power. They come from far and wide to be with Jesus, and follow him wherever he goes. Even if they seem to desert him at the last, certain individuals from this character group remain loyal. He is served even in death by folk as diverse as the eminent Joseph of Arimathea and a group of seemingly insignificant women who had been with him since his days in Galilee (15.40-47). In sharp contrast, we find that the disciples *pledge* to remain loyal (14.29, 31), despite Jesus' prediction (14.27, 30), but in fact they do not. Hard on the heels of their vehement protestations comes their short trek to Gethsemane where they cannot even keep watch with Jesus 'one hour' (14.37). When the arrest takes place there is a brief token resistance before all the disciples desert Jesus and flee (14.46-50). Peter does endeavour to remain loyal, but finds himself denying Jesus as per prediction (14.54, 66-72). At the cross, the disciples are conspicuous by their absence: only the little people have endured to the end—the women and Joseph of Arimathea. Then, too, there is the centurion who affirms Jesus' true identity.

34. Rhoads and Michie, *Mark as Story*, pp. 129-36.

One final point to be made about the 'little people' is that, individually at least, they do not function as characters in their own right, but rather as narrative elements or factors in the behaviour of the chief characters. For instance, although Herod may strike us as a weak, superstitious character, his main purpose is to raise the question as to who Jesus is (6.14-16)—and, moreover, in a manner that foreshadows the resolution to that question in 8.27-30. Similarly the centurion, of whose character we know nothing, is nevertheless accorded the privilege of delivering the one-line climax to the entire Gospel (15.39). And the many sick people or their friends and relatives, by their demonstration of faith enable Jesus to heal them, thereby allowing him to reveal something of his divine nature. In all these cases, the character of the individual is rather less important than his or her narrative function.

9. *Summary*

We began this chapter with the assertion that literary characters can never be identical with real persons, even when they are intended to represent such persons. Jesus, John the Baptist, Peter, and so on, were no doubt real historical figures, but in Mark's Gospel they take on individual literary characters which need not, and indeed do not, conform to their characters as real persons. We have little exact knowledge as to what Jesus was like as a person in history, and even less about many of the other Gospel figures; but for the literary critic there is no disadvantage here, since he or she is interested only in the way in which the *evangelist* presents them in the context of the Gospel narrative as a whole. We saw that each of the chief characters manifests a pattern of behaviour known as a character trait, and explored how these emerge from the story. These traits can be disclosed directly by the implied author, or indirectly through the narrative action—in what a character does or says, by means of a description of physical appearance, and even through setting—or through a combination of these.

Following the ground-breaking work of E.M. Forster, we next explored the distinction between flat and rounded characters—in other words, between those who exhibit a limited number of largely predictable character traits, and those who exhibit a large number of diverse ones. In surveying the different characters in Mark's Gospel, we found that many are relatively 'flat' because their behaviour is predictable. This is especially true of Jesus' opponents as a composite group; we always know what they are aiming to do. On the other hand, both Jesus and his disciples are essentially 'rounded' characters because their behaviour is diverse and unpredictable. Perhaps this would not be so true of the disciples as individuals, except Peter, but it is certainly the case with the Twelve as a whole.

Chapter 3

MARK'S GOSPEL: THE PLOT

1. *Plot: Some Literary-Critical Principles*

What is a plot? That question has been posed by generations of literary critics,[1] and more recently by biblical scholars too.[2] Any attempt to formulate an answer must inevitably begin with Aristotle whose response appears, at first glance, to be disarmingly simple: 'By "plot" [μῦθος]', he says, 'I mean here the arrangement of the incidents.' The demonstrative 'here' (τοῦτον) is an important qualification, for μῦθος had a wide range of meanings, and Aristotle is careful to explicate its use in this instance. But to describe 'plot' as an arrangement of incidents still begs the question as to what principles or criteria the arrangement is based on. After all, any story is a series of incidents: what is it about arrangement that makes a plotted story different, and enables us to assert that plot is somehow free from identity with mere story? In answering this question we need to take account of at least four factors: the causal factor, the affective factor, the character factor and the conflict factor. It is my purpose now to discuss each of these independently, and later to assess how each might contribute to a consideration of plot in Mark.

a. *Plot-Related Factors*
i) *The Causal Factor.* Above all else, the incidents in a story must be causally related. According to Aristotle,

> the component incidents must be so arranged that if one of them be transposed or removed, the unity of the whole is dislocated and destroyed. For if the presence or absence of a thing makes no visible difference, then it is not an integral part of the whole.[3]

1. K. Egan, 'What Is a Plot?', *NLH* 9 (1977–78), pp. 455-73; R. Scholes (ed.), *Approaches to the Novel* (San Francisco: Chandler, 1961), p. 218.
2. F.J. Matera, 'The Plot of Matthew's Gospel', *CBQ* 49 (1987), pp. 235-36.
3. Aristotle, *Poetics*, 8.4.

A little later, he elaborates:

> Of simple plots and actions, the worst are those which are 'episodic'. By this I mean a plot in which the episodes do not follow each other probably or inevitably.[4]

Clearly, then, for Aristotle causality is indispensable, and its importance has been emphasized by many modern literary critics. In what may seem to some to be astonishingly simplistic terms, E.M. Forster defines plot as,

> a narrative of events, the emphasis falling on causality. 'The king died and then the queen died' is a story. 'The king died, and then the queen died of grief' is a plot. The time-sequence [characteristic of story] is preserved, but the sense of causality overshadows it.[5]

Whatever the shortcomings of this statement may be, it does stress that events must be arranged in some kind of unbroken sequence if they are to be understood as plot, and it should be added that causal sequence must result in some kind of closure in which resolution of some sort is achieved. Aristotle's dictum that every work should have a beginning, a middle and an end[6] may sound banal, but it is not in fact as self-evident as it appears; for Aristotle makes this statement in the context of a discussion on plot and causality:

> We have laid it down that tragedy is a representation of an action [πρᾶξις] that is whole and complete... A whole is what has a beginning and middle and end. A beginning is that which is not a necessary consequent of anything else but after which something else exists or happens as a natural result. An end on the contrary is that which is inevitably or, as a rule, the natural result of something else but from which nothing else follows; a middle follows something else and something follows from it. Well constructed plots must not therefore begin at random, but must embody the formulae we have stated.[7]

In fiction the aim of the plot is to represent a process of change in the protagonist—from good fortune to bad, for instance—which is not completed until the final episode or plot unit. The important point is that this end situation is reached naturally via the process of cause-and-effect. Moreover, this process should lead from possibility through probability to

---

4.   Aristotle, *Poetics*, 9.11.
5.   Forster, *Aspects of the Novel*, p. 87.
6.   Aristotle, *Poetics*, 7.3.
7.   Aristotle, *Poetics*, 7.2-7.

inevitability,[8] so that as the story progresses options which are open at the outset are gradually closed down until none remain.

An 'end', therefore, is not, in literary-critical terms, the inevitable final episode of a work—not that alone, at any rate; it is the proper closure of the plot by means of an acceptable resolution. Authors do not achieve this automatically.

ii) *The Affective Factor*. A second important feature in the construction of plot is the affective or emotive factor: a plot must be capable of effecting a particular emotional response in the audience or the reader. In the words of Friedman, 'The end of a plot...is to represent some completed process of change in the protagonist for the sake of the sequence of emotions which that process evokes in the reader.'[9] In fact, according to Egan, this 'determinate affective response' on the part of the reader is precisely what is implied by causality.[10] Plot does not always embrace a logical causal process, but it is bound by an emotive one, in which case the source of causality is to be found in the reader rather than the text.

Once again, the inspiration for all this is Aristotle. Speaking specifically of tragic drama, he asserts that the proper emotive response to such a play should be one of fear (φοβερός) and pity (ἐλεεινός), and that these twin emotions should be aroused by means of the plot alone:

> Fear and pity sometimes result from the spectacle and are sometimes aroused by the actual arrangement of the incidents [plot], which is preferable and the mark of a better poet. The plot should be so constructed that even without seeing the play anyone hearing of the incidents happening thrills with fear and pity as a result of what occurs.[11]

This feeling of fear and pity itself stands at the end of a dynamic process. The audience or reader should not experience it at the outset, but should be led to it causally as the end to which the plot is directed. Only if the audience/reader at last experiences these emotions can the

---

8.   An observation made by P. Goodman, quoted by S. Chatman (*Story and Discourse*, p. 46) and again, via Chatman, by Matera ('Plot', p. 239): 'In the beginning, anything is possible; in the middle things become probable; in the ending everything is necessary.'

9.   N. Friedman, 'Forms of the Plot', in P. Stevick (ed.), *The Theory of the Novel* (New York: Free Press, 1967), p. 150.

10.   Egan, 'What Is a Plot', pp. 469-70.

11.   Aristotle, *Poetics*, 14.1-2.

tragic plot be said to have succeeded. In that sense, it is perfectly legitimate to assert that the affective plot should initiate an emotional
pilgrimage on the part of the reader.

iii) *The Character Factor*. Some of the most severe criticism levelled at
Aristotle by modern critics has been in respect of his treatment of plot
and character as separate entities. While character is necessarily related
to plot since all human action is performed by living persons to whom is
attributed certain qualities of character,[12] plot is nevertheless superior to
character:

> The most important of these [constituent parts[13]] is the arrangement of
> the incidents [plot], for tragedy is not a representation of men but of a
> piece of action, of life...and the end aimed at is the representation not of
> qualities of character but of some action; and while character makes men
> what they are, it is their actions and experiences that make them happy or
> the opposite. They do not therefore act to represent character, but character-
> study is included for the sake of the action... Moreover, you could not
> have a tragedy without action, but you can have one without character-
> study.[14]

But is character as independent of, and subservient to the action as
Aristotle suggests?[15] Although the word 'independent' should be used
guardedly in that in practice it is not feasible to discuss plot without
referring to character and other factors (such as diction and thought), it
is nevertheless a fact that Aristotle treats plot alone as the first among a
hierarchical dynasty of features composing a complete drama or epic.[16]
More recent critics, such as R.S. Crane,[17] have endeavoured to expand
the definition of plot to embrace the possibility that factors other than
action—character and thought, for instance—might sometimes take
over the dominant rôle. Given that the plot represents a completed

12. Aristotle, *Poetics*, 6.7.
13. According to Aristotle (*Poetics*, 6.9), the six constituent parts of tragic drama
are: plot, character, diction, thought, spectacle and song.
14. Aristotle, *Poetics*, 6.12-14.
15. Henry James (*The Art of the Novel* [London: Scribner, 1935]) has declared:
'What is character but the determination of incident? What is incident but the
illustration of character?' See M.H. Abrams, *A Glossary of Literary Terms* (New
York: Holt, Rinehart & Winston, 5th edn, 1988), p. 139.
16. Cf. R.S. Crane, 'The Concept of Plot', in Scholes (ed.), *Approaches to the
Novel*, pp. 233-43 (234-35).
17. Crane, 'Concept of Plot', pp. 233-43.

transformation in the protagonist from one state to another—its opposite—such transformation need not be in respect of action alone. It is true that in Sophocles' tragic masterpiece, *Oedipus Rex*, the controlling principle of the plot is action 'determined and effected by character and thought';[18] but equally, there are plots in which these determinants become the dominant principle. In some works (say, James's *Portrait of a Lady*, or Austen's *Emma*) the change in the situation of the protagonist is in no sense related to overt practical factors, but rather to a change in his or her character as 'precipitated or molded by action, and made manifest both in it, and in thought and feeling'.[19] Similarly, a transformation in the protagonist's thought and feelings may be 'conditioned and directed by character and action.'

While ancient fiction tends to be dominated by plots of action, so that we would not expect Aristotle to have regarded factors such as character and thought as plot dominants, their potential to control plots, of which the modern critic has made us aware, should not be too lightly dismissed.

iv) *The Conflict Factor*. Finally, there is the concept of conflict. Unlike character, conflict is not indispensable to plot: it is possible, though perhaps not frequent, to construct a plot without the presence of conflict at all.[20] Where conflict does exist, it can take any one of several forms:

1. conflict with the supernatural, such as God or evil
2. conflict with human beings
3. conflict with other living entities
4. conflict with non-living entities
5. conflict with natural forces such as time, the physical world (for example, geographical phenomena) or the biological world (for example, disease and death)
6. conflict with social forces such as economic conditions, political situations, religious principles, and so on
7. conflict with the inner self, whether conscious or unconscious

Some works, of course, embrace more than one of these forms simultaneously. Melville's *Moby Dick*, for instance, is the story of

---

18. Crane, 'Concept of Plot', p. 239.
19. Crane, 'Concept of Plot', p. 239.
20. As Abrams (*Literary Terms*, p. 139) has noted, Thornton Wilder's play, *Our Town*, is a classic example of this.

conflict between the protagonist and a whale (3, above) at one level, but at a deeper level also traces a conflict with evil (1, above), an abstract force which the whale is made to represent. Moreover, it is possible to have any number of subsidiary conflicts or rivalries which may or may not interplay with the main one. In Lawrence's *Sons and Lovers*, for example, Paul Morel is in conflict with Baxter Dawes, while Mrs Morel is pitted against both her husband and, more covertly, against Miriam Leivers. But the overall conflict which the plot seeks to resolve is an inner one which rends the protagonist, Paul, and is centred on the dilemma over his attraction towards his mother on the one hand, and other women, especially Miriam, on the other. The purpose of the plot is to resolve a situation which is only finally settled by the mother's death. The subsidiary conflicts serve to underpin this main one in various ways and at different levels. The largely subconscious rivalry between Mrs Morel and Miriam, for instance, tends to sharpen Paul's inner dilemma; for we discover here that it is not simply a matter of his attraction towards two very different and incompatible women, but of their separate attraction towards him: the fact that both earnestly desire him makes his dilemma all the more difficult to resolve.

The resolution of a conflict dominating the plot as a whole usually occurs via a series of cameo conflicts within the individual plot units. In other words, progress is made towards resolution by means of the particular emotional response made by the protagonist to conflict situations suggested by the independent episodes. It is this response which gives rise to certain expectations within the reader. If the response to a whole series of these conflicts is consistent, the reader may feel confident in anticipating the nature of future responses. The author is then at liberty, if he or she so wishes, to occasion surprise by having the protagonist behave contrary to expectations, particularly as a means of finally resolving the plot.

b. *Plot Construction Theory*

So much, then, for the significant plot-related factors—causality, affectiveness (emotion), character and conflict. But how are plots constructed? It is generally agreed that events must be arranged in plot-units or narrative blocks, and that each unit must contain an event which is indispensable to the progress of the plot. This event should normally force the protagonist into a certain decision or emotional response. In practice, of course, any substantial narrative will contain episodes of various kinds (digressions, for example) which are not essential to the plot. Chatman has distinguished between the essential and subsidiary elements by employing the terms 'kernel' and 'satellite'.[21] Kernels 'are narrative moments that give rise to cruxes in the direction taken by events, [and] cannot be deleted without destroying the narrative logic', whereas 'satellites can be deleted without disturbing the logic of the plot, [even] though their omission will…impoverish the narrative aesthetically. Satellites entail no choice, but are solely the workings out of choices made at the kernels.'[22]

The kernels, then, form the skeleton of the plot. They are not disconnected bones, but are necessarily causally related. The response made by the protagonist to one 'crux' situation conditions the nature of the following kernel to which he or she must make a further response.

The final plot-unit should contain the climax of the narrative. The protagonist is put to the test for a final time, and his ultimate response determines the resolution of the plot. The obstacle which here hinders the protagonist's purpose will be the most formidable of all, demanding a climactic affective response through decisive action. It is here, too, that the emotional response of the reader/audience should be evoked most strongly. To use a musical analogy, the closure situation of a traditional plot should be akin to a symphony which, after many musical adventures, arrives decisively in its dominant key. Whatever emotions the reader/audience is subjected to during the narrative, he or she must be allowed to experience the intended emotions (fear and pity in the case of tragedy) as the work reaches its climax.

2. Application to Mark's Gospel

Having discussed the chief principles underlying the composition of plot, we consider now their application to Mark's Gospel. Two preliminary points should be taken into account. First, it must be remembered that Mark was writing long before the rise of modern literary criticism, and that to apply such principles to his work is to invite the charge of anachronism. We are far safer working with Aristotle, whose *Poetics* predates Mark's Gospel by some four centuries; though even then, we should not imagine that he was some omniscient guru to whose literary principles all dramatists and poets subsequent to him were expected to conform. To some degree, he was airing his own preferences for what

21. Chatman, *Story and Discourse*, pp. 53-56.
22. Chatman, *Story and Discourse*, pp. 53-54.

he believed to be superior technique, rather than establishing a set of universal principles by which all writers were to be judged. The point is that many of the literary precepts of which he speaks had already become well-established among dramatists and poets before Aristotle passed judgment upon them. Nevertheless, Mark does appear to adhere quite closely to Aristotelian principles, so it is better to read him in that light, on the whole, rather than to impose modern literary principles which, in any case, are most probably ultimately derived from Aristotle. If we do take account of modern developments, we should do so judiciously, using them to provide insights into Mark's literary technique rather than expecting to find them there.

The second point is that ancient and modern literary critics alike are concerned primarily with fiction, whereas in Mark's Gospel we are faced with a work which purports, at least implicitly, to be historical. And a historian—albeit an ancient and theologically-oriented one—could not be expected to be as flexible in his plot construction and characterization as a poet or dramatist working with what was generally agreed to be mythological material.[23] The incorporation of historical events into a work is bound to affect the literary outcome to some extent, and in Mark's case is likely to be one of the chief reasons why the Gospel tends to be more episodic than Aristotle would no doubt have preferred.

a. *Plot-Related Factors and the Markan Plot*
i) *The Causal Factor.* With these preliminary points in mind, it is time to engage once more the issue of causality. Is Mark's Gospel purely episodic, or does it contain a fully-developed plot—or maybe something between the extremes? There are certainly some causal elements, but they are not tightly woven. The dilemma of the religious authorities who are seeking to destroy Jesus will serve as an illustration. The opponents' opposition is broadly comprehensible from the perspective of cause and effect. Jesus feels that the Spirit of God has come upon him, and that by this Spirit he is to proclaim the gospel in word and deed. As he thus preaches, the people recognize in all this the word of authority (1.27) which, as the implied author stresses, directly challenges the authority of the religious leaders (1.22). Naturally, the opposition occurs as a

---

23. We have only to compare the various dramatic treatments of the Orestes myth to appreciate how freely the playwrights worked the material.

consequence of this—a fact confirmed by later passages in which the
bone of contention is legitimate authority (2.5b-10a; 11.27-33). So the
opponents' desire to destroy Jesus (3.6; 11.18; 14.1) is causally established; but how do they progress from the desire to the deed? Clearly,
they are quite impotent until Judas arrives on the scene. Yet Judas seems
to arrive from nowhere; his sole purpose is to betray Jesus to the
authorities so that they can fulfil their plan to bring him to the cross, but
the reader is never enlightened as to the traitor's motives. Ideally, some
action by the protagonist ought to cause Judas to take the action he
does. Beyond the scope of the narrative, suggestions to this effect have
been made,[24] but from within, the reader never learns why Judas turns
traitor; he discovers only that he is instrumental in Jesus' death. Why
should Mark have wished to conceal this information from the
reader?—perhaps because he felt that in stating the reasons for Judas'
action he would have weakened the antagonistic effect he wanted him to
exert upon his audience.

In this instance, then, we find a curious mixture of well-plotted
narrative and disparate episodes which seem designed to get the plot out
of an impasse without themselves being interwoven with it. Whether this
is good literary practice is no doubt a matter for debate. We should
reiterate, however, that Mark was to some extent constrained by historical
circumstances (did he know what Judas' motives really were?), and
must have been conscious that however much he endeavoured to adhere
to dramatic techniques he was, in the last analysis, engaged on a project
quite different from pure drama.

ii) *The Affective Factor*. How, then, does Mark fare in regard to the
evocation of emotion? Different types of plot are designed to illicit
different emotional responses in the reader/audience. Aristotle tells us
that in the case of tragic drama, the response should be one of fear and
pity. The Markan plot, as we shall argue in more detail later, is essentially a tragic one, so we should expect to find a tragic appeal of the kind
Aristotle describes. And this, in fact, is what we do find. We are invited
to feel pity for a good man (better, in fact, than the ideal tragic protagonist, who has human limitations and is thus subject to tragic error, or

---

24. The most common solution is that Judas was a Zealot who, by arranging for
Jesus' arrest, hoped to force him into an act of violent resistance, at which point the
momentum for his becoming the warrior messiah expected by the masses would be
too strong to be denied.

hubris[25]) who is convinced that he has been commissioned by God to preach the good news of God's incoming kingdom, and who resolutely carries out his mission despite progressively bitter opposition to his campaign and the foreknowledge that his persistence in this matter will lead directly to his death. The reader understands the divine inspiration for the mission to be authenticated by what Jesus does and says, and can only wonder and lament at the manner in which men—particularly those who are supposed to be the guardians of Israel's religious consciousness—reject both proclamation and proclaimer. Our sense of pity increases in proportion to the growing magnitude of hostile forces which crowd in upon the protagonist with slow, deliberate inevitability.

So much, then, for pity; but there is also fear—not so much fear in the sense of terror, although there is a hint of that, but more in the sense of awe. A man who raises the dead, feeds multitudes with a few morsels of food and walks on water is bound to evoke a fearful response. Again, this sense of awe is built up through a narration of the incidents until a climax is reached in the empty tomb episode. This is not the climax of the *plot*—that honour goes to the utterance of the centurion at the moment of Jesus' death (15.39)—but it is the point of greatest intensity in relation to one of the emotions which the author is seeking to arouse. Many incidents are calculated to illicit a feeling of awe in the reader as he or she comes face to face with the mystery of the protagonist, but none can serve the purpose so well as the empty tomb. The Gospel *must* end here; one more word after the final ἐφοβοῦντο γάρ ('for they were afraid') would spoil the effect. The reader is meant to share the mystified awe of the women as they flee from the empty tomb.

According to Aristotelian principles the desired emotional effect should emanate from the plot itself—that is to say, from the nature of the events and their arrangement. Although, as we have seen, there is evidence of this in Mark, the author drives home the emotional tenor of his work in the language he employs. Thus, he uses a wide range of words expressing fear and astonishment. The people who witness the exorcism at Capernaum are astonished (ἐξεπλήσσοντο) and amazed (ἐθαμβήθησαν) at Jesus' teaching (1.22, 27); when he stills the storm,

---

25. Cf. Aristotle, *Poetics*, 13.5, where the ideal tragic protagonist is said to be 'the sort of man who is not pre-eminently virtuous and just, and yet it is through no badness or villainy of his own that he falls into misfortune, but rather through some flaw (ἁμαρτίαν) in him, he being one of those who are in high station and good fortune...'

the disciples are 'filled with awe' (ἐφοβήθησαν φόβον μέγαν, 4.41)[26]; those who encounter the Gerasene demoniac in his right mind are afraid (ἐφοβήθησαν, 5.15), while Jesus' compatriots at Nazareth are astonished (ἐξεπλήσσοντο) at his wisdom (6.2); after the healing of the deaf mute the bystanders are 'astonished beyond measure' (ὑπερπερισσῶς ἐξεπλήσσοντο, 7.37); and the disciples are both amazed (ἐθαμβοῦντο) and 'exceedingly astonished' (περισσῶς ἐξεπλήσσοντο) at their Master's hard teaching concerning those with riches entering the kingdom (10.24, 26); similarly, those who accompany Jesus on the way to Jerusalem are amazed (ἐθαμβοῦντο) and afraid (ἐφοβοῦντο, 10.32); after the cleansing of the Temple the multitude is astonished (ἐξεπλήσσετο) at his teaching (11.18); even his most implacable enemies are amazed (ἐξεθαύμαζον) at him (12.17), and Pilate wonders (θαυμάζειν) at his silence (15.5).

It is clear, then, that while Mark does follow Aristotelian principles by allowing the appeal to the emotions to exude from the plotted narrative itself, he also underscores the specific emotions he hopes to illicit from the reader by recourse to an appropriate vocabulary.

iii) *The Character Factor.* As to the question of character, it is evident that, in common with most other ancient works, the actors tend to serve the plot. In Crane's terms the plot is one of action, and the rôle of the characters is to help it along. Thus it is that we know nothing of Judas as a character in his own right; his sole purpose, as we have seen, is to cut through the dilemma about how Jesus might be arrested, and so free the plot from the doldrums in which it has been becalmed.

Peter, too, is a functional character in this sense. Although we know much more of him than we do of Judas, and are presented with certain character traits pertaining to him, he also is instrumental in keeping the plot on the move. Half way through the Gospel, at 8.27-30, the plotted narrative has reached a point beyond which it cannot proceed without a particular intervention. Jesus is demanding to know what people say of his identity, and the disciples respond with all the usual stock answers. But the next question is, 'Who do *you* say that I am?' Unless Jesus receives the correct answer to this, the plot cannot progress. It is Peter who provides it: 'You are the Christ', he declares (8.29). And once that has been understood, Jesus is able to explain what manner of Christ he

---

26. ἐφοβήθησαν φόβον μέγαν is literally 'they were afraid with a great fear'.

is, and the plotted narrative is able to resume.

Mark, then, has little interest in the characters themselves; they are simply instruments enabling the plot to function. Even the protagonist is more interesting for what he represents than for any particular character traits he might have. In a novel in which character dominates the plot (as in Austen's *Emma*) the interest lies in the manner in which the fortunes, and perhaps the prejudices, of the protagonist are transformed by events. *Emma*, in fact, is a prime candidate for classification as a character novel in which the principle of the plot is, in Crane's words, 'a completed process of change in the moral character of the protagonist, precipitated or molded by action, and made manifest both in it, and in thought and feeling'.[27] The Markan Jesus, on the other hand, is somewhat iconic. It is true that he reacts in various ways to other characters and events; and, in one sense, he is a very human figure. But, unlike Aristotle's ideal protagonist, he does not undergo a process of change brought about by the frailties in his own character. Sophocles' Oedipus brings catastrophe upon himself because he cannot resist his own curiosity: he must know, and the tragic reversal occurs when he finds out. Jesus, however, is in a sense monolithic: whatever activity is going on around him, he will not be budged from his ultimate purpose. Despite hostility from family, acquaintances and religious authorities, and misunderstanding on the part of his disciples, Jesus remains resolute in his aim of proclaiming by word and deed the good news of God's kingdom: nothing deflects him from this aim, even the inevitability of his death. But this is to lay emphasis on what Jesus has come to do rather than on his character. In the last analysis, character, like everything else, simply serves the ends of the plot.

iv) *The Conflict Factor*. The last of the four factors we discussed—conflict—while not essential to the plot, is nevertheless the linchpin of Mark's narrative. Of the seven types of conflict possibility listed above, most appear in one form or another in Mark. Jesus' conflict with demons would constitute an obvious example of conflict with the supernatural (1); conflict between humans (2), Jesus' controversies with the religious leaders for instance, is widespread, while the cursing of the fig tree (11.12-14, 20-21) may signify confrontation with another living entity (3), even though its purpose is symbolic; conflict with natural forces (5) is to be found in Jesus' dealings with the sea (4.35-41), disease

27. Crane, 'Concept of Plot', p. 239.

and death (5.21-43); the religious controversies (2.1-3.6; 7.1-23; 11.15-18; 12.13-17, and so on) are all instances of conflicts over religious principles and, to some extent, political situations (6), while conflict with the inner self (7) is represented in debates such as that in 11.27-33, where the inner deliberations of the religious authorities are really representative of how an individual mind might address the dilemma.

Essentially, though, the Markan plot is centred on a human conflict which takes place at two levels, both against a supernatural backcloth. Since we hope shortly to discuss this plot in outline, we need not anticipate that discussion here other than to indicate briefly what the essential conflicts are. First, there is the conflict with human opponents which is set up as early as 1.22, proceeds through some deceptively innocuous debates about legal principles (2.1–3.6), and gradually hardens into an earnest quest for Jesus' death. Secondly, there is a conflict with the disciples over Jesus' identity and the true nature of messiahship. Finally, running as an undercurrent to these is a cosmic conflict in which Jesus, endowed with the Spirit of God, clashes with God's arch-rival, Satan (1.13) and his entourage. These three narrative lines are free to develop independently of one another in one sense, but are inextricably linked as well. The view that the human opposition is a manifestation of the demonic, for instance, may have something to commend it.

b. *Plot Construction in Mark*

Finally, there is the question of plot construction. F.J. Matera has resolved to use the Chatman model of units composed of a kernel and several satellites to inform his understanding of Matthew's plot.[28] On this basis, he contends, the entire structure of the Gospel can be ascertained. But Matthew is, in any case, well-organized around a system of narrative and discourse units, as has for long been recognized;[29] it is, therefore, a Gospel which is susceptible to the kind of treatment that Matera suggests. Mark, it has to be said, is more episodic, and despite a clear outline structure, the delineation of the sub-units is not always easy to achieve. Nevertheless, without endeavouring to apply Chatman's model in any rigid sense, there are at least two points in Mark where the principle is clearly applicable. The first is at 1.14-15 where Jesus calls people to repent and believe in the gospel. This is a crux because it calls

---

28. Matera, 'Plot', pp. 233-53.

29. Cf. B.W. Bacon, *Studies in Matthew* (London: Constable, 1930), pp. 165-249.

people to decision. It is not the protagonist who is called to decision, notice: since the Spirit of God has already been conferred on him (1.10), he cannot but do the will of God in total obedience. It is the message which calls to decision, and the bulk of the Gospel is concerned to show how people respond to it—whether positively, like the disciples in 1.16-20, or negatively like the religious leaders in 2.1–3.6. So, no proclamation, no plot!

The other obvious kernel is, of course, the great confession (8.27-30). Again, there is no question that the protagonist must engage the crux; it is, on this occasion, the disciples who are required to do so. Jesus questions them about his true identity and, as we have already intimated, the future course of the plot depends upon their response. Regardless of misunderstandings, they must acknowledge that Jesus is messiah—whatever that may mean—before the narrative can advance.

3. An Outline of the Markan Plot

a. The Markan Prologue and the Plot

Mark states the purpose he has in writing his Gospel right at the outset: it is to demonstrate that Jesus Christ is the Son of God. If the text is pristine,[30] the first verse sums it up: the beginning of the gospel of Jesus Christ, the Son of God. At the climax to the narrative, where the plot is resolved, the centurion is made to confess Jesus, using this title. The essential business of the plot, then, is to lead in causal stages from Mark's initial declaration to the centurion's confession. How does an obscure, itinerant rabbi from Nazareth come to be confessed as Son of God as he hangs on a cross? That is the question the plot is required to answer. As the plot develops, the reader is expected to take account of the information supplied by the omniscient author—information which, it must be remembered, is not freely available to the characters in the story. It is this special privilege of being able to share the author's insights that enables the reader to entertain particular impressions of the characters he or she meets. For instance, the reader may perceive the

---

30. The text critical problem is whether the phrase 'Son of God' was part of the original text. It is omitted by some manuscripts, including Sinaiticus (though the phrase is there inserted by a later hand). But since 'Son of God' is certainly, for Mark, a christological title which appears at strategic points in his narrative (3.11; 15.39), and given that there is a strong textual tradition of inclusion (ABDLWf[1]f[13] 565 700 latt sy co Ir[lat]), the authenticity of its appearance in 1.1 is probable.

disciples as dull-witted, but then they do not share his or her omniscient viewpoint; the reader may regard the religious leaders as negative characters who endeavour to thwart Jesus' purposes, but they, without access to the reader's special knowledge, feel that they are doing God a service by preserving the true religion of Israel from the wiles of apostates.

But I digress: 'point of view' properly belongs to the next chapter; let us return for the moment to plot. The action in Mark stems from Jesus' awareness that the Spirit of God has come upon him, and that he has a divine mission which he must fulfil in word and deed. The narrative then goes on to explore the different ways in which others react to this mission—especially the opponents and the disciples. Finally, underpinning these two threads is a cosmic struggle between Jesus, in whom God's Spirit dwells, and Satan and his demonic forces.

Mark 1.1-15 is essential as a basis for the entire narrative. The Old Testament citation in 1.2-3 (cf. Mal. 3.1; Isa. 40.3) is the only one which the author presents directly—that is to say, without ascribing it to one of his characters. Clearly, he wishes to show that the events he is about to relate are consequent upon Old Testament prophecy. By Mark's day, the tradition that Elijah would herald the coming of messiah was well-established (cf. Mal. 4.5 [Hebrew text, 3.23]), so the evangelist depicts John the Baptist as playing that rôle. He wears the same kind of clothes as Elijah (1.6; cf. 2 Kgs 1.8) and later he is openly identified with him (Mk 9.11-13). As Elijah is to messiah, so John is to Jesus: the conclusion to be drawn from this is obvious. Mark, however, goes further still; everything that occurs in relation to John foreshadows what occurs in relation to Jesus. John appears in the wilderness (1.4), which is precisely where Jesus goes after his baptism (1.12); John preaches 'a baptism of repentance for the forgiveness of sins' (1.4), and Jesus, too, calls people to repent (1.15); John baptizes with water, Jesus baptizes with the Holy Spirit (1.8); sometimes people confuse the identities of John and Jesus (6.14-16; 8.27-28). Most significantly of all, John's execution prefigures that of Jesus. He is arrested for condemning Herod's adultery with Herodias, executed at the behest of Herodias and her daughter, despite the king's reservations, and laid in a tomb by his disciples (6.17-29). Similarly, Jesus is arrested, having antagonized the Jewish leaders, executed despite Pilate's reservations, and laid in a tomb by Joseph of Arimathea. The parallels may seem minimal, and the sequence, arrest–execution–burial, is perhaps unavoidable in an account of death by execution, but in the parable of the wicked husbandmen (12.1-9) the relationship seems to be deliberately underlined. There, the tenants (= Jewish leaders) kill the servants (= prophets) of the absent vineyard (= Israel) owner (= God), and wound another in the head (surely a reference to the beheading of John), before finally disposing of the son (= Jesus).

It is against this background, then, that Jesus arrives for baptism. Given what we already know, we can say that baptism here is a confirmation of the relationship between John and Jesus; John, in baptizing Jesus, is acknowledging him as the greater one who comes after, 'the thong of whose sandals I am not worthy to stoop down and untie' (1.7). Jesus' status is confirmed when, on emerging from the water, the Spirit of God descends upon him in visible form, and a heavenly voice declares, 'Thou art my beloved Son; with thee I am well pleased.' At this point Jesus must be aware of his own divine sonship. The references to the senses shows that there can be no mistake. 'Sight' and 'hearing' stand like the two concurring witnesses required for a successful indictment in Jewish legal proceedings, and it is significant that the voice here addresses the recipient in the second person singular (Σὺ εἶ ὁ Υἱός μου ὁ ἀγαπητός, 1.11), not in the demonstrative (Οὗτός ἐστιν ὁ Υἱός μου ὁ ἀγαπητός) as at the transfiguration (9.7). Armed, therefore, with this self-knowledge of his divine commission, Jesus begins his work. We note that he is *driven* (ἐκβάλλει) into the wilderness by God's Spirit (1.12), and we may surmise that he proclaims the gospel in the same dynamic manner: it is not that he has any choice in the matter; he is compelled by the Spirit within. John, the forerunner, having completed his task, is removed from the stage, leaving Jesus to proclaim, 'The time is fulfilled, and the kingdom of God is at hand; repent and believe in the gospel' (1.14-15).

b. *The Rôle of the Opponents in the Plot*
Immediately after this key episode (a plot kernel, if we may use Chatman's term) the two chief threads of the plot are introduced, namely the response to Jesus made by the disciples on the one hand, and the authorities on the other. In 1.16-20 Jesus calls four fishermen to follow him, and to do this really involves responding to his proclamation. The invitation is taken up unhesitatingly: Jesus calls, and 'immediately they [leave] their nets and follow him' (1.18). This, then, initiates the disciples' involvement with the plot.

Next, the seed of opposition is sown. In 1.21-22 Jesus enters the synagogue in Capernaum and teaches as one with authority, 'and not as the scribes'. And this is the nub of the issue. The Spirit of God which is vested in Jesus makes authoritative all that he does and says; but the scribes, too, claim authority. Traditionally, a special rabbinic authority, *reshut*, was conferred on successive generations of scribes by the laying-on of hands—a practice which, it was claimed, could be traced back to Moses' conferring of authority upon Joshua (Deut. 34.9).[31] Thus, the popular recognition of the authority in Jesus' teaching was bound to threaten the scribes' rôle as authoritative teachers of the law. Herein lay the root of their opposition to Jesus. Henceforth the debates which take place between these opposing parties, whatever their superficial content, are essentially concerned with the question of whose authority comes from God—that of Jesus or that of the scribes?

During the early stages of opposition in Galilee the controversies tend to revolve around points of *halakhah*—eating with tax-collectors and sinners (2.15-17), fasting (2.18-20), Sabbath observance (2.23–3.6) and ritual purity (7.1-5, 14-23). Although, at this stage, there is little serious attempt to destroy Jesus, his fate is nevertheless prefigured. In 2.7 he is accused of blasphemy—the very charge which leads directly to his death in 14.61-63; the removal of the bridegroom, which is to be the occasion for fasting (= mourning)(2.20), is also a foreshadowing of Jesus' crucifixion; and, of course, the appearance of the Pharisees and Herodians who conspire to destroy Jesus (3.6) anticipates their reappearance during Passion week (12.13), when Jesus' opponents collectively are making a concerted effort to 'destroy' him.[32]

Even at this stage, events are arranged in such a way as to show a steady intensification of opposition. Initially, the battle lines are drawn: Jesus is set over against the scribes in the matter of his teaching with authority (1.22); it is in 'their' synagogue that he exorcises one possessed (1.23); and it is 'to them' that the leper must show himself cleansed after sacrifice (1.44).[33]

31. Cf. D. Daube, 'ἐξουσία in Mk 1:22 and 27', *JTS* 39 (1938), pp. 45-59; *idem, The New Testament and Rabbinic Judaism* (London: Athlone Press, 1956), pp. 205-23.

32. The word ἀπόλλυμι is used of Jesus' destruction in both 3.6 and 11.18. Other rubrics which reveal the opponents' plan to remove Jesus occur at 12.12; 14.1-2.

33. The RSV rendering, 'to the people', is really an inference based on Old Testament regulations—a leper would be exiled from the community until pronounced clean, at which point he would be readmitted to the camp. In Mk 1.44,

The first face-to-face encounter occurs in 2.1-12, where Jesus forgives the paralytic his sins, but the scribes can only murmur disapprovingly (2.6); it is Jesus who takes the initiative in raising the matter openly. Next, Jesus is found eating with tax collectors and sinners (2.15-17), and the opponents do object openly to that; but they can only manage to address the disciples about their Master's behaviour; they do not address Jesus himself. The fasting episode (2.18-20) seems to lack the hostility of its context. True, Jesus is addressed directly for the first time in the controversy series, but the indeterminate pronoun makes it impossible for the reader to establish who asks the question: it cannot even be ascertained beyond doubt that this pericope is a genuine controversy; form-critically it is closer in nature to a *Schulsgespräch*. In the cornfield incident (2.23-28) the authorities (the Pharisees, on this occasion) do at last verbally confront Jesus, but only about the behaviour of his disciples (even though a rabbi would have been responsible for his disciples' actions[34]). Finally, when Jesus heals on the Sabbath (3.1-5), the opponents appear to revert to the brooding, conspiratorial attitude with which they began: they watch him in order to accuse him. But, in view of Jesus' stinging initiative (3.4), they take counsel over the matter of how they might destroy him (3.6).

Despite the malice of the final verse, the controversy cycle in 2.1–3.6 is concerned chiefly with legal wrangling—matters of *halakhah*. But in the Beelzebul controversy (3.22-30) hostility is intensified to the extent that it is Jesus' own person that comes under attack. No longer is the dispute over his words and actions alone, but over the authority by which he operates. A ministry inspired by the Holy Spirit (3.29) is taken by the authorities to be the outworking of Satan (3.22). The seriousness of this charge is underlined by the fact that those who make it are described as 'scribes who came down from Jerusalem'—the very people, in fact, who will later conspire with the chief priests and elders to bring about Jesus' death. At this stage, however, there is no indication that the accusation is being made in Jesus' presence. Mark 3.20-35 also intensifies the opposition quantitatively: now it is not only the Jewish leaders who object, but Jesus' family. From this point, Jesus faces opposition on three fronts—the official, the domestic and the demonic.

however, the pronoun αὐτῶν is ambiguous, and could refer to the religious authorities.

34. D. Daube, 'Responsibilities of Master and Disciples in the Gospels', *NTS* 19 (1972–73), p. 5.

The complex of controversies in 7.1-23, particularly that in 7.1-5, appears to return us to the world of 2.1–3.6. As in 2.23-28, for instance, religious officials make a direct approach to Jesus to object, in question form, to the behaviour of his disciples (2.24; 7.5), and in his response Jesus appeals to the authority of Scripture (2.25-26; 7.6-7), applying it to the immediate situation in a pithy summary saying (2.27; 7.8). The content of 7.1-5 is also quite close to that of 2.15-17: both deal with the law of purity within the context of an 'eating' episode. But the presence once again of the 'scribes...from Jerusalem' (7.1) functions both retrospectively and prophetically. On the one hand it recalls their appearance in an earlier controversy (3.22-30), while on the other it anticipates their later conspiracy with the chief priests and elders in Jerusalem. This group, therefore, is meant to tie together the various controversy blocks or cycles into a continuous story.

The next relevant pericope, 8.11-12, takes an ominous turn. Though set in Galilee, the arena of legal controversy, there are signs that the encounters are becoming ever more acrimonious. There is a return to the issue of Jesus' authority—he must show his messianic credentials if he is to be taken seriously. But there is also a new and sinister element: the Pharisees are out to 'test' (πειράζειν) him—the word is the same as that used of his temptation by Satan in 1.13. And this effectively carries the story forward into its next stage in which the authorities' attempts to 'test' or 'entrap' Jesus constitute a significant feature.

The transition between the Galilean and Judean phases of opposition is effected by the passion predictions. Strikingly, the first of these, at 8.31, is uttered at the furthest point (symbolically, at least) that Jesus ever gets from Jerusalem. The geographical distance is paradigmatic of the conceptual distance: at the point where Peter confesses Jesus to be Messiah the latter's death on the cross must seem as conceptually remote as Caesarea Philippi is geographically remote from the Holy City. No wonder Peter turns to rebuke! But then comes the long trek south, and the formally similar repetition of the Passion prediction at 9.31 and 10.33-34, along with other passages of foreshadowing at 9.12; 10.45, set up a fateful yet driving rhythm which carries the story of opposition right across the border between Galilee (literally, Samaria) and Judea.

Yet the actual traversal does not go unnoticed. It is as if, at 10.1, Jesus is crossing the Rubicon. Now he finds himself in truly hostile territory—the domain of the 'scribes from Jerusalem'—where a whole array of opposition groups gather like wolves for the kill. Once across the border he is plunged straight into another controversy by Pharisees seeking to put him to the test (10.2-9). The nature of the dispute is a legal one, divorce, as we might expect of pharisaic involvement, but the Pharisees are no longer content simply to triumph in the argument as in 2.23-28; now they are seeking to bring their distinguished opponent to grief.

When he arrives in Jerusalem, Jesus keeps the momentum going by his act of cleansing the Temple (11.15-18). This act is in response to the cultic system of Israel, of which the chief priests are the guardians, just as the scribes and Pharisees are the guardians of the legal system. But Jesus reacts against a state of affairs which allows commercial transactions to take place in the Temple precincts. Two things emerge from this episode: first, the resurrection of the authorities' desire to destroy Jesus (11.18), and secondly a preoccupation with the judgment of Israel (11.12-25; 12.1-12, 38-40). There is no small irony here. In proclaiming the judgment of Israel—its cultic (11.12-25) and legal (12.38-40) perversions— and by announcing condemnation for the religious leaders (12.1-9, 38-40), he is inevitably bringing his own condemnation upon his head. The double irony, of course, is that this condemnation leads directly to his exoneration, and the religious leaders, who seem at first to have triumphed, are confounded.

Mark 11.27-33 heralds the so-called 'day of questions' in which all the leadership groups endeavour in vain to bring Jesus down in debate. As he strolls through the Temple, he is accosted by the tripartite group of chief priests–scribes–elders (11.27) who, as we have already gathered, are destined to bring him to the cross. The question of authority is raised again: 'By what authority are you doing these things, or who gave you this authority to do them?' It is the second form of the question which is really pertinent, for it signals the re-emergence of the old struggle for power: Who is acting on God's authority—Jesus or the leaders? By consistently linking the ministry of Jesus to that of John (cf. 1.2-15; 6.14-16; 9.11-13) Mark implicitly provides the answer: those who are convinced that John's baptism was 'from heaven' (merely a circumlocution for God) are obliged also to acknowledge Jesus' ministry as emanating from the same source. 'These things' (ταῦτα), while referring initially to the cleansing of the Temple, extend ultimately to the entire ministry; for the question of divine authority has been an issue from the outset.

After the judgment parable, which incites the authorities to redouble their efforts to secure Jesus' arrest (12.12), there follows the tribute question (12.13-17). This signals the reappearance of the Pharisee–

Herodian alliance (cf. 3.6), but now they are 'sent'. By whom? One supposes by the last-named leadership group, the chief priests–scribes–elders: in Jerusalem they are the ones to direct operations. Nevertheless, under that direction it is the Pharisees and Herodians who endeavour to 'entrap [Jesus] in his talk'. This strange alliance may be especially apt here given that the tax question raises both religious and political issues. The word ἔξεστιν ('it is/is it lawful?', 12.14), used also in 2.24, 26; 3.4; 10.2 where matters of law and tradition are at issue, indicates that payment of taxes was, in part, a religious problem: it raised the question of who was really king—Caesar or God? But the motive is political: a negative answer would have been likely to lead to a charge of treason under Roman law. The Jewish religious authorities are by now prepared to use any means at their disposal to secure Jesus' condemnation.

With the successful response to the previous question, the authorities' efforts appear to be on the wane. The next issue, brought by the Sadducees (12.18-27), could hardly do more than ridicule Jesus' position. In rabbinic terms the case of levirite marriage, purely hypothetical in its application here, is no more than a *boruth* question designed simply to ridicule the opponents' position. Jesus replies that the debate in this instance arises purely out of the Sadducees' failure to understand the Scriptures.

The next episode (12.28-34) is not strictly a controversy story at all; the scribe appears to be genuine in his question about the greatest commandment. It seems odd that the conflict element should be absent, until we recognize that in none of the final three episodes in the Jerusalem conflict series (12.13-40) do the opponents seize the initiative; on the contrary, in 12.35-37, 38-40, it is Jesus who goes on the offensive. The message seems to be that, in debate with opponents in both Galilee and Judea, Jesus has beaten all comers; he has vanquished the opposition to such an extent that even a scribe—traditionally an arch-enemy—must now acknowledge his supremacy.[35] From his new position of strength, he then feels able to round on his assailants to deliver a crushing judgment on both their teaching (12.35-37), which cannot, therefore, be 'with authority', and their practices (12.38-40). Surely Jesus has triumphed, sending his opponents to ignominious defeat! For no-one dares to ask him a further question (12.34).

---

35. That this is a specifically Markan programme may be evident from the fact that in the Matthean parallel (Mt. 22.34-40) the questioner *is* an enemy.

The point about the story of the righteous scribe is that it forms a climactic moment in Jesus' dealings with his legal opponents. We almost forget, amid the euphoria, that they have one card left up their sleeve—namely, their alliance with the chief priests. And so, in 14.1, those chief priests make their ominous re-entry. In language reminiscent of earlier rubrics (11.18; 12.12; cf. 3.6), Mark informs us that they are still seeking a way to kill Jesus. Defeated on religious grounds they may be, but the political option remains open to them. Even so, all seems lost until Judas arrives on the scene. The rubrics in 3.6; 11.18; 12.12; 14.1-2 seem collectively static: the authorities are perpetually wondering what to do; the use of subjunctives such as 'might destroy' (ἀπολέσωσιν, 3.6; 11.18) and 'might kill' (ἀποκτείνωσιν, 14.1) reflect their indecisiveness; they want to seize him, but they fear the multitude with whom Jesus still enjoys a high degree of popularity. It is precisely when they are at their wits' end that the solution comes. Using his characteristic intercalation technique,[36] Mark poses the problem, inserts the story of the anointing at Bethany (14.3-9), then provides the answer to the problem, namely, Judas' offer to betray Jesus—an act which has been foreshadowed for the reader as early as 3.19. Indeed, it is not until the reader knows that the betrayal has been arranged that the relevant actors become privy to it (14.18-21). By that time, of course, the die has been cast: nothing can stop the inevitability of Jesus' crucifixion...

...Or can it? At least I need to qualify my last statement. We should be aware that the readers/hearers of Mark's Gospel would already have been well-acquainted with the story of Jesus—at least in outline—so the death of Jesus in Mark's narrative would not have been unexpected. What suspense there is, lies not in any ignorance of the outcome of the plot, but in a certain uncertainty as to how that end might be achieved. In this respect the reader shares the perplexity of the chief priests and their allies. This uncertainty is kept afloat right up to the last as Jesus is presented with various channels of escape. First, at the moment of arrest in Gethsemane, there is brief resistance from one of Jesus' companions

36. On which, see E. von Dobschütz, 'Zur Erzählerkunst der Markus', *ZNW* 27 (1928), pp. 193-98; H.G. Wood, 'The Priority of Mark', *ExpTim* 65 (1953–54), pp. 17-19; J.R. Donahue, *Are You the Christ? The Trial Narrative in the Gospel of Mark* (SBLDS, 10; Missoula, MT: SBL, 1973), pp. 42-43, 58-63; J.R. Edwards, 'Markan Sandwiches: The Significance of Interpolations in the Markan Narrative', *NovT* 31 (1989), pp. 193-216; T. Shepherd, 'The Narrative Function of Markan Intercalation', *NTS* 41 (1995), pp. 522-40.

(14.47), but instead of taking his cue from that, he submits passively. At the trial before the High Priest, the witnesses cannot even agree among themselves, and the case for the prosecution is in disarray. It is surely an irregularity for the High Priest to cut through the customary procedure by asking directly, 'Are you the Christ, the Son of the Blessed?' (14.61). Jesus needs only to maintain his prudent silence in order to be acquitted; yet he chooses to affirm his messiahship (14.62), thus bringing about his condemnation. Again, at the trial before Pilate it appears as though Jesus might be released, for the governor is unable to find fault with him; but the priests begin to poison the crowd against him, so that when Pilate offers to release a prisoner they cry for Barabbas (15.11). Now Jesus is taken to Golgotha and crucified there. The bystanders hurl insults: 'Aha! You who would destroy the Temple and build it in three days, save yourself, and come down from the cross!' The chief priests and scribes, leering in triumph, sneer, 'He saved others; he cannot save himself. Let the Christ, the King of Israel, come down now from the cross, that we may see and believe.' And the reader senses here a bitter irony: of course, Christ could indeed cheat death by descending from the cross. Then why does he not do so? At the last, Jesus utters his cry of dereliction. Misinterpreting the Aramaic, the bystanders believe that he is calling Elijah (15.34-35). Might not Elijah save him, even at this late hour? But no! Jesus utters a loud cry and dies (15.37). All hope seems lost: surely the forces of opposition have triumphed. But the centurion utters his great christological affirmation (15.39), and the final episode (16.1-8) leaves the reader with the women at the empty tomb, wondering.[37]

c. *The Rôle of the Disciples in the Plot*
The response of the religious leaders to Jesus' proclamation of the gospel is to bring him eventually to the cross; what is the disciples' response? Initially, it is one of obedience. Jesus calls, and they follow (1.16-20). They bear the rebuke of the authorities for Jesus' unorthodox behaviour (2.16), and he bears theirs (2.24). He appoints them 'to be with him, and to be sent out to preach and have authority to cast out demons' (3.14-15)—a mission which is fulfilled in 6.7-13. It appears that Jesus is at liberty to confer his authority upon 'those whom he desire[s]' (3.13), just as the scribes hand down their authority to others in the laying-on of

37. My case for regarding the religious authorities as actors in an unfolding tragic drama is presented more meticulously than is possible here in S.H. Smith, 'Role of Jesus' Opponents', pp. 161-82.

hands. The disciples are Jesus' loyal assistants (3.9); neither does their loyalty go unrewarded, for they are considered to be among the insiders to whom 'has been given the secret of the kingdom of God' (4.11). The parables, which appear to confound those outside, are meant to provide insight for the disciples.

But it is precisely at this point that clouds appear on the horizon; for the disciples do *not* understand, and Jesus must furnish them with explanations (4.13-20, 33-34). Hard on the heels of the parables section comes the storm on the lake (4.35-41), and the disciples' terror makes it evident that they are oblivious to Jesus' true identity—'Who, then, is this, that even the wind and sea obey him?' (4.41).

A number of incidents now occur which ought to result in enlightenment. Peter, James and John are privileged to witness Jesus raise Jairus' daughter from the dead (5.21-24, 35-43); the disciples are sent on a mission, with power to exorcise (6.7-13), and they find that they are able to do so (6.13); on their return, Jesus feeds five thousand people with five loaves and two fish (6.35-44); despite their initial lack of understanding (6.37), he even allows the disciples to assist in the miracle by distributing the bread (6.41). Yet in the very next episode they are terrified to see Jesus walking towards them on the sea (6.45-51). Mark 6.52 is a fitting summary to what precedes: 'And they were utterly astounded, for they did not understand about the loaves, but their hearts were hardened.' Now we see that the disciples are becoming more like the religious leaders. Of the latter, Jesus was said to be aggrieved because of their hardness of heart (3.5); here, the disciples are guilty of that same obduracy. The verb πωρόω, 'to harden', is merely the verbal equivalent of the nominal πώρωσις, 'hardness', in the earlier passage. Yet at least in the case of the opponents, their hostility seems to be of their own making. In the disciples' case, on the contrary, the passive form of the verb 'hardened' indicates that they are as powerless to do anything to relieve their obduracy as are the outsiders in 4.11-12. Indeed, after further failures to understand, first about the parable about purity (7.14-23), and then the second feeding miracle (8.1-10), Jesus' frustration with his disciples reaches a crescendo in the boat incident (8.14-21). Still they do not understand about the loaves, and the succession of short, brusque rhetorical questions on the lips of Jesus (8.17-21) reflects his exasperation. But what is of greatest significance here is that the language of 8.17-18, by recalling that of 4.12 (and hence Isa. 6.9-10, on which it is based), has the effect of classifying the disciples with the outsiders. They seem to have lost their privileged position, and to have been cast out in the cold.

In the next pericope (8.22-26), however, there is a hint of trans-formation, for the two-stage healing of the blind man is really paradig-matic of the disciples future restoration. Like the man at Bethsaida, they too are blind—metaphorically so—but like him they will come to see aright, if only partially at first. As a matter of fact, this anticipated change begins almost at once. In an obviously intentional juxtaposition to the blind healing episode, Peter's confession at Caesarea Philippi (8.27-30) demonstrates that the first stage of restoration has been reached.Peter (and, by implication, all the disciples) does at last see that Jesus is messiah. As we have seen, this recognition is necessary in order to advance the disciples' rôle in the plot. But, of course, it does not go far enough: the original failure to understand simply becomes a misunder-standing of what messiahship means. This is clear initially from Peter's reaction to the first Passion prediction (8.31-33): he cannot accept that messiah must suffer and die.

The section on discipleship which follows (8.34–10.52) is concerned chiefly with the tension between Jesus' understanding of messiahship and that of his disciples. I cannot afford myself the luxury of going into detail, but basically the pattern is one of the disciples' misunderstanding followed by Jesus' corrective teaching. Peter and the others want to reject the way of suffering (8.31-33), but Jesus teaches that the true disciple must renounce the world with its promises of glory, deny self and take up the cross (8.34-38). With these words ringing in their ears, Peter, James and John are taken to be witnesses at the transfiguration. The voice first heard at Jesus' baptism is now heard again, delivering the same message (9.7), but the addressee is different—no longer Jesus, but the disciples. To them the voice bears authoritative testimony to who Jesus is. God approves his Son, but more significantly under the circum-stances, also approves what he does and says. The teaching about self-denial cannot be wrong because God himself justifies it in saying, 'This is my beloved Son; listen to him.'

But, in descending the mountain, it is clear that nothing has changed. Jesus again speaks of rising from the dead (9.9), but still the disciples have no idea what he means; and when they arrive at the bottom they find that the other disciples have been unable to exorcise a demon from an epileptic boy (9.17-18), despite the fact that they had successfully used the authority given them by Jesus to do such things earlier (6.13). Again, misunderstandings abound. The second Passion prediction is met with incomprehension and fear (9.30-32), and followed immediately by the futile discussion on greatness (9.33-37). Indeed, it seems as though Jesus' concern for the way of suffering and death is more than misunderstood by the disciples: they are completely oblivious to it.

The remainder of the section picks up again the dominant pattern—misunderstanding followed by correction. The disciples are elitist, but the Christian community should be inclusivist (9.38-41); they are self-important when they should be humble (9.33-37; 10.13-16); they crave for positions of power and prestige when it should be their place to serve (9.35; 10.31, 35-45); and they appear to share the values of the rich man who is bidden to sell what he has and give to the poor (10.17-30). In the midst of all this comes the third Passion prediction (10.33-34), but again the disciples seem quite oblivious to its gravity or significance.

By contrast, a blind beggar along the road exhibits a degree of insight. The irony is that, although physically blind, he does see metaphorically—he sees that Jesus is Son of David (10.47). No prompting is required as in the case of the Twelve: Bartimaeus knows instinctively who Jesus is. And so, once he has been healed, he follows Jesus along the way (10.52), not as one who is 'amazed' or 'afraid' (10.32) but as a model of what real discipleship should be.

The most striking feature of the section on discipleship is its static quality. Despite repeated misunderstandings and the requisite corrective teaching, there is no improvement in the disciples' disposition. They are as wrong-headed about messiahship in 10.35-45 as they are in 8.32-33. This does not augur well for Passion week, for the narrative already stands on the threshold of Jerusalem, and the cross looms large. Nevertheless, some positive features do remain. The disciples still endeavour to assist Jesus whenever they can (11.2-7; 14.13-16), and he persists in teaching them. The character of the teaching now, though, is different from that in the previous section. Instead of seizing on the disciples' misunderstandings and correcting them, Jesus now tends to teach in a less intense manner, in terms of object lessons, in fact. From the withered fig tree (11.12-14, 20-25), he is able to make a point about faith and prayer; he uses the sight of the widow contributing her whole living to the Temple (12.41-44) as an object lesson on real as opposed to false piety; and, appropriately, the Temple is in view throughout the eschatological discourse (13.1-37).

But this sense of calm and orderliness in Jesus' relationship with the Twelve acts as a foil for the negative traits which are about to break the surface. The first upset is Judas' betrayal. Although this seems to come like a bolt from the blue, it does, in a way, make logical sense in the context of the plot. Jesus, as we have seen, has been unable to convince his disciples that messiahship is necessarily (δεῖ, 8.31) bound up with suffering and death: they have never looked like comprehending this. And because they are not committed to this view, we can hardly expect them to remain resolute when the going gets tough. Judas has already defected, and although it is left to the reader to infer why, it is not difficult to surmise that his betrayal of Jesus is an earnest attempt to tempt him at the eleventh hour to accept a worldly view of messiahship (one of violent resistance, which would need to be forthcoming now, if Jesus hoped to avoid capture), just as Peter had done in 8.32-33. The reader's perception, according to the implied author, should be that Judas' action (14.10-11) is simply a more desperate and extreme form of Peter's earlier temptation.

From then on, things go rapidly downhill. Peter, and all the other disciples, vow to remain loyal (14.29-31) but, just as Jesus predicts (14.27, 30), Peter denies him (14.66-72) and the rest flee (14.50). Indeed, the three in Gethsemane just prior to the arrest cannot even stay awake while Jesus agonizes over his fate (14.32-42). There are no disciples at the cross, nor afterwards at the empty tomb and, within the parameters of the story, they do not receive the message delivered to the women (16.7).

The causal connection between the disciples' apostasy and their Master's fate lies in the latter's failure to persuade them to adopt his point of view regarding the nature of his messiahship. Had he been able to do that, he would have thwarted the efforts of the Jewish leaders to bring him to the cross because, in all likelihood, Judas would have stayed loyal and consequently would not have provided a way for the opponents to make good their plan. Thus, it is precisely by embarking on the way of suffering and death that Jesus signs his own death warrant. Yet in order for that death to take place, both the opponents and the disciples must be essential elements in the plot.

d. *The Rôle of the Demons in the Plot*
Running as a kind of undercurrent beneath the chief elements of the plot is the story of cosmic struggle between Jesus, in whom dwells the Spirit of God, and Satan, the source of all evil. I referred in the previous chapter to the view that Jesus bound Satan at the temptation (1.12-13)

and, as the victor, was then able to deal with his minions at will (1.23-27, 32, 39; 3.11-12, 15; 5.1-20; 6.7, 13; 7.24-30; 9.14-29). While this appears to be a story in itself, it is clearly meant to interact with the surface elements of the plot. There are times when the human opponents, and even the disciples, seem to be depicted as personifications of demonic forces. Twice, as we have seen, the Pharisees are said to 'tempt' Jesus (8.11; 10.2) just as, in 1.13, Satan 'tempts' him; and Jesus himself regards the tax question, posed by the Pharisees and Herodians to entrap him, as a temptation (12.15). Again, when Peter attempts to dissuade Jesus from taking the way of the cross, he is called Satan, his vociferous appeal being taken as a demonic temptation.[38] There are further instances in which the idea of such temptation is implicit—in Jesus' prayer in Gethsemane (14.36), for instance, and also, perhaps, in Judas' motive for betraying Jesus (if we are right about that), and in the token resistance that accompanies the arrest (14.47). Jesus' own awareness that demonic forces underlie the events in Gethsemane may be reflected in his exhortation to the disciples: 'Watch and pray that you may not enter into temptation' (14.38).

Finally, we may recall Danker's insightful analysis of the cry of dereliction which he thinks represents a final, decisive exorcism of the demonic from Jesus' own person. Whether or not we can agree with every detail of this thesis, it is noteworthy that soon after Jesus' great cry (15.34) the centurion proclaims his divine sonship (15.39), as if he is somehow affirming a final victory of the Spirit of God, as manifested in Jesus, over Satan and his demonic forces.

This demonic presence in the narrative, working through demons and humans alike, actually helps to strengthen the plot, for if the reader/hearer is to be filled with pity for the plight of the protagonist, the full weight of opposing forces must be shown to be pressing in on him inevitably. In the end, Jesus faces overwhelming odds—opposition from Jewish leaders,

---

38. E. Best (*The Temptation and the Passion: The Markan Soteriology* [SNTSMS, 2; Cambridge: Cambridge University Press, 1965]) argues that Jesus decisively defeated Satan at the temptation, and that all later references to temptation (πειράζω / πειράσμος) are to the purely human variety. But in that case, Mark's insistence on using the same term for both types causes considerable confusion and, of course, Peter is explicitly identified with Satan at one point. The view of J.M. Robinson (*The Problem of History in Mark* [SBT, 21; London: SCM Press, 1957]), pp. 35-38, that in 1.13 Satan is subdued but not finally vanquished, and that his influence persists in both demonic and human opposition, seems preferable.

opposition from relatives and acquaintances, misunderstanding from the disciples and, as if all that were not enough, opposition from demonic forces. At the cross, Jesus faces total desertion and dereliction, and with this the plotted narrative draws to a close.

e. *The Markan Epilogue and the Plot*

Where does the plot end? Assuming that the original ending of the Gospel itself was at 16.8,[39] are we to understand that the story and the plot are coterminous? Although the numinous aura of the empty tomb episode is a clear reflection of the mood in the Gospel as a whole, and is anticipated in passages such as 8.31; 9.9, 31; 10.34; 14.28, it is not the consequence of the plotted events. Of course, the women flee from the tomb in fear (16.8) and, as we have seen, fear is an emotion which tragic plotting endeavours to arouse, but in the present case this fear is not engendered by the causal sequence of events, but by an episode which does not follow on logically from what has preceded it. The sole end of the plot is unquestionably the death of Jesus on the cross. We have already discovered how the course of events leads him there. The climax is reached at 15.39 where, having beheld the manner of Jesus death, the centurion makes his celebrated acclamation, 'Truly this man was the[40] Son of God', and the burial (15.42-47), which is naturally consequent upon death, is the final plotted action. Where, then, does that leave 16.1-8? It is certainly no mere afterthought, though superficially it may read like one. It is, in fact, a clear instance of the classic *deus ex machina* device in which the protagonist makes good his escape or his upturn in fortune not as a result of plotted causality, but by means of literary contrivance. In Mark's case we are continually forewarned of the rising from the dead, but not of the means by which it is to be achieved; therein lies the suspense and the mystery. In one sense the end, when it does come, is commendably subtle. There are no 'risen Lord' manifestations

39. One of the best known exponents of the view that 16.8 marks the author's intended conclusion is R.H. Lightfoot, *Locality and Doctrine in the Gospels* (London: Hodder & Stoughton, 1938), pp. 1-48; *idem, The Gospel Message of St Mark* (Oxford: Clarendon Press, 1950), pp. 80-97. Since his day, this position has become more common, but continues to be opposed by many conservative scholars. Although now somewhat dated, the review article by F.F Bruce ('The End of the Second Gospel', *EvQ* 17 [1945], pp. 169-81) conveniently outlines the chief solutions to the problem.

40. In the Greek text, the title is without the definite article.

as in Matthew and Luke, only an empty tomb which fosters in characters
and readers alike a sense of numinous awe—precisely the effect which
Mark has been intent on achieving all along. In a purely literary—and,
specifically, Aristotelian—sense, however, the ending is unsatisfactory
precisely because it *is* contrived, rather than the result of what precedes.
The 'young man' (16.5) appears as if from nowhere to deliver his
message, and Jesus' prediction in 14.28 seems to have been designed to
make the shock of 16.7 more credible. Once again, however, it cannot
be stressed too strongly that my criticism here is a purely literary one: if
Mark had reliable historical tradition at his disposal, then the element of
surprise occasioned by the lack of causality behind the empty tomb
episode would naturally be controlled by that factor, and not by any
literary inadequacy of the author.

f. *The Markan Narrative: Episode or Plot?*
We have now traced the various elements of the narrative in their
entirety. How do we respond to the charge that they are too episodic to
be regarded as the backbone of a properly plotted story? In a sense their
episodic nature is inevitable because, as we have just pointed out, Mark
inherited his material from the tradition, and was restricted in what he
could do with it. His chief task was that of redaction, by which is meant
editing, selecting, summarizing, linking and arranging—but not, by and
large, creating (although Mark 8.14-21 could be a Markan composition).
Nevertheless, despite the fact that many of the pericopae are arranged
topically (controversies, miracles, parables, eschatology, and so on) it
would not be true to say that this was the sole criterion by which Mark
worked; the principle of contingency is operative, too. One example will
have to suffice. Mark 2.1–3.6 is widely regarded as a catena of controversy stories collected on topical grounds. Indeed, the cycle may already
have pre-existed Mark,[41] who then felt obliged to preserve the order, or

---

41. See Albertz, *Die synoptischen Streitgespräche*, pp. 5-16; B.S. Easton, 'A
Primitive Tradition in Mark', in S.J. Case (ed.), *Studies in Early Christianity* (New
York: Century, 1928), pp. 85-101; Knox, *Mark*, pp. 8-16; H.-W. Kuhn, *Ältere
Sammlungen im Markusevangelium* (SUNT, 8; Göttingen: Vandenhoeck &
Ruprecht, 1971), pp. 53-98; I. Maisch, *Die Heilung des Gelähmten* (SBS, 52;
Stuttgart: KBW, 1971), pp. 111-18; Cook, *Mark's Treatment*, pp. 29-51; R. Pesch,
Das Markusevangelium (vol. 1; Freiburg: Herder, 1976), pp. 149-51; W. Thissen,
Erzählung der Befreiung: Eine exegetische Untersuchung zu Mk. 2:1-3:6 (FzB, 21;
Würzburg: Echter Verlag, 1976); A.J. Hultgren, *Jesus and his Adversaries: The*

decided to retain it on literary grounds. But this is not to say that it does not suit the causal element of the plot. True, 2.13-17 cannot be said to follow logically from 2.1-12, nor 2.18-22 from 2.13-17, and so forth; but the cycle as a whole can be taken as a concerted response to Jesus' 'teaching with authority'. The five individual pericopae may represent the responses of different groups (scribes, Pharisees, Pharisees–Herodians, and so on), the persistence of which is made necessary by Jesus' flair for defeating his opponents in debate. Each controversy that elicits an authoritative response from Jesus is bound to keep the debate about authority on the boil.

4. *Mark as Tragic Drama*

Having established how the Markan plot operates, we come now to the question, What kind of plot is it? As Friedman[42] has shown, there are many different forms (he enumerates fourteen). However, it is hardly necessary to evaluate all these in order to conclude that Mark's Gospel is written in a tragic style. The only contentious issue is whether it resembles pure tragedy or tragicomedy. D.O. Via, Jr has argued for the latter on the basis of the resurrection story;[43] but quite apart from doubts as to whether the empty tomb episode really qualifies as such an account, the insurmountable difficulty for Via is that the plot is concluded at 15.47, so that even if the *story* could be classed as tragicomic (which I rather doubt), the plot, strictly defined, cannot. We should recognize, too, that in attempting to classify the Markan plot, we should be endeavouring to do so, as far as possible, on the basis of pre-Markan (which is to say, for all practical purposes, Aristotelian) literary principles. We know what literary criteria were taken to underlie tragic drama: how closely does Mark adhere to them?

a. *Aristotle and the Tragic Plot*
Although there is a good deal to be said about Mark as tragic drama, and much that has been said already,[44] it is important that I should be

Form and Function of the Conflict Stories in the Synoptic Tradition (Minneapolis: Augsburg, 1979).

42. Friedman, 'Forms of the Plot', pp. 157-65.

43. D.O. Via, Jr, *Kerygma and Comedy in the New Testament* (Philadelphia: Fortress Press, 1975).

44. E.W. Burch, 'Tragic Action in the Second Gospel: A Study in the Narrative

clear and incisive in my remarks. With this in mind, I ought to make two cautionary or provisory points before embarking on a more extensive discussion of this issue. The first is that we should be judicious in our use of Aristotle's *Poetics* for assessing plot structure in Greek tragedy and other works of a kindred spirit. There is no doubt, of course, that Aristotelian precepts do make for an obvious point of departure, and that the broad structural principles elucidated there are in general conformity with what we find to be the case in the extant tragedies of Aeschylus, Sophocles and Euripides. Nevertheless, we should appreciate that the standardization of such principles as an expression of literary-dramatic theory arose out of the historical development of drama in fifth-century Athens, and not from the fourth-century pen of Aristotle. He, at best, can be no more than a literary adjudicator or critic passing opinion upon the principles that had already been established. As Standaert has rightly observed, some of the subtleties behind Aristotle's assessment of the 'ideal' play might better be ascribed to the subtlety of his own thinking.[45]

On the other hand—and here is my second point—there is a sense in which some scholars have not read Aristotle closely enough, in that they fail to make a clear distinction between the structure of the play (or Gospel) and that of the plot. Standaert, for instance, treats of 'prologue', 'recognition' and 'epilogue' in direct sequence, as if they all operate at the same structural level.[46] Now, we may accept as fundamentally sound Standaert's desire to demonstrate that in Mark the prologue is related in substance to the epilogue, and both these elements to the central recognition scene (8.27-30): this is to be faithful to Aristotle's dictum that every literary whole must have a beginning (ἀρχή), a middle (μέσον) and an end (τελευτή). But, on further examination of the *Poetics*, we discover that there 'recognition' is regarded as part of the *plot* structure (complication—δέσις; recognition—ἀναγνώρισις; dénouement—λύσις),[47]

of Mark', *JR* 11 (1931), pp. 346-58; C. Beach, *The Gospel of Mark: Its Making and Meaning* (New York: Harper & Row, 1959), pp. 48-51; G.G. Bilezikian, *The Liberated Gospel: A Comparison of the Gospel of Mark and Greek Tragedy* (Grand Rapids: Baker, 1977); F.G. Lang, 'Kompositionsanalyse des Markusevangeliums', *ZTK* 74 (1977), pp. 1-24, esp. 19-22; B. Standaert, *L'évangile selon Marc: Composition et genre litteraire* (Brugge: Sint Andriesabdij, 1978), esp. pp. 30-34, 82-108.

45. Standaert, *Marc*, p. 33.
46. Standaert, *Marc*, pp. 83-106.
47. Aristotle, *Poetics*, 10.3, 4; 18.1-3.

whereas 'prologue' and 'epilogue' properly belong to the dramatic elements of the play structure (prologue—πρόλογος; episode—ἐπεισόδιον; exode—ἔξοδος; parode—πάροδος; stasimon—στάσιμον)[48] which, of course, extends beyond the limits of the plot.

With these points in mind, we can now proceed to review the relevant sections of Aristotle's text, Of course, it would be instructive to show how many of the salient features of tragic drama according to Aristotle— the ideal character of the protagonist, and the concept of tragic error or hubris, for instance—are to be found in the plays themselves and, indeed, in Mark's Gospel; but for the present we must confine ourselves to the issue of plot.

The most effective plots, Aristotle tells us, are those in which the sequence of cause-and-effect is at its tightest, and where the incidents are not simply in loosely connected episodes.[49] The tragic plot should consist of two basic movements with a recognition scene between them which causes a change in direction. The first movement is the 'complication' or 'binding' (δέσις) in which the rising action takes place. The fortunes of the protagonist seem to go from strength to strength (though the reader may be forewarned of catastrophe from an early stage). Then comes the recognition scene (ἀναγνώρισις) in which something not hitherto known by the protagonist comes to light and changes the whole situation. This point in the drama is all the more striking if it coincides with a sudden and complete reversal (περιπέτεια) in the protagonist's fortunes,[50] as it does in Sophocles' *Oedipus*. The remainder of the drama is the 'dénouement' or 'unravelling' (λύσις) of the plot which consists of the falling action or downturn in the protagonist's fortunes. Whatever happens now smacks of the inevitability of his or her fate. It is important that this movement should occur on a causal basis, with each incident spawning the next, and not be dependent on a *deus ex machina*, as Euripides' *Medea* seems to be.[51]

b. *Sophocles'* Oedipus Rex

Before returning to Mark's Gospel to consider how far it takes on board

48. Aristotle, *Poetics*, 12.1-3.
49. Aristotle, *Poetics*, 9.11-13.
50. Aristotle, *Poetics*, 11.5.
51. Aristotle, *Poetics*, 15.10. I would want to maintain that the *deus ex machina* is used here, despite the disclaimer of J. Ferguson, *A Companion to Greek Tragedy* (Austin: University of Texas Press, 1972), p. 410.

these Aristotelian precepts, we must pause to see how they are reflected in one of the best known of all Greek tragedies, the *Oedipus Rex*. My choice of that play, as an illustration of how the principles of plot operate, is not entirely arbitrary: its plot structure was much admired by Aristotle, and he cited its text more than that of any other tragedy. The characterization is exceedingly powerful, and the recognition scene most striking.[52]

Briefly, the story of the *Oedipus Rex* concerns a king whose parents expose him at birth because they have learned through a prophecy that he will kill his father, Laius. But the child is saved and reared by Polybus and Merope in the palace at Corinth. One day, in a drunken argument, someone questions Oedipus's legitimacy, which moves him to establish the truth (or otherwise) of this charge by consulting the Delphi oracle. Although he receives no clear answer therefrom, he is told that he will kill his father and marry his mother. In an effort to defy the oracle he resolves not to return to Corinth (since he believes Polybus and Merope to be his real parents) but to travel instead to Thebes. On the way there he kills a man in an argument over who should have right of way on the road, and on his arrival in Thebes frees the city from the curse of the monstrous Sphinx by solving its riddle. In gratitude the citizens make Oedipus their king, and he marries the wife of the former monarch who has been murdered.

All this precedes the play itself: it is information afforded by the prologue. And now, years later, we find the city bedevilled by a rampant plague. Again the oracle is consulted, from which it transpires that the only way to lift the curse is to identify and banish the man who killed the former king, Laius. Of course, it turns out that Oedipus himself is the unsuspecting culprit, and the plot works towards the self-recognition of his crime.

i) *Complication*. The complication straddles the mythological presuppositions of the play and its internal action. In other words, the action embodied in the complication is founded on and develops the spectator's understanding of events which occur prior to the opening of the drama. Against this background the protagonist is presented at the outset as a humane, benevolent monarch who cares deeply for the welfare of his

52. One wonders whether it is merely coincidental that the motif of physical and metaphorical blindness by which the *Oedipus* is characterized is also a prominent feature of Mark.

subjects; but he is also something of a 'know-all',[53] and this turns out to be the tragic flaw that leads to his demise, for as he strives to discover the identity of the murderer, so he is drawn inevitably into an obsessive quest for his own identity. Other characters are reluctant to divulge information, or try to dissuade the protagonist from delving any deeper into the matter (Suspense! If only Oedipus would take heed, he could escape his fate): but Oedipus must *know*, and it is that thirst for knowledge—knowledge of Laius' murderer and of his own identity— which leads inexorably to the catastrophe.

ii) *Recognition.* Typically in Greek tragedy, the recognition scene is anticipated in those which precede. This is particularly striking in the *Oedipus* where, piece by piece, the jigsaw puzzle is solved as the protagonist interacts with the characters around him. The seeds of doubt are first implanted in the mind of the super-confident Oedipus by Tiresias, the blind prophet, who accuses him of Laius' murder (1. 362). Although, naturally enough, the king regards the charge as preposterous, a change comes over him; he becomes tetchy and suspicious, accusing Tiresias and Creon, the queen's brother, of conspiracy (1. 378). Before long, in dialogue with his wife Jocasta, Oedipus learns that the place where he once killed a man in an argument corresponds to the spot where Laius was murdered. The king must know the truth. He seeks confirmation— or exoneration—from a shepherd who was a witness to the events…the very shepherd, indeed, who will eventually provide the vital clue to the king's true identity (ll. 765, 1119-85).

Meanwhile, a messenger arrives from Corinth with news of Polybus' death. In the course of the scene (ll. 924-1073) Oedipus discovers that the old king and his wife Merope were never his true parents, but that they reared him after the messenger himself had saved the infant king from exposure after receiving him from a shepherd from the house of Laius. Immediately, Jocasta perceives that Oedipus is not only her husband but her son, and the remainder of the scene is dominated by her frantic efforts to prevent him from discovering the truth.

Now the shepherd arrives on the scene. He had been called originally to establish whether or not Oedipus was Laius' murderer: by identifying him as Laius' son the whole horrific situation is made clear; Oedipus is

53. Although the name Oedipus ('swell-foot') is derivative of the child's being discovered with his feet pinned together, it can also be taken as a pun on the verb οἶδα, 'to know'.

guilty of both parricide and incest—all that was prophesied of him has come to pass. Thus we see how, in this play, the entire compilation is concerned to collate, from various independent character-sources, the information necessary for leading the protagonist to his awful self-recognition. The climactic power of this ἀναγνώρισις is dependent upon the gradual revelation to Oedipus of the circumstances behind the dramatic situation.

In common with many Greek tragedies the recognition scene in the *Oedipus* is preceded by a preparatory scene in which the messenger from Corinth makes the important double disclosure that Oedipus' real parents were not Polybus and Merope, and that he was handed over by a shepherd in Laius' employment. Immediately, Jocasta realizes the awful truth that Oedipus is her son, and tries to prevent him from questioning the shepherd because she knows that he will confirm Oedipus' identity (ll. 1056-71).

iii) *Dénouement.* The length of the dénouement in Greek tragedy varies in accordance with the relative position of the recognition scene. In the *Oedipus* it is comparatively short (ll. 1223-1530): we are simply told of the effects of the recognition—the suicide of Jocasta, the self-blinding of Oedipus, and his poignant farewell to his children before he is banished. The real centre of interest in the play lies not so much in the dénouement as in the complication where it is shown exactly how the oracle given to Oedipus regarding his incest and parricide is fulfilled. In Aeschylus's *Choephoroi*, on the other hand, the recognition occurs very early in the play (ll. 164-263) because the centre of interest in that work lies in the dénouement, where the conspiracy of Orestes and Electra to murder Aegisthus and Clytaemnestra is developed.

c. *Tragic Plot in Mark's Gospel*
If we now compare the Markan plot structure with that of the *Oedipus*, which Aristotle praised so highly, we shall be able to see that, in essentials at least, the Gospel conforms rather well to the literary tradition underlying the tragic genre.

We saw that in the *Oedipus* the prologue is used to set the scene for the plotted action. Through the characters, including the protagonist, Sophocles provides all the information necessary for an understanding of the action. The important motif of metaphorical blindness, ignorance and knowledge, is also introduced here: words such as 'blind', 'see' and 'know' abound.

A glance at the Markan prologue (1.1-13)[54] shows us that it functions in a similar way. To begin with, Mark himself exploits his position as omniscient author to disclose to the readers information of which most of the characters are unaware. Within the parameters of his rôle as messenger he introduces to us two others—John the Baptist and God, both of whom are given speaking parts. These speakers are given something momentous to disclose about Jesus—that he is mightier than any human, even prophetic, figure (1.7, 8)—indeed, is the very Son of God (1.11).

Further, just as in the prologue of the *Oedipus* the frequent references to knowledge and blindness/sight foreshadow the course of the plot (the path from metaphorical blindness to metaphorical sight, and from physical sight to physical blindness), so Mark 1.1-13 is similarly characterized. Themes and motifs which are expanded in the plotted narrative are introduced there. Thus, the messenger motif, which appears at the outset (1.2), is found also to bring the Gospel to a close (16.5-7). Part of the quotation, 'Prepare the way (ὁδός) of the Lord', not only testifies to John's rôle as the one who is preparing for the coming of Jesus, but also anticipates the whole central section of the Gospel (8.27-10.52), where the 'way' motif is of paramount importance (cf. 8.27; 9.33, 34; 10.32, 52). The description of John in 1.6, and his function as herald (1.8), is intended to cast him in the rôle of Elijah (cf. 2 Kgs 1.8), so it is no surprise to find him appearing again in that guise in 9.11-13. Again, the words of the divine voice in 1.11 not only find an echo in Ps. 2.7, but serve as a foreshadowing of that same voice on the Mount of Transfiguration (9.7). Finally, the story of Jesus' temptation in the wilderness (1.12, 13) sets the scene for a sustained conflict between Jesus and the forces of evil (1.23-26, 34, 39; 3.11, 15, 22-27; 5.1-20; 6.13; 7.24-30; 8.31-33; 9.14-29, 38, 39), and in particular presages the aftermath of the recognition scene where Peter endeavours to tempt Jesus away from his divinely appointed course and is given the name Satan (8.31-33).

---

54. The extent of the Markan prologue has been much debated. The choice seems to lie between 1.1-13 (Standaert, *Marc*, pp. 82-89; Lang, 'Kompositionsanalyse', pp. 10, 12) and 1.1-15 (L.E. Keck, 'The Introduction to Mark's Gospel', *NTS* 12 [1965–66], pp. 352-70; H. Anderson, *The Gospel of Mark* [London: Oliphants, 1976], p. 58). But if we accept the dramatic structure of Mark, we have to say that the prologue must conclude at v. 13, for the following verse initiates the action by introducing the activity of the protagonist.

Thus, we see that the form and purpose of the Markan prologue is in basic conformity with that in the *Oedipus* and, indeed, with the majority of those to be found in the extant Greek tragedies.

i) *Complication.* The Markan complication (1.14–8.26) follows a course somewhat similar to that of the *Oedipus*. Jesus sets out with a specific aim (1.14-15) which he is determined to carry through, and at first things seem to go well. He gathers about him a loyal, obedient band of followers, and his programme of teaching and healing proves extremely popular among the masses. But as with Oedipus, so with Jesus: the more resolutely he engages in his task, the nearer he draws to catastrophe; for it is precisely this teaching and healing activity, particularly the former, which causes the authorities to begin plotting his downfall (3.6). After the first cycle of controversy stories, Jesus retires to the Sea of Galilee (3.7), not only because it is the place of his popularity (2.13; 3.7; 4.1; 5.21) but because it provides sanctuary from his opponents. They engage him in house, synagogue and Temple, but the seaside is the domain of the doting crowds; Jesus must not be exposed too early to the hostile forces that lurk around him.

One of the chief diversions of Mark's Gospel from Greek tragedy is that there is no clearly definable tragic flaw in the Markan Jesus other than that he refuses to be deflected from his course despite the inevitability of the fate to which it leads.[55] We have seen that in Aristotelian terms it is the protagonist's human limitations which cause his hubris. Thus, Oedipus' quest to discover who murdered Laius, while commendable in itself, actually leads to his downfall because, unlike the audience who would already be familiar with the story, he does not realize that the trail will lead to himself. And he is unable to foresee how the quest will end precisely because of the human limitation of his knowledge. He is not, like the gods, omniscient: he must make step-by-step discoveries.

The Markan Jesus is different. Although the evangelist goes to great lengths to stress his humanity, he emphasizes his divinity as well. Jesus may be subject to human emotions, but there are strong hints that he foresees his own fate in a manner that Oedipus cannot. Moreover, Jesus is not the model tragic protagonist, for although he conforms to the tradition that such a character should encounter misfortune 'through no

---

55. And if this be reckoned as a tragic flaw at all, it is certainly not a moral one (cf. the note to Aristotle, *Poetics*, 13.5 in the Loeb edition [trans. W. Hamilton Fyfe; Cambridge, MA: Harvard University Press, 1982], p. 117).

badness or villainy of his own', he certainly does not fulfil the requirement of being 'the sort of man who is not pre-eminently virtuous or
just'. Nevertheless, he clearly is a tragic protagonist of sorts, albeit an
unorthodox one.

ii) *Recognition.* In the Gospel of Mark, the recognition scene (8.27-30) is
anticipated in just the same way as in Greek tragedy. People begin to
recognize the distinctiveness of Jesus from the beginning of his ministry
(1.27-28). The disciples, in particular, are privy to his secret teaching
(4.10-20; 7.17-23; 8.14-21) and marvellous signs (1.29-31; 4.35-41; 5.35-
43; 6.45-52). Potentially, all this provides them with an opportunity to
recognize who Jesus is, but they fail to do so, and Jesus becomes
increasingly exasperated at their lack of understanding (4.13, 40; 7.18;
8.17-21). Indeed, the very exhortation to understand is a heartfelt plea
for an understanding of Jesus' messianic identity. Just as in the *Oedipus*,
so every unit in Mk 1.14–8.26 has its fixed place and purpose in
pointing to the recognition scene; but two, in particular, may presage it
more than any other. First, the fact that in 6.14-16 some are identifying
Jesus with John the Baptist, or Elijah, or one of the other prophets,
clearly foreshadows 8.28 where the disciples deliver the same report.
Then, too, the Pharisees in 8.11-12 are attempting to do what the
disciples are doing in 8.27-30—namely, establishing who Jesus really is.
But both Herod and the Pharisees get it wrong: no wonder they are
juxtaposed in Jesus' saying about the leaven in 8.15. The failure of these
two contrasts sharply with Peter's assessment at Caesarea Philippi, thus
making the recognition there all the more striking.

As we have noticed above, it is common for recognition scenes in
Greek tragedy to be directly preceded by a specific preparatory scene.[56]
Although there is no preparatory dialogue in Mark as there is in tragic
drama there is, nonetheless, a preparatory episode. It is not, as has been
suggested by some,[57] the discussion about Jesus' identity in 8.27-28—
that is properly part of the recognition scene itself—but the healing of
the blind man in 8.22-26. It is commonly observed that the two phases
of the healing in this pericope are paradigmatic of Peter's imperfect
recognition of Jesus:[58] he sees that Jesus is the messiah but does not

56. Sophocles' *Oedipus*, ll. 1098-1173 and *Electra*, ll. 1126-70 will serve as
typical examples.

57. So Burch, 'Tragic Action', p. 352.

58. Cf. Lane, *Mark*, pp. 286-87, and n. 54. On the structural relationships

appreciate what messiahship entails. The paradigm assures us that, like the blind man, Peter and the other disciples will one day see clearly, but that phase of understanding is projected beyond the parameters of the dramatic action.

Next, how well does Mk 8.27-30 correspond to Aristotle's view of what a good recognition scene should be like? In one sense it fares rather well because, as in the *Oedipus*, recognition and reversal coincide. In the first 'act' of Mark, Jesus' teaching and healing activity make him a popular figure, and the religious leaders are frustrated in their opposition. But as soon as the recognition takes place, Jesus is obliged to teach a suffering messiahship in which the true disciple is expected to share—a teaching which, not surprisingly, is not so well received. Many adherents fall away, even the inner circle finds it hard to accept, and the authorities redouble their efforts to bring Jesus down. At the end he is left desolate, having been deserted by all—even, it seems, by God (15.34).

But if Mark conforms to Aristotelian principles in this respect, the manner by which the recognition scene is constructed is less satisfactory; for, unlike the ideal scene which arises directly from the plot, the episode in Mark is contrived by the author, and does not emerge effortlessly from what precedes.[59] Jesus, in fact, has to initiate the action by asking his disciples about people's opinion of his identity. Only then is the discovery made.

The above comments remind us that, despite the obvious similarities between 8.27-30 and recognition scenes in Greek tragedy, we should not underplay the differences. It is as well to note that in the latter we generally find that it is the protagonist who experiences the recognition, and the discovery which he himself makes results in a change in his own fortune. But in Mark it is the protagonist who invites others to recognize *him*, and his change of fortune occurs chiefly because, once recognized, he finds that he must adapt his teaching about himself to meet the new situation.

---

between 8.22-26 and 8.27-30, cf. M.-A. Beavis, 'The Trial Before the Sanhedrin (Mark 14:53-65): Reader-Response and Greco-Roman Readers', *CBQ* 49 (1987), pp. 581-96 (589-90).

59. In this respect the Markan recognition scene is rather like that in Euripides' *Iphigenia in Tauris*, which Aristotle criticizes (*Poetics*, 16.6-7) because the scene is contrived: Orestes, rather than the plotted circumstances, reveals himself to Iphigenia (ll. 800-30).

iii) *Dénouement*. In Mark, the complication (311 verses) and the dénouement (351 verses) are virtually co-extensive, so that equal weight is given to both 'acts' of the drama. We have just seen how the recognition episode forces Jesus to adopt a style of messianic teaching which causes him to lose popular support, thus giving his opponents fresh impetus. They harbour a more malicious intent now (8.11; 10.2; 11.18; 12.12, 13; 14.1-2) and the elders–chief priests–scribes, who are to be instrumental in Jesus' downfall, appear—significantly—for the first time as a composite group in the very first verse of the dénouement (8.31). The shadow of the cross looms large over these chapters (8.31, 34-38; 9.12, 30-32; 10.32-34, 45; 12.1-9), for this unravelling of the plot is concerned, above all, to demonstrate the inevitability of the protagonist's death.

5. *Summary*

My purpose in this chapter has been to discuss some important aspects of plot theory, and to apply them to Mark's Gospel in the hope of gaining some insights into its structure. I uncovered four plot-related factors (causal, affective, character and conflict) which were found to be largely essential to the plot, and sometimes dominant over the plot *per se*. I also briefly examined Chatman's kernel-satellite model for plot construction—the idea that every plot is composed of units which are essential to its development (the kernels), and those which are subsidiary to it (the satellites).

In the following section, I applied Chatman's model to the text of Mark. The effectiveness of this, I argued, rather depends on which end of the spectrum we begin our enquiry. Do we accept Chatman's model as a set of rules to which texts subsequent to it should be made to conform? If so—and it must be admitted that Chatman's theory has only modern literature in view—the legitimacy of applying them to ancient texts could no doubt be questioned. On the other hand, insights into characteristics common to ancient and modern plot structure might well be gained. My application of Chatman's model to the narrative of Mark's Gospel was intended as an experiment as much as anything, yet I showed that the ancient text conformed surprisingly closely to the modern theory. The chief plot factors noted above all stand out very clearly in Mark, and the plot kernels (such as those in Mk 1.14-15 and 8.27-30) are readily recognizable.

On the basis of my discussion of plot theory, I proceeded to a consideration of the Markan plot in general. Having outlined it according to the aforementioned principles, I then applied the literary-critical canons of Aristotle, of which the flesh-and-blood author of the Gospel may well have been aware, and to which he might sub-consciously, if not consciously, have conformed.[60]

60. Here, of course, we are faced with an important distinction between our consideration of modern literary theory on the one hand, and ancient literary theory on the other—a distinction which cannot be too greatly emphasized. My discussion of Chatman's model and its application to the Markan narrative has been carried on at a purely literary level; there is no suggestion that Mark himself would have been aware of such principles even if, coincidentally, his text is not at odds with them. This phase of my discussion was not, in any case, concerned with Mark as flesh-and-blood author, but only with his second self implied by the text and formed out of its intercourse with reader and author alike.

As soon as we began to deal with *ancient* literary criticism, as represented by Aristotle, however, we were faced with questions of history as well as literature, because we had to consider the possibility that the historical Mark may have been consciously constructing his plot in accordance with well-known literary principles. Certainly, the Markan narrative conforms remarkably well to the typical plot structure of classic Greek tragedy, as I have demonstrated.

Chapter 4

MARK'S GOSPEL: TIME AND SPACE

Narrative critics tend to refer to time and space in a work as components
of the setting. Strictly speaking, we should also add socio-cultural
background to these two factors, but since this would take us further
from the purely narrative considerations of Mark than it is possible to
venture at present, and given that sociological and cultural aspects of the
gospels have been widely dealt with by others, I shall confine myself
here to time and space alone.

1. *Time*

In a sense, time is a rather slippery customer to handle, given that
discussion of it can be approached from a number of directions. On the
one hand, there is the purely philosophical discussion: What is the nature
of time? How do we experience it? Ricoeur has endeavoured to introduce something of this debate into the field of narrativity.[1] Then there
are the more purely literary issues of time in the text. At the outset, we
have to clarify what 'time in the text' means. We have to distinguish, for
instance, between the time it takes a reader to devour the text, the time-
frame implied in the story (story-time), and that implied in the plot
(plotted time). None of these are likely to be identical. And then, to take
plotted time alone, we need to consider what sub-divisions are needed. Is
it, perhaps, appropriate to begin with Aristotle's dictum that every plot
requires a beginning, a middle and an end?[2] Dan Via, certainly, appears
to make this assumption the basis for his study of ethics in Mark 10.[3]

1. P. Ricoeur, 'Narrative Time', *Critical Inquiry* 7 (1980–81), pp. 169-90; and
now see *idem, Time and Narrative* (3 vols.; Chicago: University of Chicago Press,
1986–88).
2. Aristotle, *Poetics* 7.2-7.
3. D.O. Via, Jr, *The Ethics of Mark's Gospel: In the Middle of Time*
(Philadelphia: Fortress Press, 1985).

Then there is the question, ably addressed by Genette,[4] as to precisely how narrative time is handled according to arrangement, duration and frequency. And finally, overlapping these concerns, is the matter of tension between mundane (or historical) time and monumental (or cosmic) time—*chronos* as opposed to *kairos*. Our thinking on this matter now benefits from the imput of Bruce Malina who argues that in order to properly appreciate the phenomenon of time as understood by the evangelists, we need to be alert to the gulf between the first-century and the modern concepts of time.[5] Nor do the questions end there. What about the different perspectives on narrative time experienced by the story-world characters, the author and his or her immediate audience, and future readers?

Obviously, it will be impossible to discuss these many issues at length. I have already had occasion to refer specifically to plotted time as opposed to story-time in my chapter on plot, so we need not concern ourselves too deeply with that issue now. This leaves us free to consider the tripartite view of time espoused by Via, and the observations of Genette regarding the author's manipulation of time for rhetorical purposes. In each case, of course, we shall consider how these proposals apply specifically to Mark's Gospel. Finally, it will be worth considering the extent to which perspectives on time depend on which of the constituent parties in or to the narrative (character, author, first reader, modern reader) is in question.

a. *Dan O. Via*

The title of Via's book, *The Ethics of Mark's Gospel: In the Middle of Time*, at once testifies to his view that while Mark's plot is concerned primarily with the middle of time, it also presupposes a beginning and an end with which the middle is inextricably bound. As we have seen, the tripartite nature of the dramatic plot was advocated by Aristotle as a literary essential, and, of course, it was the bread-and-butter of the structure of tragic drama. Indeed, Via appears to suggest that the tripartite literary structure is based on the pattern of life itself which, of course, it represents:

---

4. G. Genette, *Narrative Discourse: An Essay in Method* (trans. J.E. Lewin; Ithaca, NY: Cornell University Press, 1980).

5. B.J. Malina, 'Christ and Time: Swiss or Mediterranean?', *CBQ* 51 (1989), pp. 1-31.

> ...the self is a whole whose unity resides in the unity of a narrative that links birth-life-death as narrative beginning-middle-ending.[6]

The tripartite form found in Greek tragedy, espoused by Aristotle and adopted by Mark, therefore, is none other than *mimesis*—representation of life itself. But how is it utilized in the Markan narrative? As with Conzelmann's understanding of the structure of salvation-history (*Heilsgeschichte*) in Luke,[7] Via feels that the three plotted elements in Mark—1.1-13; 1.14–14.52; 14.53–16.8—represent three epochs respectively: the time from the beginning until John the Baptist, the time of Jesus, and the post-resurrection era. Historically, these are distinct periods, but the Markan plot takes account not only of mundane or mortal time, but of cosmic time too; and this time—God's time—invades mortal time in such a way that, cosmically, the three areas interpenetrate one another to the point where beginning and end are indistinguishable.

Via points to Genette's comment that in one sense, the first time is always the last time, for once an act has been accomplished—for instance, the first kiss, the first sight of the sea, the first night at a certain hotel—the newness and spontaneity is lost and can never be recovered.[8] Such experiences seem to echo T.S. Eliot's statement, 'In my beginning is my end',[9] and to be anticipated in the traditional Jewish understanding of apocalyptic. According to Deutero-Isaiah, the divine purpose was plotted from the beginning (Isa. 40.10; 48.12) and thus was evident not only at the creation (Isa. 44.24; 45.18) but throughout history (Isa. 42.6; 43.28; 45.1; 46.3, 11) until the end (Isa. 51.6).

The key passage, for Via, is Isa. 51.9-11 where the first time of creation, the time of the exodus, and the new exodus (from Babylon) of the eschaton, of which Isaiah believes himself to be on the verge, are synchronically linked; that is, they are all events of the one time, even though historically separate. As Via has it,

> It is not simply that three distinct times or events are connected with the same place... It is, rather, that three widely separated moments of time— the primordial past, the salvation historical past, and the salvation-historical-eschatological future—are made simultaneous with one another by being connected to the same fusion of time and space...[10]

---

6. Via, *Ethics*, p. 13.
7. Conzelmann, *Theology of St Luke*.
8. Genette, *Narrative Discourse*, p. 72; cf. Via, *Ethics*, p. 29.
9. T.S. Eliot, 'East Coker', *Four Quartets*, 1.1.
10. Via, *Ethics*, p. 29.

Mark has both similarities to and differences from this scheme. Like Isaiah, there is a sychronicity about his vision of cosmic history; the end-time is none other than a recovery, or 'reactualization', of the first time, and both these epochs encroach upon the middle time. Indeed, the only thing that separates the first from the last time is humanity's fallenness. It is the human condition which, in Genette's terms, denotes the loss of the new; but whereas for Genette this loss is irrecoverable, for Mark, Jesus Christ stands as a new beginning through whom man can recover his pristine past.

All this seems to echo the cosmic scheme implied in Zechariah, some of whose prophecies the Markan Jesus fulfils (Mk 11.1-10). Zech. 14.6-8, Via notes, portrays the eschatological return to paradise. In Genesis, God creates the cosmos by means of binary opposites—light/darkness, water/dry land, summer/winter. But Zechariah envisages an end-time when all these will be broken down to form total unity—everlasting light, ever-flowing streams, and so on. The newness of the first time, therefore, is recovered in the end-time.

To return briefly to our comparison between Isaiah and Mark, it will be seen that the latter has a greater sense of the diachronic than the other. While Isaiah stresses that all salvation-historical events really cohere in the one act, Mark is more concerned to demonstrate that synchronicity must work through diachronicity. The first time can certainly be recovered synchronically in the last time, but this can occur only through a diachronic understanding of history:

> While Second Isaiah can and does distinguish moments of history, his metaphor suggests that all times participate equally in the power of the first time. Mark knows that is not the case. It may well be that every segment of the Markan story is defined in some way by the presence of the kingdom of God. But sometimes the kingdom manifests itself by redemptively transforming the situation, and at other times it is met by rejection and misunderstanding. And while Mark can affirm the overlapping of history and the kingdom, he can also distinguish this age and the age to come (Mark 10:29-30). By failing, or refusing, to synchronize all times completely into a comprehensive metaphor Mark preserves temporality—the chronological and diachronic—more securely, and more realistically, than did the prophetic metaphor.[11]

Let us now see what Via makes of the three stages of the Markan plot—beginning, middle and end.

11. Via, *Ethics*, p. 32.

The term 'beginning' (ἀρχή) is used by Mark four times (1.1; 10.6; 13.8, 19), usually to refer to some rather indeterminate time within God's cosmic plan. Thus, in 10.6 Jesus speaks about what God intended from the beginning of creation. ἀρχή here does not denote a specific time in history, but the first time, when all was perfect—a time which could not be sustained because of man's 'hardness of heart' (10.5). Mark 13.8, on the other hand, speaks of a different kind of beginning—the beginning of the end. The apocalyptic signs mentioned here indicate that the restoration of the first time, its reactualization in the end time, is about to take place. And just as earlier Isaiah had counted himself to be on the threshold of the eschatological event, so now it is with Mark. In 13.19 he overtly connects beginning and end, again using the word ἀρχή, by asserting that the end-time experiences will be quite unlike anything that has happened in the world since the beginning of creation. Thus, in this one verse, Mark stands back from his canvas to take stock of the whole panorama of God's cosmic plan.

Where, then, does Mk 1.1 fit into this scheme?—for it, too, envisages a beginning—the beginning of the gospel of Jesus Christ. It has been noticed that the term ἀρχή is the same as that used to open the book of Genesis and the Gospel of John, but whereas in these latter cases the word clearly refers to primordial time, in Mark it is the beginning of the gospel of Jesus Christ (ἀρχή τοῦ εὐαγγελίου Ἰησοῦ Χριστοῦ) which is envisaged. This could be taken subjectively—the gospel proclaimed by Jesus; or objectively—the gospel about Jesus. Opinion is divided, but if Mark's use of εὐαγγελίου here is to be consistent with his usage elsewhere in the Gospel (8.35; 10.29; 13.10; 14.9) it seems that an objective meaning is preferable—the good news is something that Jesus proclaims initially, but the long-term understanding of the church is that the Christian is expected to preach *concerning* Jesus. If that is so, the question arises as to what the beginning of the good news is: does it refer only to the prologue (1.1-13) or to the entire Gospel? Since there is a break between v. 13 and v. 14, between the ministry and arrest of John and the beginning of Jesus' ministry, it is most natural to assert that this beginning refers specifically to the prologue in which the stage is set through Old Testament prophecy (1.2-3), the ministry of John (1.4-8) and Jesus' own preparation (1.9-13). Nevertheless, Via feels that, at another level, the entire plotted narrative, which is restricted to the ministry, death and resurrection of Jesus, can also be regarded as a beginning—the beginning of the Church in the world, whose work is to be carried on until the end of time. Plotted time, in other words, serves as the beginning of a story time which is projected into the indefinite future.[12]

It is interesting to note at this point how smoothly this beginning leads into the middle of time. Old Testament prophecy (Mk 1.2-3; cf. Mal. 3.1; Isa. 40.3) is fulfilled in the coming of John the Baptist whose own prophecy concerning the one who is to come (Mk 1.7-8) is immediately fulfilled by the arrival of Jesus for baptism (1.9-11). Jesus then announces the imminence of the kingdom—a reality which is inaugurated in the middle of time and consummated in the end-time (1.14-15). Thus, within the space of fifteen verses, Mark has introduced us to time in all its facets—to story-time as both an historical (*chronos*) and a cosmic (*kairos*) concept, and to the mundane, worldly time of the plot.

The most important point about the middle of time (represented, according to Via, by Mk 1.14–14.52) is that both beginning and end encroach upon it. It is related to the beginning in that the potentialities of 1.1-13 are actualized in the narrative middle. But this relationship is not merely historical; it is cosmic, too. In 10.2-9, for example, Jesus calls on his hearers to live in the present as if they were living in the first time, before humanity's fallenness had set in.[13] Similarly, at the other end of the scale, Jesus' healing and exorcising activity is a demonstration of his proclamation in 1.15 that the kingdom of God has drawn near—in other words, that the end time has invaded the middle time. Given this, it appears that the middle of time according to the Markan plot is essentially about the loss and subsequent recovery of God's time:

12. Via, *Ethics*, pp. 46-47. A convenient discussion of the many issues raised by Mk 1.1 can be found in R.A. Guelich, *Mark 1–8:26* (WBC, 34A; Dallas: Word Books, 1989), pp. 5-14.

13. Perhaps the use of ἀρχή in Mk 10.6, unlike that in 1.1, is meant to be seen in the light of the 'beginning' mentioned in Gen. 1.1. The 'beginning' in this latter passage is to be seen not in terms of a specific beginning in history, but rather in terms of 'first principles' (cf. A. Wikgren, 'ΑΡΧΗ ΤΟΥ ΕΥΑΓΓΕΛΙΟΥ', *JBL* 61 [1942], pp. 16-19). Thus, God's creation in Genesis denotes not the making of history, but something God does with his eternal present. God's creation is a perfection which characterises that present. Historical time arises as soon as humanity falls; for humanity's knowledge is about more than nakedness (Gen. 3.7); it is about mortality. Tasting the fruit of knowledge (Gen. 3.6) brings recognition of past and future which is of the essence of human history. In light of this, the truth of Mk 10.5-6 may be that, but for human hardness of heart, redemption would have been unnecessary, since time would always have been in-the-beginning time—an experience of God's eternal present.

Since Jesus calls on his hearers to live both in the eschatological kingdom
and in the primordial time, the former must be the recovery of the latter.
The kingdom which dawns in the mid-time is the actualization, with
qualification, of both ultimate terminal points.[14]

The final stage of the Markan plot, according to Via, commences at
14.53, and thus includes the trials, crucifixion and resurrection, but it is
the last of these events on which he focuses. The resurrection, it is said,
stands on the threshold between plotted time and story time. The plot
ends there, but the story frequently implies a time beyond which will be
deeply affected by the story of the empty tomb. The time of the plot and
the post-resurrection era anticipated in the story are linked by the
concept of 'concealed revelation'. In the plot, there is a constant tension
between moments of insight (1.11, 24; 3.11; 5.7; 8.22-26; 9.7; 10.46-52)
in which Jesus is revealed for who he is, and the more general tendency
to concealment through dullness or hardness of heart. The resurrection
story exhibits this same tension because, contrary to the case in the
other Gospels, Jesus never appears, and the narrative ends on a note of
flight and fear. There is a revelation of a kind, but it is ambiguous, and
this ambiguity extends into the life of the church:

> After the resurrection, concealment still diminishes the effect of the
> resurrected Jesus upon his followers and the world. The failure of Jesus'
> disciples to understand his teaching about the death and resurrection of
> the Son of man belongs to the plot. But because this teaching is given in
> terms of the church's proclamation, the time of the disciples and the time
> of the church are assimilated to each other. There will be failures to under-
> stand *after* the resurrection.[15]

Finally, however, there is discontinuity as well as continuity. Just
as the kingdom is both present and future, so revelation is both given
and withheld. 'The resurrection does not introduce a radically new
departure',[16] but for the disciples it is a watershed experience which tips
the balance in favour of enlightenment. Whereas prior to this event
concealment is the dominant factor, after it revelation goes into the
ascendency, although, of course, the two are still in tension.

---

14. Via, *Ethics*, p. 47.
15. Via, *Ethics*, pp. 55-56.
16. Via, *Ethics*, p. 56.

b. *Bruce Malina*

An important recent study of the biblical concept of time is that of Bruce Malina. The title of the article, 'Christ and Time: Swiss or Mediterranean?' is an accurate reflection of the concern with which he is dealing—that our modern understanding of time is all too frequently superimposed upon the concept of time embraced by agrarian societies in antiquity. This, he claims, is an underlying weakness in such ground-breaking studies as Cullmann's *Christ and Time*.[17] Given that Mark and his community were likely to have shared this ancient, traditional view of time,[18] it is worth pausing here to take stock of what Malina is saying.

There are two areas of particular relevance for measuring the differences between modern technological time, and ancient traditional time. Modern time is abstract and future-oriented, while traditional time is either experienced or imaginary, and present-oriented. Again, modern time is linear and separable, while ancient time is cyclical and procedural. Let us examine these categories more closely, assessing as we do so how they might apply to Mark's Gospel.

Industrialized, technologized Western culture tends to measure time in terms of future goals or schedules. I may, for instance, take on an important speaking engagement which has been booked for a specific time on a specific date, say three months hence. From the moment of acceptance, the course of my life tends to be dictated by that distant goal: I have to arrange my time so as to allow me to write my speech or paper, and I may spend many hours working on how I should present myself and my speech. Modern time is 'non-personal' and 'non-organic'. That is to say, the individual must adapt to the time-schedule rather than vice versa. Ancient time, on the other hand, is quite the opposite, being moulded to personal need: the only consideration in deciding what should be done is whether or not it is felt to be the right time for doing it.

Ancient time is of two varieties—experienced and imaginary. Experienced time is that which each individual experiences as a present reality; but this present is not necessarily punctiliar, in which events occur

---

17. O. Cullmann, *Christ and Time: The Primitive Christian Conception of Time and History* (trans. F.V. Filson; Philadelphia: Westminster Press, 1964).

18. While Mark's Gospel was probably destined for a city-dwelling community rather than for a strictly agrarian society, Malina has argued that in fact all peasant/pleb communities shared the agrarian understanding of time as an on-going present. Only the Roman elites, he says, had a somewhat different concept—a past-oriented one based on their ancestrism (see Malina, 'Christ and Time', pp. 5-6, and n.15).

at a particular instant; rather, it is frequently an on-going or extended period of time. Mark 9.1 and 13.30, which are generally regarded as apocalyptic passages, illustrate this principle well-enough. The first of these reads:

> Truly, I say to you, there are some standing here who will not taste death before they see the kingdom of God come with power.

According to the ancient concept of time, this passage does not speak of some indeterminate future at all, but of an on-going present which is part of the listeners' experience. The reality of experienced time did not extend beyond the parameters of the present generation, so the coming with power of God's kingdom is, for Jesus and his hearers, a totally present experience—realized eschatology indeed.

Mark 13.30 bears a similar interpretation:

> Truly, I say to you, this generation will not pass away before all these things take place.

'These things' (ταῦτα), which certainly include at least *some* of the events described in 13.5-27,[19] must in some way be understood as part

---

19. Just what 'these things' are, and when they would take place is ambiguous, and the matter is far too involved for discussion here. Some events, like those in 13.5-23, are clearly meant to be experienced by 'this generation' (13.30). The references to false Christs in vv. 5-6, 21-23 form an *inclusio*, suggesting that all the signs or events mentioned within these parameters (vv. 7-20) belong to the same time-frame. Verse 24 then introduces a new situation—a time 'after that tribulation' (presumably the hardships mentioned in vv. 14-20) in which the heavenly bodies are to be disordered. This, it seems, is the advent of the end itself, the winding up of history which is heralded by the coming of the Son of man (v. 26). But who sees it? 'This generation'? At v. 26, Mark slides from second- into third-person plural, which could mean that some future generation is envisaged as a witness, or even the heavenly bodies themselves (cf. R.H. Gundry, *Mark: A Commentary on his Apology for the Cross* [Grand Rapids: Eerdmans, 1993], p. 783); but this would hardly square with Malina's contention ('Christ and Time', p. 7) that ancient communities would not have conceived of generations beyond their own. Others feel that the change of person may indicate that v. 26 is an interpolation, or is at least drawn from a different source; the repeated 'and then' (καὶ τότε) + future verb could further support this view. The little parable in vv. 28-29, with its climactic double saying in vv. 30-31, could also be a later addition. Events have already reached a climax at vv. 26-27, and so, as M.D. Hooker (*The Gospel according to St Mark* [London: A. & C. Black, 1991], p. 320) notes, '"these things" in v. 29 cannot refer to the events in vv. 26f, since they were themselves the climax to the period of waiting'. It is worth remembering, too, that the events of the very end could not, according to the

of the present, on-going experience of 'this generation', and yet, as Malina has noted, they are regularly interpreted futuristically by modern Western Christians. The point is that events which were felt to occupy the horizon of present experience would not have been conceived by Mark as having a future aspect at all, since that lay beyond the world of experience entirely.

Imaginary time, as understood by ancient agrarian societies, is any time other than that which is experienced, and includes the indeterminate past and future. It is solely the domain of God for whom all things are possible (Mk 10.27), and only he can know what occurs in imaginary time (Mk 13.32)—the time beyond 'this generation'. There is thus a sharp distinction between what is *forthcoming* (the future which is actualized in the present) and what is *imaginary* (the possible future which lies beyond the world of experience):

> ...for members of [the early Christian community] God's kingdom was forthcoming, Jesus' emergence as Messiah with power was forthcoming, the transformation of social realities in favor of God's people was forthcoming. Yet for the audiences of Mark, Matthew and Luke, things obviously changed. The coming of Jesus is moved now into imaginary time. For the coming of the Son of Man with power in Mark and Matthew, for example, was now future, a piece of imaginary time known only to God: 'But of that day or that hour no one knows, not even the angels in heaven, nor the Son, but only the Father' (Mark 13:32; Matt. 24:36)...[Thus], in the NT writings, we can see how the forthcoming became future, how the experienced became imaginary.[20]

The forthcoming, therefore, was something that was already embodied in the world of present experience, a potentiality necessarily arising out of what already existed. These potentialities, argues Malina, were bound to be realized among real or actual people, and not in any indeterminate way. 'There was no reference to future possibility or probability, only to what was going to be and must be because it already is.'[21] This is well

---

ancient mind, have been envisaged as belonging to the world of the extended present, since they are clearly part of the future which no-one but God can know (cf. v. 32): the coming of the apocalyptic Son of man was not a forthcoming experience, but beyond the world of experience altogether.

The whole vexed question of Mk 13 cannot be addressed without careful reference to the standard commentaries and monographs (cf. the brief bibliographical note in Lane, *Mark*, p. 444).

20. Malina, 'Christ and Time', p. 15.
21. Malina, 'Christ and Time', p. 16.

illustrated in passages such as Mk 1.15 and 8.31. In the first of them, the
kingdom of God has drawn near simply because it emerges out of what
is present, namely Jesus' appearance in Galilee in readiness for his
proclamation of the gospel.

Similarly, the Passion prediction in 8.31 is born out of necessity: the
Son of man *must* (δεῖ) suffer. Jesus' suffering would arise from his present circumstances, and so was an essential part of them. The crucifixion
was at this juncture a forthcoming event, not one possibility among
others. Malina says,

> What distinguishes the forthcoming rooted in the potential and the future
> rooted in the possible is not greater or lesser remoteness from the directly
> perceived present...[but] the degree of immediate and direct organic
> connection with some presently experienced person, event, or process.[22]

It appears that circumstantial changes constitute the catalyst for
transforming the forthcoming into the non-experienced future. Thus, the
kind of eschatological statements seen to be actualized by the earliest
Christian community (Mk 1.15; 9.1; 13.30, for example) have for us
become open-ended and indeterminate, and thus belong to the indefinite
future known only to God.

The other significant temporal axis is that occupied by modern, linear,
separable time on the one hand, and traditional, cyclical, procedural time
on the other. Contemporary Western society operates largely on the
basis of clocks, schedules and promptness. Such time is monochronistic,
demanding the individual's total attention to one task at a time. Time is
its own master, and is no respecter of persons. None of this applied to
first-century agrarian culture. Time for the Palestinian peasant or Roman
pleb was social, personal, cyclical, procedural, non-directional and poly-
chronic. This is well illustrated, according to Malina, by the well-known
saying of Jesus in Mt. 6.34:

> Therefore, do not be anxious about tomorrow, for tomorrow will be
> anxious for itself. Let the day's own troubles be sufficient for the day.

What mattered most for ancient agrarian communities was to do what
was necessary at the right time. Life revolved around the seasonal cycle
with its wet and dry season. Planting was done at the appropriate time,
and the crops were harvested in due season. This can be seen in some of
the Markan parables. The farmer puts in the sickle 'when the grain is

---

22. Malina, 'Christ and Time', p. 17.

ripe...because the harvest has come' (4.29). Likewise, the vineyard owner sent servants to get some of the produce 'when the time had come' (12.2). This principle applies as much to the spiritual (1.15) as to the physical world. The underlying sense here is always καιρός, the right time, not χρόνος, a particular time.[23]

The parable of the secretly-growing seed (4.26-29) again epitomizes the cyclical nature of time. The sleeping/rising, night/day antitheses are mirrored in the gradual, stage-by-stage growth of the seed: both are repetitive, cyclical processes. This same principle, however, extends to other areas of life, particularly the cultic. The Temple was the centre from which cyclical time in its cultic manifestation was regulated. 'Temple-time simply concretized the recursive and divinely-controlled quality of cyclical time'.[24] It could be argued, no doubt, that Jesus' attack on the Temple and its cult (11.12-22) was essentially an attack on the religious leaders' monopoly on cultic time. Given that cyclical time was based ultimately upon the motion of the heavenly bodies, all such time, in the last analysis, belonged to God, and there was a sense in which the religious leaders had wrested cultic time from his control and were using it to consolidate their own positions of power. As Malina remarks,

> ...it was in the interest of Jerusalem elites to mark time, to be in control of the time signalling system and thus to control time and the people who marked time by the Jerusalem temple.[25]

Jesus himself, no less than his peers, is presented by Mark as being subject to cyclical time in his everyday life. His ministry is full of repetitive processes such as prayer (1.35; 6.46; 14.32, 35, 39) and teaching (1.21, 22, 27; 2.13; 4.1, 2; 6.2, 6, 34; 8.31; 9.31; 10.1; 11.17, 18; 12.14, 35, 38; 14.49). Even in the Temple, where cyclical time predominates in the hands of the religious leaders, Jesus observes his own form of it by teaching daily (καθ' ἡμέρα) there.

The other aspect of traditional time is its procedural nature. The emphasis here rests not on repetitive processes, but on single or infrequent events which nevertheless chart the appropriate course of things. Birth, marriage and old age, for instance, are all once-only events or

---

23. Mark uses the term καίρος five times (1.15; 10.30; 11.13; 12.2; 13.33), which compares with just two instances of χρόνος (2.19; 9.21).

24. Malina, 'Christ and Time', p. 22.

25. Malina, 'Christ and Time', p. 22.

processes whose experience is marked by a sense of completion. Mark's Gospel contains several instances of this aspect of time. The Markan Jesus speaks of the right time for proclaiming the gospel: πεπλήρωται ὁ καιρός (1.15); and immediately, the first disciples sense that it is the appropriate time to respond to the call (1.16-20; 2.14). Like Qoheleth (Eccl. 3.1-8), the evangelist sees that everything must occur in due course or order, whether it be the stages in the agricultural year (Mk 4.26-29), or the signs of the eschaton (13.5-27).

I must draw this section to a close. Enough has been said, however, to show that we cannot take Mark's understanding of time for granted. It is clear that future studies of biblical time will not be able to reckon without Malina's contribution.

c. *Gérard Genette*

One of the most helpful and influential of modern studies of narrative time for literary critics of the Bible is that of Gérard Genette. Basic to his thesis is that this concept falls broadly into text-time and story-time, and that on this basis it can be dealt with under three fundamental principles— order, duration and frequency. In elucidating these principles and applying them to Mark, it should be appreciated that limitations of space will not permit a full excursion through the Gospel text. Nevertheless, it is hoped that sufficient illustration can be given to demonstrate how Genette's classifications may be applied.

i) *Text-Time and Story-Time.* Text-time refers to the time involved in actually reading the text syllable by syllable, word by word, sentence by sentence. This time, which conducts the reader from point A to point B, is always linear. Rimmon-Kenan has pointed out that occasionally attempts have been made to disturb the predictability of this process.[26] He refers to Cortázar's *Hopscotch* in which the reader is directed to read the chapters in a somewhat (but not totally) haphazard order. But even here, text-time is proceeding apace. It may be possible to alter the order in which the chapters are read, but not the ultimate linearity of time itself.

Story-time, on the other hand, is more flexible. While the text-time may occupy only a few hours, the story (and, indeed, the plot within the story) may range over many years, and there is no compunction upon the author to ensure that time is sequentially-arranged. The story might

---

26. Rimmon-Kenan, *Narrative Fiction*, p. 45.

legitimately begin near the end, and then flash back to an earlier period; or it may speak of a time that the reader could never be physically a part of (such as a distant past or future), or of a time-span that no single human life could bridge.

We can see that in Mark's Gospel, these two levels of time present a striking contrast. The simple act of reading (text-time) takes only about two hours, but the story-time embraces not only the plotted events of Jesus' ministry (covering roughly two years), but also the much broader sweep of cosmic time. There are references to conditions 'from the beginning' (10.6; 13.19), to periods of Old Testament history (2.25-26; 12.26), to prophecies (1.2-3), and to the apocalyptic future (13.5-37).

Again, unlike the text-time, the story-time in Mark does not adhere absolutely to the principles of linearity. On the whole, of course, there is a progression from beginning to end, but there is little indication of how the various pericopae relate to each other temporally. Apart from the odd rubric (that the Transfiguration [9.2-8] occurred six days after Peter's confession [8.27-33], for instance), most of the units are loosely connected, and their order seems to be dictated more by theological than by temporal considerations. It is significant, for instance, that Peter's confession comes hot on the heels of the healing of the blind man (8.22-26), not because the events necessarily happened in that order, but because the restoration to physical sight becomes a paradigm for Peter's eventual acquisition of metaphorical sight.

ii) *Order*. While the reader is accustomed to beginning at the start of the text and working through to the end, story-time need not be totally sequential. Some episodes may be placed later in the narrative than might be expected, while others may appear earlier than expected. Genette refers to this technique as *analepsis* and *prolepsis*. Each of these categories can be divided into sub-types. External analepsis/prolepsis refers to an event which lies entirely beyond the beginning or end of the narrative, whereas internal analepsis/prolepsis denotes any event which one would normally expect to find earlier or later within the story-time. A mixed analepsis is an episode which starts by preceding the narrative itself, but extends into the narrative world, while a mixed prolepsis denotes an event which begins within the narrative, but extends beyond the end of it.

Some of these categories can be sub-divided further. An external analepsis, for instance, may refer to an episode in history prior to the narrative, or to some pre-historical occurrence; and an external prolepsis, similarly, can anticipate some occurrence in future history posterior to the narrative, or to the eschatological future.

Again, there is a distinction, according to Genette, between 'repeating analepses', which simply serve to recall earlier portions of the narrative, and 'completing analepses' which actually fill in information which was left out of account earlier. The same distinction can be made for prolepses, too.

It should be noted at this stage, however, that analepses and prolepses are not necessarily identical with retrospection and foreshadowing in general. Taking Mk 2.20 as an example, although this passage is a fore-shadowing of the crucifixion, it cannot be regarded as a true prolepsis which is a clear foretelling of a specific event prior to its expected time. The passage about the bridegroom does not manage this, but simply introduces an air of foreboding into the narrative without specifically referring to the event it is foreshadowing. Similarly, the reader might well be urged, on reading the healing of blind Bartimaeus in 10.46-52, to recall the earlier blind-healing in 8.22-26, but since the later passage does not constitute a specific reference to the earlier one, it cannot be a true analepsis. In Culpepper's discussion of analepsis and prolepsis as applied to John's Gospel,[27] this distinction appears not to have been made, so that some of the instances given as 'repeating prolepses', which he admits are ambiguous (for example, Jn 1.50; 6.27; 7.38), appear to be nothing more than instances of foreshadowing (of a kind labelled *amorce* by Genette).

Now let us take one or two examples of these figures as they appear in Mark. No attempt will be made at a full classification of types. Indeed, there is room for only the odd random illustration. The diligent reader will no doubt be able to find other instances not alluded to here.

The most striking analepsis in Mark is the account of the death of John in 6.17-29. We are told as early as 1.14 that John had been 'delivered up' before Jesus began his ministry, and so, according to the actual order of events, we should expect to find the detailed story of John's death at that point. Instead, Mark delays it for some five chapters. Opportunity for the narration finally arises when rumours begin to spread about who Jesus is. In 6.14-16 (which itself can be seen as a repeating prolepsis of 8.28), the alternatives are presented: John the

27. Culpepper, *Anatomy of the Fourth Gospel*, pp. 54-70.

Baptist, Elijah or one of the prophets. Herod decides upon John *redivivus*. Then, with an explanatory γάρ (6.17), Mark is able to relate precisely how the Baptist met his death. Thus, we are provided with a good example of an internal, completing analepsis—'internal' because its referent (1.14) lies within the narrative; and 'completing' because it supplies information which was lacking in the initial passage.

But why did Mark decide to tell this story analeptically instead of in its logical sequence? Two reasons spring to mind: (i) The function of Mk 1.1-15 is clearly to announce themes which are to be developed later in the Gospel.[28] Telling the full story of John's death at that point would have diverted attention away from that primary purpose. (ii) In its present position, the story serves two functions—one narratival and one theological. It serves as the 'meat' in one of Mark's 'sandwiches' (or intercalations). Jesus sends out the Twelve on their mission (6.7-13). King Herod hears about what Jesus is doing, and decides that he is none other than John *redivivus* (6.14-16). This, in turn, leads to the story of how John was executed (6.17-29); and finally, the Twelve return from their mission (6.30-31). The effect of the intercalation of the story here is to separate the sending out of the Twelve from their return, and thus to present the illusion of the passing of time.[29] Theologically, the ruminations of Herod about Jesus' identity, which lead into the story of John's death, make a striking contrast with the similar episode in 8.28. Here, the king ponders the question and draws the wrong conclusion (Jesus is John), whereas at Caesarea Philippi the same question is pondered by the disciples with at least superficial success (Jesus is the Christ).

Briefer instances of analepses include 3.30 and 6.52. The first of these follows Jesus' saying about the unforgiveable sin. Any sin would be forgiven except blasphemy against the Holy Spirit (3.28-29). At this point, the reader is left to ponder just what this means; but then Mark adds analeptically, 'For they had said, "He has an unclean spirit."' Light begins to dawn: blasphemy of the kind mentioned here has something to do with attributing evil to what is perfectly and divinely good. The indeterminate 'they' in 3.30 may also suggest that Mark is classifying Jesus' family and the scribes together as outsiders. His family had accused him of being beside himself (3.21), and the scribes had accused

---

28. On the rôle of the prologue as an introduction to the essential themes in Mark, cf. M.D. Hooker, *The Message of Mark* (London: Epworth Press, 1983), pp. 1-16.

29. Wood, 'Priority of Mark', pp. 17-19.

him of being possessed (3.22), so both these parties could be implied by
the condemnation in 3.30. In a sense, this verse is a completing analepsis
because it provides the key both to the interpretation of the otherwise
enigmatic 3.28-29, and to the reason as to why the Beelzebul controversy
(3.22-27) is intercalated into the story of Jesus' family and their hostility
towards him (3.20-21, 31-35).

Mark 6.52 is a redactional verse which concludes the story of Jesus'
walking on the water (6.45-51): it testifies to the fact that the disciples
were astounded (v. 51) because they did not understand—not about the
walking on the water, as might be expected, but about the *loaves* (cf.
6.35-44). After a previous nature miracle, the stilling of the storm (4.35-
41), they express awe immediately (4.41), but in this later case, their
reaction is delayed for an entire pericope. Why? Perhaps Mark is
attempting to say that if the disciples failed to understand about the
loaves, they would be no wiser about the walking on the water.

Instances of prolepsis in Mark can be found throughout the text. As
early as 3.19, for instance, Judas is described as the one who betrayed
Jesus, even though the account of the betrayal does not appear, appropriately enough, until much later in the text (14.10-11, 43-46); and this
same event is again treated proleptically when Jesus foretells it (14.18).
Thus, by means of this device, Mark divests the reader of all possible
suspense. The only question is how the foreshadowed event will take
place.

Generally, however, prolepsis becomes more significant and substantial
the further the narrative proceeds. The three central Passion predictions
(8.31; 9.31; 10.33-34) are, of course, proleptic of the Passion itself. There
is no ambiguity as in the inference in 2.20. Indeed, after the first prediction, the narrator adds, 'And he [Jesus] said this plainly' (8.32a).
From this point, the reader is exhorted to look forward, and to ponder
just how this prediction might be fulfilled; the entire narrative takes on a
passionward slant. These particular prolepses are of the 'repeating' kind,
for they simply reiterate what is later to take place; they do not tell us
anything other than we learn from the Passion story itself.

Another internal prolepsis occurs at 11.12-14, where the story is told
about Jesus' condemnation of the fruitless fig tree as he journeys from
Bethany to Jerusalem. On his arrival in the city he 'cleanses' the Temple
by wreaking havoc among the money-changers and pigeon-sellers
(11.15-18), then returns to Bethany (11.19). At this point, these two
pericopae could easily be regarded as being complete in themselves, for

the outcome of Jesus' curse on the fig tree might have been left to the reader's imagination. But, in fact, using one of his rare specific time rubrics (11.20), Mark picks up on this story by declaring, 'As they passed by in the morning, they saw the fig tree withered away to its roots.' Thus, the Temple-cleansing becomes the filling for yet another Markan sandwich (intercalation).

The question now arises, Why does Mark decide on this arrangement here? After all, Matthew is content to relate the two stories consecutively (Mt. 21.12-17, 18-22). The short answer is that Mark, by means of his intercalation technique, wants to show that they are meant to interpret each other. The fruitless fig tree is symbolic of fruitless Israel, and Jesus' curse in 11.14 is essentially a prophecy about Israel's fate. The intercalation which follows discloses the reason for the condemnation: the religious leaders who were supposed to be the custodians of the Temple (and thus of Israel's cultic life), had allowed corruption to creep in, so that Israel's cultic worship was no longer fit to offer to God. Worse still, they were preventing others from engaging in true worship (11.17). In light of this, 11.20-21 announces the fulfilment of the 'prophecy' in 11.14: the fig tree (Israel) duly perishes as a result of its fruitlessness.

In this complex, we have a double prolepsis—one internal and one external. Jesus' condemnation of the fig tree is, as we have seen, an enacted prophecy, the fulfilment of which is noticed next day. But from the perspective of Mark and his community, it (and perhaps also the Temple-cleansing) is also externally proleptic of the fall of Jerusalem and its Temple which at the time of writing was either imminent or had already happened.

Another very important proleptic passage, which we can do little more than allude to here, is the so-called Little Apocalypse (Mk 13.5-37). The prolepsis is external throughout, but while the events of which Jesus speaks lie completely outside the time frame of the narrative, from the Markan perspective they are of two varieties: events which have occurred between the end of the story and the time in which it was being written; and events which had still to take place. It is likely that the sufferings and hardships mentioned throughout 13.5-12 were occurring at the time of writing, and certainly these were seen as signs of the end; but the sign *par excellence*, the 'desolating sacrilege' (13.14) is notoriously difficult to interpret. If it refers to the fall of Jerusalem in AD 70, it is difficult to know whether or not Mark was writing of it with hindsight. The consensus seems to be that it had yet to happen, but was so inevitable that Mark could confidently speak of it as if it has already happened. It does seem, however, to be an event set apart from those preceding it.

With the words 'in those days' (ἐν ἐκείναις ταῖς ἡμέραις, 13.24) we seem to be projected onto a new time plane, the time of the end itself. It comes 'after that tribulation' spoken of in the previous verses, and, while it is keenly expected, there is no certainty about when it will be (13.32-35). Thus, Mark carefully distinguishes between the time of the end, and the events leading up to it which have a firm footing in history.

iii) *Duration*. Whereas it is possible to compare the linearity of the text with the order of the story events, it is impossible to compare text duration with story duration in the same way. This is because different readers take different lengths of time to negotiate the text. A quicker reader of Mark, for instance, may take one and a half hours; another, slower, reader could take two and a half hours. To overcome this difficulty, it is customary to compare the story duration (in terms of hours, days, months or years) with the proportion of a text taken to cover a particular period. This takes account of the pace at which the narrative is told. If the events covering a month are narrated in the space of five pages, while those covering a week are narrated in ten, it is likely that the first passage is being told at a much quicker pace than the second. Maximum constancy of pace would occur if each page covered the same period of time (a page per day, for example). But constancy is frequently changed deliberately for rhetorical effect. Slowing the pace down may be indicative of a particularly significant point in the story.

Deceleration can be achieved in various ways—by devoting a long segment of text to a short period of the story, as we have seen; by developing static devices, such as dialogue, at the expense of action; and (in modern literature, at least) by increasing sentence length. The minimum speed possible is achieved by means of a *descriptive pause* where the action is suspended while something is described or ruminated upon. In the New Testament, long chapters of discourse like that in Mark 4 and 13 and John 14–17 have this effect.

Acceleration, naturally, is achieved by the reversal of these processes—short portions of text to cover long periods of the story, plenty of action, and short sentences. The maximum possible speed is *ellipsis* where a certain section of the story is covered by zero space. An obvious example is Luke 2–3 where the story of Jesus' birth is told in some detail, but nothing else is heard about him until his appearance in the Temple at the age of twelve (Lk. 2.41-52), and then nothing again until the time of his baptism (3.21-22) at the age of about thirty (Lk. 3.23).

Between these extremes, the pace of the narrative can be freely regulated by means of scenes and summaries—the one to decelerate and the other to accelerate.

How does Mark handle narrative pace? The most striking point to note is that the first ten chapters present a marked contrast with the final six. Mark begins his narrative at breakneck speed, and ends it at a virtual standstill. There is a pronounced deceleration after chapter ten, but this is not to say that the first ten chapters all proceed at the same hectic pace; there are subtle variations, and an overall deceleration, though perhaps it is more insideous than that which grips the final chapters. A few specific observations may help us to justify these assertions:

1. Mark's use of the word 'immediately' (εὐθύς) has often been noted. Obviously, it is a word which conveys the idea of movement and action: everything happens at once. It is interesting to note the distribution of this term throughout the Gospel. Of Mark's 42 uses, no fewer than 36 occur in the first ten chapters, of which eleven appear in ch. 1, while only six are to be found in the final six chapters. If we sub-divide chs. 1–10 into two, we find that chs. 1–6 contain 29 instances of εὐθύς, while chs. 7–10 contain only seven. This tends to show that while Mark uses this term to help regulate the pace of the narrative, its use starts declining (implying deceleration) long before ch. 11 is reached, although the decline becomes more pronounced after that point. It should be noted, too, that while many of the occurrences in the early chapters are strictly redundant, and are present only to help the pace along, those in chs. 11-16 are generally required to enhance the description of the episode in question.

2. While it is not easy to estimate the length of Jesus' ministry on the basis of Mark's time signatures, it is fair to suggest that a span of at least two years is implied. Virtually the whole of this period is covered by Mark 1–10, while chs. 11–16—about one-third of the text—is devoted to the final week of Jesus' life, of which 14.12–15.39 covers the 24 hours up to his death. On the basis of proportionality, then, it is evident that the pace of the narrative decelerates as the cross looms ever larger.

3.   In the earlier part of the gospel, the pericopae tend to take the
      form of short, vivid scenes, each complete in itself. (Mk 1.16-
      45, for instance, contains five such scenes: 1.16-20, 21-28, 29-
      31, 35-39, 40-45). This leaves ample opportunity for the
      judicious use of ellipsis and summary. We are told, for instance,
      that Jesus spends forty days in the desert (1.13), but learn
      nothing of what happened there other than that Satan tempted
      him; he is left unable to enter a town in 1.45, but in the
      following verse is found returning to Capernaum 'after some
      days' (2.1); and he ascends the Mount of Transfiguration six
      days after Peter's confession—nothing is mentioned of what
      lay between. Summary passages about Jesus healing activity
      (1.32-34; 3.7-12; 6.53-56) hurry the action. In the final few
      chapters these techniques begin to evaporate. Naturally, the
      odd ellipsis is inevitable, but they tend to cover shorter periods
      of time, and the summary passages disappear. Further, after
      13.1, the short, self-centred units give way to long discourse
      (13.5-37) and narrative (14.12–16.8) complexes in which the
      source materials are more tightly interwoven than previously.

4.   Mark never measures mundane time by units of longer than
      the day (1.13; 2.1; 8.2, 31; 9.2; 14.1, 58; 15.29, for example),
      and he frequently mentions parts of the day—morning (1.35;
      11.20; 15.1; 16.2), evening (1.32-34; 4.36; 6.47) and night (6.48;
      13.35-37; 14.37-41). As the Passion approaches, however, and
      the narrative becomes more detailed, Mark favours the hour as
      the time measurement most appropriate to setting the pace of
      the story (14.35, 37, 41) which, at the last, proceeds by three
      hour intervals (15.25, 33, 34)—almost at funereal pace.[30]

All these factors suggest an inexorable deceleration of the narrative
pace as it reaches the Passion until, at the climax, time, for one brief
moment, seems to stand still. At the third hour Jesus is crucified; at the
sixth hour darkness descends. Finally, at the ninth hour, there is Jesus'
cry of dereliction (15.34), his death (15.37), the rending of the Temple
veil (15.38) and the centurion's cry of affirmation (15.39)—all this, it
seems, in one time-ceased moment. And Mark's handling of the time
duration factor appears to be directed primarily to achieving this effect.

---

30. Much of this has been observed and briefly discussed by Powell (*What is
Narrative Criticism?*, pp. 78-82).

iv) *Frequency*. The last of Genette's categories deals with the number of times an event occurs in the story compared with the number of times it appears in the text. There are three broad classes of frequency:

1. Singulative—telling once what happened once. Obviously, the vast majority of a narrative is told on this basis, and no further comment is necessary.

2. Repetitive—telling more than once what happened once. It is often the case that an event which occurs once is related two or more times—perhaps by the same character each time, or perhaps by different characters adopting different points of view. The repeated accounts may be exactly the same, or they could have some variation. An obvious biblical example of this device is Paul's conversion which appears in Acts three times (9.1-19; 22.4-16; 26.9-18), once told by the narrator and twice by the Lukan Paul. Repetition may be used for various reasons. In modern literature it may lead to a sense of staticity or stagnation, but in ancient texts it is more likely to denote an event of outstanding significance, as in the example above. Such appears to be the case in Mark where the Passion is told three times in cameo (8.31; 9.31; 10.33-34) before the final, detailed narration. The significance of the feeding miracles, too, seems to be established through repetition. It is commonly held, nowadays, that the two accounts are really variants of a single event. Some insist that Mark was aware of this, or even that he created one of the episodes himself.[31] Even should this not be so, he clearly *does* refer to the feedings again in 8.19-21.

3. Iterative—telling *once* what happened more than once. Mark's various summary passages may provide some instances of what is meant here. In 10.1 we are told that Jesus taught the crowds, 'as his custom was'. Although Jesus as teacher is mentioned frequently by Mark, it is true to say that this passage is iterative in that its one reference to Jesus' activity clearly implies innumerable instances of teaching. Similarly, in 14.49 Jesus tells his opponents, 'Day after day I was with you in the temple teaching...' In fact, the only real insight we receive regarding this apparently customary activity is in 11.27–12.44,

---

31. Fowler, *Loaves and Fishes*, pp. 37-38.

where Jesus spends the day debating and teaching in the Temple precincts—a kind of 'day in the life...' which is representative of many such days.

d. *Typological Time in Mark*

Powell has noticed that while many of Mark's time references are chronological—both locative (15.25, 33, 34) and durative (1.13; 2.1; 8.2; 14.58; 15.29)—others are typological; in other words, they refer to the kind of time at which an action takes place—evening, night, morning, Sabbath. In these cases, it is appropriate to look for themes and motifs underlying each type. Evening, for instance, given that it marks the beginning of the Jewish day, is appropriately a time of preparation or new ventures for Jesus. He begins a healing mission then (1.32-34), prepares for a boat journey (4.35), prays (6.47) and shares the Passover meal with his disciples (14.17-25)—a meal which Jesus himself sees as an act of preparation (14.25).

Night is a time of trouble or danger. The disciples find themselves beset by high winds on the Sea of Galilee in the middle of the night (6.45-51). It is a time of anguish for Jesus in the Garden of Gethsemane (14.32-42), and the time of his betrayal, arrest (14.43-52), trial before the High Priest (14.55-65) and denial by Peter (14.54-55, 66-72). It is to be noted that Jesus taught in the Temple day after day (14.49) but was never arrested then; his opponents had to wait until darkness, the time of evil.

Mornings, Powell observes, are, for Mark, nearly always *early* mornings. It is at this time that Jesus is frequently on the move. He is found praying in preparation for a preaching tour (1.35), or he is on his way from Bethany to Jerusalem (11.20), or he is being transferred from Jewish to Roman custody (15.1). It is also the time when the women discover the empty tomb (16.2), and are told by the young man that Jesus is going ahead of his disciples to Galilee.

One final category of typological time is the Sabbath. Clearly, while this is meant to be a day of rest, it turns out for Jesus to be one of conflict—conflict with demons and disease (1.21-34), with the religious authorities (2.23–3.6) and with his own townspeople (6.1-6).

Powell argues that there is a correlation between the instances of mundane time noted above and Mark's understanding of monumental time expressed in passages such as 1.14; 10.6; 13.7, 9, 13. The middle of mortal time, it is said, is night, since evening begins the Jewish day, and morning succeeds night. Two things can be said about this middle period: as noted above, it is a time of trouble, hardship and danger; and it shades into the following period—the morning. Indeed, the phrase πρωῒ ἔννυχα λίαν (1.35) means literally, 'the morning during the night'. The morning, then, encroaches on the darkness. A similar pattern to this can be traced in monumental time. The middle of this time, too, is a period of apostasy, hardness of heart and tribulation, but the end time encroaches on the middle. It is significant that the empty tomb is discovered at this same intersection between night and morning (16.2), as if the resurrection is meant to serve as a gateway leading from the present (middle) to the future (end). Powell concludes as follows,

> Mark's overriding concern regarding temporal settings is to emphasize that all time belongs to God... [C]hronological times (days and hours) are known to the Father, and the most significant of these, only to the Father (13.32). In the same way, God's rule is active 'night and day' in ways that are often unknown (4.26-27). The directive to people who live in the middle of time is to keep watch during every kind of time: 'in the evening', 'at midnight', 'at cock-crow', and 'in the morning' (13.35). All time belongs to God and God's new beginning may come suddenly at any time.[32]

e. *Time and the Reader*

An intriguing yet infrequently discussed question is that concerning how the time of the narrative relates to that of the reader. Since the factors involved are in a state of constant flux, the possibilities seem endless. A.A. Mendilow has explored how the time of writing can relate to the time of the story-world in the case of secular literature.[33] One can think, for instance, of the historical novel written from the perspective of the modern author and readers, or of the novel written by a contemporary author about contemporary events, or of the novel written in an earlier age about events that were contemporary then, or of the novel written in history about an even earlier period. And when we bring the future into the equation, the picture becomes more bewildering still. There are novels written in the past or present about an indefinite future, or, as in the case of Orwell's *1984*, about a specific future era. And this latter case opens up the possibility that future readers of the book might find themselves living in the period projected in it. Saga novels are characterized by their ability

---

32. Powell, *What is Narrative Criticism?*, p. 82.

33. A.A. Mendilow, 'The Position of the Present in Fiction', in Stevick (ed.), *Theory of the Novel*, pp. 255-80.

to cover long periods stretching from the past into the present, while some works, like *2001: A Space Odyssey*, attempt even more, embracing entire aeons—from the primeval past to the indeterminate future.

Many of these permutations are embodied in Mark's Gospel. We can say that at the time of writing, the evangelist's narrative was essentially about events in recent history on which events of the more distant past and also of the eschatological future impinged. But precisely which events belong to which epoch depends on the perspective in question. For Mark and his first readers, living in the post-resurrection era, the entire Jesus story, together with the Old Testament prophecies taken to refer to this period, was already past event. According to the narrative, Jesus made a number of prophecies, some of which had already been fulfilled by the time the Gospel was written. The Passion predictions (8.31; 9.31; 10.33-34) are an obvious instance of this. Other predictions, however, are more difficult to place. The enigmatic saying in 9.1 is a case in point: 'There are some standing here who will not taste death until they see the kingdom of God come with power.' When, exactly, was the prophecy fulfilled, if at all? There are so many imponderables that it is impossible to know whether it still awaited fulfilment at the time of writing. A similar difficulty is presented by those passages which seem to symbolize the end of the Jewish nation as the legitimate people of God (11.12-21) and the destruction of the Temple (13.14). Scholars seem to be divided on whether these events were imminent or already past at the time Mark's Gospel was written. What was it, exactly, that Mark wanted his readers to understand? (13.14).

On the other hand, some events were clearly still in the future, though perhaps imminent. It seems likely that Mark considered the various apocalyptic signs to be occurring at that very time, so that the Parousia (13.26) would not be long delayed, even if its arrival could not be accurately predicted (13.35).

For Mark, then, it appears that past, present and future aspects of his narrative derive their ultimate meaning from the perspective of his own community.

Of course, the perspective on past, present and future changes as we move back into the story-world, or forward into the world of the later reader. Naturally, the characters do not know as much as the author's community, not simply because the author is omniscient and shares that privilege with his readers, but because from the perspective of the story world, they cannot possibly know whether Jesus' predictions about the Passion and beyond will come to pass.

At the other end of the spectrum stand those readers who are subsequent to Mark's own community. They, of course, are in a position to know all that the Evangelist and his community knew, and perhaps even more. If we cannot be certain whether or not Mark stood anterior to the fall of Jerusalem in AD 70, we can be sure that his subsequent readers were aware of it as a cataclysmic event.

Another point of difference between Mark's community and subsequent (especially comtemporary) readers concerns apocalyptic expectation. The apocalyptic discourse (Mk 13) is one of the most time-conscious passages in the Gospel, being full of references to 'that hour', 'that day' or 'those days' (13.11, 17, 19, 20, 24, 32) and other temporal references (13.7, 8, 19, 35). There are repeated warnings to keep on constant alert (13.33, 35, 37), and a tension between the imminence of the end (13.30) and the not-knowing-when (13.32). Clearly, Mark's community was living in daily expectation of the eschaton.

Some nineteen hundred years later, Mark's current readers find that they are still living in that limbo between the resurrection and the end time; they share in the not-yet of the original community. Historical, social and cultural differences may mean that a modern reader's eschatological expectations are different from those of the first readers, but in their ability to participate in the narrative action, all readers are one. How is this feat achieved? Mendilow declares that in reading a narrative the reader exchanges the actual present for a 'fictive present'. The narrative action may occur in the past, but by identifying with a story character, the reader can be fictively present—present, that is, in imagination:

> Not only…is the reader's actual present, his own time-locus, absorbed into the fictive present of the action, but that fictive present itself constitutes an imaginative shift from the past tense in which it is recorded. To put it more concretely, someone may today be reading a novel written in the past tense about events that took place on a certain day in the year 1789, and feel as though they were happening now at his moment of reading, in his presence and presentness. The relation of the tenses used in the novel to those felt by the reader is that of *oratorio obliqua* to *oratorio recte*: the past of the narration—*he went*—is translated in imagination into *I am going* or *I go*; the pluperfect—*he had gone*—into the present perfect—*I have gone*, or the past—*I went*; and the conditional—*I would go*—into the future—*I shall go*.[34]

---

34. Mendilow, 'Position', p. 266.

The ability of the reader to immerse him or herself in the story-world depends on the degree to which the narrative is 'shown' rather than 'told'. An intrusive narrator can break the spell, and some authors can make skilful use of this as a device for controlling or manipulating the reader.

Mark's characteristic vividness, his frequent use of the historic present tense, and his willingness to allow his protagonist to speak for himself all serve to draw the reader into the story-world so that, in a sense, ancient and modern readers alike share the time perspective of the characters. To return to Mark 13, we can now appreciate that from the narratival viewpoint the eschaton is perpetually 'not-yet' because the reader, while he or she remains in the story, will always be anterior to it, just as he or she will always be anterior to the signs of its coming. Briefly, however, the narratorial intrusion in 13.14 ('Let the reader understand') reminds us that whereas for Mark's own community, apocalyptic expectation was actual as well as narratival, the modern reader stands at both ends of the spectrum. Narratively, the modern reader stands shoulder to shoulder with the original reader, but theologically his or her understanding of the eschaton is somewhat different. The modern reader may be willing to play the language game which the apocalyptic myth presents, but he or she sees, too, that the underlying reality is as much a present as a future one. Existentially, Jesus comes on the clouds of heaven for all who come to the moment of decision and affirm that Jesus is Lord.

Some attempt has been made to summarize the complex relationship between the author, his story world, and his various reading communities in the accompanying diagram (p. 151).

2. *Space*

The obvious counterpart to the temporal setting of a literary work is the spatial one. As recently as 1964, D.S. Bland was lamenting that literary critics had not given sufficient attention to this matter, particularly in regard to the novel.[35] Since then, at least, it has been increasingly recognized that in the better novels spatial setting (or background description, as Bland has it) is not merely an elaboration which could easily be discarded without any fear of doing violence to the work, but is

---

35. D.S. Bland, 'Endangering the Reader's Neck: Background Description in the Novel', in Stevick (ed.), *Theory of the Novel*, pp. 313-31 (313-14).

Narrative Past		Narrative Present		Narrative Future		
Primordial Past	Historical Past	John the Baptist	Ministry of Jesus	Historical Future		Eschatological Future
				Markan Community	Post-Markan Period	
Beginning (10.6; 13.19)	Old Testament Prophecy and History (1.2-3; 2.25-26; 12.26)	(1.2-13)	(1.14–16.8)			End (13.7)
Characters of Story-World				Author/First Readers	Subsequent Readers	

Past of the Characters ←

—Past of Mark and his Community→

Implied Author ← →Implied Reader

←—Past of the Post-Markan Readers—

often indispensable to character or plot. In the view of some, indeed, that is the only time when such setting can legitimately be used:

> Scene is only justified in the novel where it can be shown, or at least felt, to act upon action or character. In fact, where it has dramatic use.[36]

Of course, there are ways and means of dealing with scene, some more acceptable than others. Bland rather frowns on the contrived method where, like Theodore in Walpole's *The Castle of Otranto*, a character actually seeks out the kind of scene which will fit his mood. Ideally, a scene should be used only to underscore the mood a character is already in.

Some of the most effective use of scene, according to Bland, is made by utilizing actual locations, and not simply imagined ones. He gives the example of Scott's *Heart of Midlothian*, where his description of the environs of Arthur's Seat by moonlight serves to create an appropriately mysterious atmosphere for the meeting of Jeanie Deans and Wilson. In the early novels of Lawrence, too, much of the evocative atmosphere is gained through reference to real towns and landscapes. The prospect of Nottingham from the vantage point of Nottingham Castle, for instance, forms the background to a conversation between Paul and Clara in *Sons and Lovers*,[37] which simply could not have taken place without it; and at the beginning of the same author's *The Rainbow*,[38] the people are shown to be at one with the land, so that the characters in the novel seem to emerge from the landscape.

Enough has been said, I think, to show that spatial setting can be indispensable to a work of modern fiction. It is high time to discover whether this same degree of significance is reflected in Mark's Gospel. I shall look first at the possibility of meaning behind Markan space generally; then I shall review Malbon's approach, in which spatial features are treated antithetically, or as binaries; finally I shall advance the view that 'threshold theology' is an important outcome of Mark's spatial settings.

a. *Markan Space and Theological Meaning*
When we compare the settings in Mark with those in a modern novel, we notice immediately just how spartan the former are. Even in those

---

36. E. Bowen, *Collected Impressions* (London: Longmans, Green, 1950), p. 254; quoted in Bland, 'Endangering the Reader's Neck', p. 314.

37. D.H. Lawrence, *Sons and Lovers* (Harmondsworth: Penguin, 1948), p. 331.

38. D.H. Lawrence, *The Rainbow* (Harmondsworth: Penguin, 1981), pp. 41-43.

⸝vels in which 'showing' takes the greatest precedence over 'telling', one expects that at least some background description will be necessary; but the settings in Mark are much more akin to the stage directions in a play-script. R.W. Funk has noticed that such paucity of description was not typical even of literature virtually contemporaneous with Mark (such as Josephus),[39] though it should be noted that the Gospel was written from the outset in a dramatic vein, and that stage-directions are perhaps more appropriate to it than rich background description. Be that as it may, despite the frequent observation that Mark is full of vivid detail, the evangelist uses hardly a word in his settings which is not directly relevant to either characterization, plot or theology. For instance, the scene in which the four men break through the roof to get their paralytic friend to Jesus (2.4) is not told simply to lend interest to the episode; it is there to reinforce the conviction that miraculous healings, far from giving rise to faith once they have been performed, actually require it. Throughout the Gospel, Jesus commends faith (for example, 5.34), and condemns the lack of it (4.40); and in the present case Jesus does not respond until he has seen their faith (2.5), which is made manifest by the lowering of the man through the roof.

Even a minute detail such as the observation that other boats were accompanying that in which Jesus lay sleeping on the occasion of the storm (4.36), may be of theological significance. According to Dennis Nineham,[40] the episode as a whole may recall the passage about God's power over the sea in Ps. 107.23-32, and that since the word for 'ship' is there in the plural (v. 23), Mark added 'and other boats were with him' in order to make the allusion to the psalm clearer.

In other cases, particular places become associated with specific motifs. The synagogue, for instance, is not the place of prayer and teaching as one might have expected, but of conflict of one sort or another (Mk 1.21-28; 3.1-6; 6.1-6), while the house is sometimes a place where crowds gather for healing or teaching (1.33; 2.1-2; 3.20, 31-32), and sometimes a retreat from the crowds, where Jesus can teach his disciples privately (7.17; 9.33; 10.10).

Yet other settings are specifically designed to incite recollection of Old Testament passages in the light of which Mark expects his own stories to

39. R.W. Funk, *The Poetics of Biblical Narrative* (Sonoma, CA: Polebridge Press, 1988), p. 141. I owe this reference to Mark Powell (*What is Narrative Criticism?*, pp. 71-72); Funk's own work was unavailable to me.

40. D.E. Nineham, *Saint Mark* (Harmondsworth: Penguin, 1963), p. 148.

be interpreted. This applies especially to references to sea, river, mountain and desert (or wilderness).

At creation, the waters are associated with chaos. Then God 'moves over the face of the waters' (Gen. 1.2) and begins to bring order, first by separating the waters of the sea from those of the firmament, and then by creating dry land, so that the seas are kept at bay. During the exodus, God again demonstrates his control of the sea by driving the waters back in order to allow the Israelites through on dry land (Exod. 14.21-29). The psalmists, too, recognize God's power over the wind and the waves, as we have seen (Pss. 77.19; 107.23-32). Thus, when we see Jesus stilling a storm (Mk 4.35-41) and walking on the sea (6.45-51), we are meant to understand that he is acting in the same way as God, and since only God is supposed to have authority over the sea, we are to infer that Jesus is, at the very least, approved by God, if not in some way identical with him. These miracles, therefore, are epiphanies, disclosing who Jesus is.

The only river to which Mark refers is the Jordan. John baptizes there (1.5), Jesus himself is baptized in it (1.9), and later must have crossed it (10.1), if Mark expects us to take this comment geographically. Of course, the fact that the Jordan is the chief river of Israel means that if Mark was going to mention any river at all, *it* was bound to be the prime candidate. However, there are theological reasons for referring to it too. Jewish readers, in particular, would have been reminded of what the Jordan meant in Old Testament times. For the wilderness people, it represented a final barrier between their wilderness wanderings and the salvation implicit in entering the Promised Land. Under Joshua (who shared the same name as Jesus—Yeshua), the barrier was broken in much the same way as at the Red Sea: the waters parted to allow the Israelites through (Josh. 3.7-17). This event, then, no less than the Red Sea crossing, was an act of divine salvation. Elijah, too, we later learn, was able to cross the Jordan when God parted the waters for him (2 Kgs 2.6-8). Thus, when John comes from the desert, wearing the kind of clothes that Elijah wore (Mk 1.6; cf. 2 Kgs 1.8), we are surely expected to link these two figures, as other passages of Mark confirm (6.14-29 [cf. 1 Kgs 19.1-3]; 9.11-13). It is here, at the Jordan, that John prophesies the mightier one who is to come, and begins to prepare people for a new salvation. For just as God saved the wilderness generation through Moses and Joshua, so Jesus would bring a new and lasting salvation by establishing the kingdom of God.

Mountains, for Mark, are seen sometimes as places of refuge and retreat (6.46; 13.14), but most strikingly as places of epiphany. Jesus ascends a mountain to be transfigured (9.2-8), and Mark clearly intends this story to reflect mountain experiences of God's people in the Old Testament. It is no coincidence that Moses and Elijah, who appear to Jesus on the mountain, are the very people who receive important epiphanies on Mount Sinai (Exod. 19; 20; 24; 1 Kgs 19), and the transfiguration account has many close correspondences with Moses' experiences in particular. In both cases, the people are left at the foot of the mountain, while the main actors venture forth (Exod. 24.2; Mk 9.2, 14), and in both, a time-span of six days is mentioned (Exod. 24.16; Mk 9.2). A cloud covers the mountain, and a voice speaks from it (Exod. 24.16; Mk 9.7). Again, Jesus' transfiguration (Mk 9.2-3) is reminiscent of the statement that when Moses came back down Mount Sinai his face shone because he had been in God's presence (Exod. 34.29, 35). Finally, it should be noted that the Jews of Jesus' day considered the feast of Tabernacles to be more than an important harvest festival: it was also used to commemorate Moses' receiving the tablets of the Law from God on Mount Sinai. This might well explain Peter's otherwise nonsensical remark that he should make tabernacles for Jesus, Moses and Elijah (Mk 9.5): Mark may well have intended the statement as an indication that the transfiguration account should be seen as a theological reflection or interpretation of the Sinai epiphany in Exodus.

Jesus' appearance on the Mount of Olives (11.1; 13.3), too, has Old Testament connotations. It probably served to remind Mark's original readers/hearers of the prophecy in Zech. 14.4 that the feet of the Lord would be planted there on the last day, when the mount would be split in two; and Jesus' descent from there on a colt in Mk 11.1 is probably meant to be understood as a conscious enactment of the prophecy in Zech. 9.9: 'Behold, your king comes to you lowly and riding on an ass, on a colt, the foal of an ass.'

The desert, or wilderness, is the place to which Jesus is driven to be tempted after his baptism (1.13), and also where he feeds the multitudes (6.35; 8.4). And, of course, in the mind of the reader, it would conjure up images of that wilderness through which Moses led the children of Israel. This is confirmed by what happens there. Jesus feeds the hungry multitude with bread as God fed his people with manna (Exod. 16). So, once again, he is acting like God, thereby disclosing, for those who can see it, his identity.

But Mark may well have in mind not only the original exodus, but the new exodus too—the return from exile in Babylon. Certainly, this is what Deutero-Isaiah had in mind when, in Isa. 40.3, he announced, 'The voice of one crying in the wilderness: Prepare the way of the Lord; make his paths straight.' After citing this verse, Mark introduces John the Baptist with the words, 'John the Baptist came in the wilderness preaching a baptism of repentance for the forgiveness of sins' (Mk 1.4). For Mark, then, Isaiah's 'voice in the wilderness' is that of John, and it is his task to prepare the way of the Lord. There is an implicit exodus theology in all this. Just as the crossing of the wilderness symbolized the way to salvation in both the first and the second exodus, so now John's appearance in the wilderness was to herald a new salvation which would be achieved by following 'in the way' (ἐν τῇ ὁδῷ,—8.3, 27; 9.33; 10.32, 52)—but this time the metaphorical way of the gospel.

There are several other aspects of Markan space which can be understood theologically, but the above examples will be sufficient, for the moment, to illustrate the evangelist's method. More will be discussed as we pass on now to consider the contribution of Malbon.

b. *The Approach of Elizabeth Struthers Malbon*
In a series of writings from the 1980s, Malbon has used literary-critical, in particular structuralist, methods to examine the concept of space in Mark. Her treatment is both diachronic (reading through the text in order to spot places where various points echo or foreshadow other points), and synchronic (taking particular themes or aspects of space to see how Mark uses them—in this case in opposition to one another). In her first contribution she focuses on Galilee and Jerusalem as binary or antithetic spaces.[41] Diachronically, it can be seen that Jesus' initial journey from Nazareth of Galilee to Judea (Mk 1.9) foreshadows his final journey to Jerusalem (9.30–11.11). Similarly, his journey back to Galilee (1.14–11.11) foreshadows his return there after his resurrection (16.7).

Jesus' journeys are important to Mark, and are often anticipated in the text. People often visit Jesus from regions which he will later visit himself. Thus, in 3.7-8, people come to Jesus from Judea, Jerusalem, Idumea, Transjordan and the Tyre and Sidon locality, every one of which, with the exception of Idumea, Jesus later visits (7.24, 31; 10.1; 11.11). Again,

---

41. E.S. Malbon, 'Galilee and Jerusalem: History and Literature in Marcan Interpretation', *CBQ* 44 (1982), pp. 242-55.

the healed Gerasene demoniac spreads news of Jesus throughout the Decapolis (5.20) long before Jesus himself arrives there (7.31). Scribes 'come down' (καταβάντες) from Jerusalem (3.22; 7.1) to observe what Jesus is doing well before he 'goes up' (ἀναβαίνοντες) thence (10.32).

The main point to note is that Galilee and Judea are placed in opposition by Mark. There is, of course, nothing new in this observation. Mark achieves his objective in various ways. Galilee is the place of feverish activity. Jesus is always on the move, rushing from village to village, or from town to country. The action is swift and breathless, and Mark makes frequent use of his favourite adverbs, 'immediately' (εὐθύς) and 'again' (πάλιν). The pattern of movement is bizarre, if taken geographically (cf. 7.31). But Rhoads and Michie rightly point out that some of these movements are beyond Jesus' control.[42] Occasionally he has to withdraw from a place owing to the threat of his enemies (3.6-7), and sometimes the crowds become so unwieldy that he can 'no longer enter a town openly' (1.45). Once he has crossed into Judea (10.1), however, all this itinerary ceases. There are no more preaching tours (1.39) or detours. Instead, we sense a resolution on the part of Jesus to reach Jerusalem by the most direct route, and the only incidents which cause any delay are those that occur 'on the way' (10.46-52).

Again, Galilee is the place of Jesus' popularity. Everywhere he goes he is thronged by excited crowds, eager to be healed or taught (1.32-34, 37, 45; 2.2; 3.7-12, 20; 4.1; 5.21, 31; 6.31-34, 54-56; 9.14). True, there is some opposition (2.1–3.6; 3.20-35; 6.1-6; 7.1-23; 8.11-12), but in the main, apart from objections raised by Jesus' 'own' (3.20-21, 31-35; 6.1-6), the chief bone of contention is *halakha*—how one should interpret the biblical laws. The only note of malice is sounded in 3.6 where the Pharisees and Herodians conspire against Jesus, but this is a literary device to foreshadow the reappearance of these same conspirators in 12.13, by which time the opponents are in greater earnest. In Galilee, much of the opposition seems to be incited by scribes 'from Jerusalem' (3.22; 7.1) for whom, one feels, the ordinary populace have a disregard, if not outright resentment (1.22). As soon as Jesus has crossed into Judea (10.1), however, opposition begins to harden. He is met immediately (10.2-9) by Pharisees who use the divorce question to 'test' him. Then Jesus arouses hostility by his actions in the Temple courts (11.15-18), so

---

42. Rhoads and Michie, *Mark as Story*, pp. 68-69.

that the opponents challenge his authority (11.27). Jesus responds by telling the parable of the wicked tenants (12.1-9) against them, and they form themselves into alliances in order to increase their chances of condemning Jesus: the scribes join with the chief priests and elders (11.18, 27; 14.1, for example) while the Pharisees conspire again with the Herodians 'to trap him in his talk' (12.13). The Sadducees enter the fray (12.18-27); but Jesus foils all his enemies, and ends by roundly condemning the scribes (12.38-40). Finally, the chief priests (and their allies, no doubt) accept the assistance offered by Judas (14.10-11), and promise to pay him for his services. It is clear that, in Judea, matters become far more acrimonious than is the case in Galilee.

In the light of what has been stated about the polarity of Galilee and Judea, Malbon reminds us that Mark, and the Markan Jesus, present us with a reversal of expectations.[43] In the social world of first-century Palestine, Jerusalem was seen as the centre of cultic life, while Galilee, ringed and influenced as it was by Gentile nations, was reckoned to be impure. Jerusalem was the place of the Temple, where God was pleased to dwell, while Galilee was both geographically and spiritually distant. In a word, Jerusalem represented order—cultic and religious life was administered and regulated from there; whereas Galilee represented chaos—distance from God. Mark, however, reverses the traditional expectations. In his Gospel, it is Jerusalem, with its hostility to Jesus, which is seen as the place of chaos, and Galilee, the place of his popularity, which is the place of order. Wherever there is chaos in his homeland, Jesus restores order. The sea may be chaotic, but he controls it (4.35-41; 6.45-51); demons may be chaotic, but he exorcises them (1.21-28, 34, 39; 3.11-12, 22; 5.1-20; 7.24-30; 9.14-29 [the last two beyond Galilee]); disease may be chaotic, but he eradicates it (1.29-31, 32-34, 40-45; 2.3-12; 3.1-6; 5.21-43; 6.53-56; 7.31-37; 8.22-26). It is to be remarked that none of these things are done once Jesus has crossed into Judea, other than that Bartimaeus is healed (10.46-52). The only other miracle which Jesus performs there is, significantly, the cursing of the fig tree (11.12-14, 20-22) which is symbolic of the destruction of the cult and its personnel.[44]

43. Malbon, 'Galilee and Jerusalem', p. 253.

44. Earlier, influential studies on the importance of Galilee for Mark had tended to be founded on historical- or redaction-critical principles. Thus, E. Lohmeyer, *Galiläa und Jerusalem* (Göttingen: Vandenhoeck & Ruprecht, 1936); Lightfoot, *Locality*, pp. 24-48, 73-77; Marxsen, *Mark*, pp. 57-116; W.H. Kelber, *The Kingdom*

In a further article,[45] Malbon turns her attention to Mark's understanding of the Sea of Galilee. It, too, is suggestive of opposites. On the one hand, we are to notice that land is the opposite of sea. The land is the place of order and security, whereas the sea represents chaos. It is the place of demons, and venturing onto it is a hazardous business. As we have seen already, only God can have control over the watery chaos, so in exerting control himself, Jesus shows who he really is: the stilling of the storm and walking on the water are acts of epiphany.

But the Sea of Galilee is not only in opposition to the land; it is a barrier or border *between* lands—between Jewish and Gentile territory. Yet it is a barrier which Jesus crosses at will (4.35; 5.1, 21; 6.51-53; 8.10, 13). These rapid comings and goings across the lake are somewhat confusing if we limit ourselves to an historical and geographical approach. For instance, on one occasion Jesus sends the disciples ahead of him to Bethsaida, on the eastern shore (6.45), but they actually arrive at Gennesaret, on the western shore (6.53). Malbon deals with this symbolically. The disciples do not understand that Jesus has enough 'bread' for Gentiles as well as Jews, so they are reluctant to journey 'to the other side', that is, into Gentile territory. The detour to Gennesaret is symbolic of this reluctance. It is significant that Mark, having just told the story of the walking on the water, adds redactionally, 'For they did not understand about the loaves, but their hearts were hardened' (6.52). Soon after this, however, Jesus engages in a Gentile mission in which he argues against the laws of ritual purity (7.1-23), exorcises a demon from the daughter of a Syrophoenician woman, after first discussing the legitimacy of a healing ministry to the Gentiles (7.24-30), heals the deaf-mute in the Decapolis (7.31-37), and miraculously feeds four thousand people on the east (Gentile) side of the lake (8.1-10). In addition, he appears to rebuff the Jewish leaders who demand a sign from him (8.11-12); in fact, he makes a special trip across the lake just to do that (8.10, 13). It is as if Mark is making a special point of comparing Jesus' attitude to the Gentiles with that of the Jewish leaders. Only after all this has been accomplished does Jesus set out again with his disciples in the

---

in Mark (Philadelphia: Fortress Press, 1974). A more recent study, that by S. Freyne (*Galilee, Jesus and the Gospels: Literary Approaches and Historical Investigations* [Philadelphia: Fortress Press, 1988]), attempts to integrate literary and socio-political insights.

45. E.S. Malbon, 'The Jesus of Mark and the Sea of Galilee', *JBL* 103 (1984), pp. 363-77.

boat (8.13), and although the latter are still 'all at sea' about the true meaning of the bread (8.14-21), they do, at last, reach their intended destination—Bethsaida.

Malbon sees the next pericope, the healing of the blind man (8.22-26) not so much as a paradigm for Peter's imperfect vision of who Jesus is (8.27-33), as most Markan scholars now contend, but rather as relating to the previous section (6.35-8.21). Just as the blind man is healed in two stages, so it takes the disciples two attempts to reach Bethsaida—that is, to recognize that Jesus has enough spiritual food for Jew and Gentile alike.

Much of the material contained in these two articles was incorporated into Malbon's 1986 book-length study of space in the Gospel as a whole.[46] In it, she again adopts literary-structuralist procedures. She discusses Markan space under three categories: geopolitical (towns, provinces, boundaries); topographical (seas, land, mountains, wilderness); and architectural (houses, tombs, synagogues, Temple). In each case, as in her articles, she presents her material both diachronically and synchronically, and is thus able both to trace these various features in sequence, and to discuss them as they appear in their polarity. Among the pairs of opposites are: Galilee/Judea, land/sea, heaven/earth, Jewish homeland/foreign lands, inhabited areas/isolated areas, house/synagogue, and tomb/Temple. Underpinning all these is the antithesis order/chaos, which applies to all the others. But, as with Galilee/Judea, discussed above, in every case traditional expectations are reversed, so that 'order' is really 'chaos', and vice versa. In the case of tomb/Temple, for instance, it is expected that the latter, with its cultic ceremony and hierarchical organization, and well-regulated administration, will represent order, while the tomb is the place of death–chaos. But by exposing the corruption of the cult and its personnel, and predicting its destruction (11.12-22) and then later demonstrating his power over the grave, Jesus reverses expectations, equating the tomb with order and the Temple with chaos.

To take just one more example, because the *synagogue* is controlled by the religious establishment, and is the custodian of Torah, and the centre for scribal teaching, one is entitled to expect it to represent the seat of order. But Mark again reverses that expectation. In his Gospel, the synagogue becomes the place of opposition, whether from demons

46. E.S. Malbon, *Narrative Space and Mythic Meaning in Mark* (Sheffield: JSOT Press, 1991 [1986]).

(1.21-28), religious leaders (3.1-6) or neighbours (6.1-6), and it is the house which becomes the place of teaching (7.17; 9.33; 10.10). As Malbon says in commenting on the healing of Jairus' daughter, 'Power is not with the ruler of the synagogue, but with Jesus in the house.'[47]

Some features of Malbon's scheme, however, are held to perform a mediating function. For instance, the mountain is meant to fill the space between heaven and earth; it is where the human and the divine meet, as can clearly be seen in the transfiguration (9.2-8).[48] We have noted already that the mountain is commonly the place for God's revelation in the Old Testament.

But the one element which Malbon thinks is central to the entire spatial scheme of Mark is 'the way' (ὁδός). Like the mountain, it too serves a mediating function, so that all other spatial elements must find their ultimate significance in it. The mediating force of 'the way' is that it lies in the space between opposites. Jesus is constantly on the move, and his disciples must follow him 'on the way' (ἐν τῇ ὁδῷ) if they are to share in the new order (cf. 9.33; 10.32, 46). 'John prepares the way, Jesus leads the way, disciples are called to follow on the way.'[49] At the end of the Gospel (which, in common with most scholars, Malbon takes to be 16.8), Jesus is still on the way—we never see him arrive; and the disciples must follow him—to Galilee, or wherever—despite hardship during the course of their journey, if they are to participate in the new order which he announces.

c. *Threshold Theology*

Do Malbon's studies succeed? Like any voyage into uncharted waters, the promise of treasure brings with it certain dangers. Unlike some of her colleagues, Malbon clearly demonstrates that structuralism can be used profitably to study an ancient text, and is not simply an abstract methodology with little scope for practical application, as one might infer from some studies. Her insights tend to shed new light on the meaning of the many spatial references in Mark's Gospel. On the other hand, we are bound to wonder whether every single reference is quite as pregnant

47. Malbon, *Narrative Space*, p. 133.

48. It is not only the Bible-writers (and biblical scholars) who take this view of mountains. The American composer, Alan Hovhaness, has said, 'Mountains are like symbols, like pyramids, of man's attempt to know God. Mountains are symbolic meeting places between the mundane and the spiritual world.'

49. Malbon, *Narrative Space*, p. 71.

with meaning as Malbon would have us believe. Surely, if there is any
history behind the Gospel at all—and it is inconceivable that there is
not—we have to accept that some spatial rubrics are present simply
because history demands them to be. This is not to say, of course, that
Mark might not have incorporated some of them into his overall
theological design.

The drawback with structuralist approaches of this kind is that we can
never be quite sure to what extent the evangelist conceived of the
scheme attributed to him. One always has that sneaking suspicion that
the scholar, with his or her sophisticated methodologies, is imposing it
on his behalf. After all, structuralism is a modern category, not an
ancient one.

Despite these weaknesses, however, Malbon's studies make good
literary-theological sense of references like Mk 7.31, which have tended
to baffle on a purely geographical understanding. In particular, she has
recognized the significance of passages which serve to mediate between
extremes of one kind or another, and which contribute to Mark's
'threshold theology'. We have seen how the mountain mediates between
heaven and earth, the Sea of Galilee mediates between homeland and
foreign land, and 'the way' mediates between one place and another.
We could add other examples. The door ($\theta\acute{\upsilon}\rho\alpha$) is an object which
shares this same function. It is not simply a physical threshold, but a
theological one, too. In 1.33, we are told that the whole city (of
Capernaum) gathered around the door so that their sick could be healed,
and their possessed exorcised. Then, in 2.2, the men bringing the
paralytic find that they cannot get to Jesus via the door because the
crowd is too large, so they find access through the roof. Mark 3.31-35
presupposes a door, even though the word $\theta\acute{\upsilon}\rho\alpha$ is not used, for Jesus is
on the inside, teaching the crowd, while his family are waiting outside. In
each of these cases, the door seems to symbolize access to Jesus; even
when access cannot be gained, as in 2.2, the door is the initial target.
Moreover, whether people are successful in crossing the threshold
depends rather on their faith. The people at Capernaum certainly get
what they want—healing and teaching; but there is no indication that
Jesus' family are admitted to the house, for they are antagonistic towards
Jesus' ministry. Indeed, Jesus appears to cold-shoulder his genetic family
in favour of those who do the will of God.

What of the remaining uses of $\theta\acute{\upsilon}\rho\alpha$? The occurrence at 11.4 has no
symbolic significance: it simply tells us that the disciples who were sent

to fetch the colt on which Jesus was to ride into Jerusalem found it tethered outside the door of the house. Mark 13.29, on the other hand, explains that when the apocalyptic signs described by Jesus actually occurred, the disciples could be sure that the Parousia was imminent, 'at the doors'. Here is a reversal of the earlier situation. During his earthly ministry, people flocked to Jesus, and the door sometimes provided access to him. Here, however, it is Jesus, as glorified Son of man, who is at the doors—and the disciples are urged to be ready for him.

Finally, Mark refers to one other door—the entrance to the tomb (15.46; 16.3), across which a stone is rolled. It appears that the time for contact between the one within and those outside is over. Yet even in death, Jesus continues to draw people to him: the women will not be denied access. But when they succeed in their quest, they find that Jesus is not in! The empty tomb means that people of faith do not need to make a pilgrimage to reach Jesus; he is freely available to them wherever they are. The reward of faith is that Jesus is always at home—in the heart of the believer.

Another 'threshold' situation, as we have seen, is Jesus' crossing from Galilee, the place of comparative security and popularity, into Judea, the place of hostility, where cultic corruption abounds, and death awaits. Mark does not let this crossing pass without a redactional passage (10.1) to mark the occasion. One receives the impression that this is Jesus' crossing of the Rubicon. On the border of Judea, he is on the threshold of an act of cosmic significance, for he knows that, once across that border, there can be no turning back. He is 'on the way'—a road which the disciples are bidden to follow.

These threshold experiences, then, are common throughout the Gospel, though the 'barrier' or the object of mediation can be of various kinds—a mountain, the Sea of Galilee, the 'way', a door or a political boundary. Is there a common denominator which is able to make sense of all such experiences? The one consideration which appears to be of significance in every case is that the threshold symbolizes a division between what is acceptable to the eye of faith and what is not. Below the mountain is the world of common earthly existence to which the faithless are bound; above it is the heavenly one for which the believer is striving; on the mountain itself the mortal is permitted a glimpse of eternity. On one side of the Sea of Galilee is the narrow, undeveloped view of faith which would restrict Christianity to the elite, and enmesh it in a web of rules and regulations and doctrinal dogmas; on the other is the ever-open door of grace through whom no seeker is denied access. At the beginning of the 'way' is the 'city of destruction', the believers' starting-point, where they must not linger; at the end is their goal, and in between them the way of discipleship which they must not cease to tread this side of eternity. On one side of the door is faithlessness and perdition; on the other side the inner peace and assurance of salvation that comes through faith in Christ. And on one side of the border is Judea—land of hostility, rebellion against God, and death—death, ultimately, for the rebel; and on the other is Galilee—land of order, security, healing and of the gospel—the call to enter the kingdom.

3. *Summary*

In this chapter, I have endeavoured to deal with some of the important questions raised by time and space in narrative through the eyes of some of the leading scholars in the field—notably Via, Malina, Genette and Malbon.

The tripartite nature of time, we discovered, is widely recognized, because it reflects the tripartite nature of life itself—birth–life–death. Aristotle saw that every plot (and every story, for that matter) must follow this same pattern—a beginning, a middle and an end. Luke, according to Conzelmann, viewed salvation history in a similar way, as consisting of a time before Jesus, the time of Jesus himself (*die Mitte der Zeit*) and the time of the Church. Jesus stands at the centre of history. It is this model, broadly speaking, which Via applies to Mark's Gospel. The same three epochs are represented in Mark by Mk 1.1-13; 1.14–14.52; and 14.53–16.8 respectively.

Malina's work is a salutory reminder of the dangers involved in superimposing our modern understanding of time upon the concept held by ancient agrarian societies around the Mediterranean. While our sense of time is linear, futuristic and dominant, theirs was cyclical, present-oriented and subservient. Time was not measured by the clock, but by the seasons, and everything had its right time—καίρος not χρόνος. This understanding particularly affects our interpretation of eschatology in the Bible, and the Markan narrative clearly displays conformity with this ancient view of time.

According to Gérard Genette, narrative-time falls into two broad categories—text-time and story-time—and can be discussed under three basic principles: order, duration and frequency. Text-time is the time required for a reader to read the text, while story-time is the time covered by the story itself and can, of course, be much more extensive than the former. Mark's Gospel, for instance, takes about two hours to read, but the story is on a truly cosmic scale, and even the plotted time extends over a couple of years.

Order is the sequence in which the story is told, while duration is concerned with the length of time devoted to each segment of the text. Mark makes full use of both these techniques. He sometimes locates a story 'out of sequence' (for example, 6.14-29) to produce a more striking narrative effect, and his masterful handling of duration ensures that his Gospel reaches its shattering climax at the foot of the cross.

Frequency denotes how often an event is recorded in relation to the frequency of its occurrence. An event which occurs once may be recorded several times, or one which happens repeatedly may be told only once. Mark, for instance records three passion predictions— predictions of a once-only event—as a means of emphasis.

The work of Elizabeth Struthers Malbon provides a bridge between time and space. She discusses the typological importance of time in the Markan narrative, and then proceeds to a consideration of spatial features as set in binary opposition, with certain mediating features. The Sea of Galilee, for instance, serves a mediating function between Jewish and Gentile territory. Basing our argument upon this view of spatiality, I attempted to isolate a stratum of Markan theology which I labelled 'threshold theology'. Doors and political boundaries both represent the threshold between the inside and the outside, between one place and another; and the common denominator of these is faith. It is faith which enables the believer to move from the outside, across the threshold, into the presence of Jesus. All would-be disciples must, like Bartimaeus, be 'on the way' in lives of faith, commitment and service if they hope to enter the kingdom.

Chapter 5

POINT OF VIEW IN MARK'S GOSPEL

According to Abrams,

> Point of view signifies the way a story gets told—the mode or perspective
> established by an author by means of which the reader is presented with
> the characters, actions, setting and events which constitute the narrative in
> a work of fiction.[1]

To put it slightly differently, point of view is the means by which an
author conveys the intended message to the reader. It is by no means a
simple matter, for it embraces a wide range of issues. For instance, Who
is speaking to the reader? Is it a third-person narrator, or a first-person
observer or character? If the former, is he or she omniscient or limited,
intrusive or unobtrusive? If the latter, is he or she peripheral or central
to the narrative? And is the narrator, irrespective of person, reliable or
unreliable? How does he or she relate to the others involved in the
narrative—the implied author, the implied reader and the characters?
Are their respective points of view compatible or not? How does the
implied author manage to control the narrative distance between these
various parties?—by means of words, or actions, or thoughts and
feelings? And whose?—the author's, the narrator's or the protagonist's?
What part do voice and mood play? Into what other categories might
point of view conceivably fall?[2] All these questions impinge, to a greater
or lesser extent, on any adequate consideration of point of view in
Mark's Gospel. I shall now endeavour to treat them systematically, using

---

1. Abrams, *Glossary*, p. 144.

2. Some of these questions are considered by N. Friedman, 'Point of View in
Fiction', in P. Stevick (ed.), *Theory of the Novel*, pp. 108-37. Voice and mood are
treated in detail by Genette, *Narrative Discourse*, while a further attempt to classify
points of view is made by B. Uspensky, *A Poetics of Composition* (trans. V. Zavarin
and S. Wittig; Berkeley: University of California Press, 1973).

the categories suggested by Uspensky and Genette[3] as a framework for my own enquiry.

1. *Boris Uspensky: Levels of Point of View*

Boris Uspensky has endeavoured to classify point of view according to different levels or planes of perception: ideological, phraseological, spatio-temporal, and psychological. Petersen has already sought to apply these categories to point of view in Mark[4] (just as Culpepper has attempted the same task in respect of John's Gospel[5]), but it will be convenient for me to use the same framework as a point of departure for my own discussion.

a. *Ideological Point of View*
Uspensky remarks first on the *ideological* point of view.[6] This is concerned with the moral or evaluative judgments made by the implied author, the narrator or the various characters, and these judgments, of course, are by no means bound to enjoy homogeneity. Conflict can arise between different characters who harbour diametrically opposed points of view, and the reader can never take for granted that the information conveyed to him by the narrator will always be reliable. Many a work hides the spectre of the unreliable or fallible narrator—that is to say, a narrator who speaks as if he or she represents the norms of the work when in fact he or she does not.[7] The point of view of an unreliable narrator will usually be found to conflict with that of the implied author and his or her readers, and in that case may serve as a foil for the reliable authorial point of view.

Happily, no such complexities exist in the Markan narrative. That work manifests only two points of view—the right one and the wrong

---

3. Uspensky, *Poetics*; Genette, *Narrative Discourse*.

4. N. Petersen, '"Point of View" in Mark's Narrative', *Semeia*, 12 (1978), pp. 97-121.

5. Culpepper, *Anatomy of the Fourth Gospel*, pp. 20-34.

6. Uspensky, *Poetics*, pp. 8-16.

7. Booth, *Rhetoric of Fiction*, pp. 158-59; *idem*, 'Distance and Point of View: An Essay in Clarification', *Theory of the Novel*, pp. 100-101. The unreliability of the narrator in James's, *The Turn of the Screw*, for instance, makes for a fascinating ambiguity in the story. Cf. Booth, *Rhetoric of Fiction*, pp. 300-16, pp. 339-74.

one.[8] The narrator clearly believes that Jesus is the Christ, the Son of God (1.1), a view shared implicitly by the author and by the characters as long as they are making reliable comments. The protagonist, Jesus, never conflicts with the status quo, and so is totally reliable. Certain minor characters—the heavenly voice (1.11; 9.7), the demons (1.24, 34; 3.11; 5.7), the centurion (15.39)—also enjoy this status, while others, notably the disciples, are reliable on some occasions and unreliable on others. We might instance the confession at Caesarea Philippi (8.27-33), where Peter reliably attests to Jesus' messiahship, but immediately betrays his misunderstanding of it. The opponents, of course, are almost wholly unreliable (with the exception of the 'righteous' scribe in 12.28-34). So then, whenever the 'things of God' (as opposed to the 'things of humans') are in view, the right point of view is being upheld, regardless of who is representing it.

b. *Phraseological Point of View*
Next comes the *phraseological* point of view,[9] the manner in which point of view can be conveyed purely by language. To quote Uspensky,

> Let us assume that an event to be described takes place before a number of witnesses, among whom may be the author, the characters (the immediate participants in the event), and some other, detached spectators. Each of the observers may offer his own description of the events... We would then expect these monologues to be distinct in their particular speech characteristics; however, the facts described by the various people—who may be in different relations to each other—would coincide, intersect, and complement each other in specific ways.
>
> Theoretically, the author, constructing his narrative, may use first one then another of these various narrations. These narrations...may merge and be transposed into authorial speech. Within the authorial speech the shifting from one point of view to another is expressed in different uses of forms of someone else's speech.[10]

Thus, a character's or a narrator's ideological point of view may be expressed by means of phraseological point of view. In the Gospels, however, it is not easy to make distinctions in this manner. Culpepper, for instance, has demonstrated that, in the case of John's Gospel, Jesus' speeches reflect the narrator's point of view not only ideologically, but

---

8.   J.L. Resseguie, 'Reader-Response Criticism', pp. 307-24.
9.   Uspensky, *Poetics*, pp. 17-56.
10. Uspensky, *Poetics*, pp. 17-18.

linguistically as well.[11] Similarly, in Mark it is notoriously difficult to distinguish between authorial language and traditional speech. Do we, indeed, have any *ipsissima verba Jesu*? Attempts have, of course, been made to address this question, but the traditional authenticating criteria[12] pay remarkably little attention to linguistic differences between authorial reporting and what is allegedly Jesus' own speech.

A major problem lies in the fact that Jesus' purported speech is so scarce in Mark. Apart from Mark 4 and 13, the little that remains consists largely of disconnected fragments. There is simply not enough material to make a fair assessment as to whether or not the language of Jesus is distinctive in its narrative context. The problem should become clearer if we briefly consider one or two areas where Jesus' speech has traditionally been accepted as authentic.

Because the phrase 'Son of man' is confined to the lips of Jesus, it has been assumed in the past that all 'Son of man' sayings must be authentic. There is, of course, a vast and still growing body of literature on this issue,[13] but the consensus now is that we must be cautiously selective in the matter of authenticity. Both the Son of man sayings in 2.10, 28, for instance, could be authorial asides—a view accepted even by some evangelical scholars.[14] Then there is the view, taken on linguistic grounds, that certain Son of man sayings have been modelled by the evangelist on other, authentic ones.[15] How is it possible to come to a decision here?

Again, it has frequently been accepted that the key Jesus logia which occur at the climax of the pronouncement stories must be authentic, but in fact there are numerous doubtful cases. We have just testified to 2.10, 28. Another instance from the same catena is 2.17: 'Those who are well have no need of a physician, but those who are sick; I came not to call the righteous, but sinners.' The first statement (v. 17a), like 2.27, seems

11. Culpepper, *Anatomy of the Fourth Gospel*, pp. 38-43.

12. Perrin, *Rediscovering the Teaching of Jesus*, pp. 39-49.

13. See the bibliography in works such as H.E. Tödt, *The Son of Man in the Synoptic Tradition* (trans. D. Barton; London: SCM Press, 1965); M.D. Hooker, *The Son of Man in Mark* (London: SPCK, 1967); M. Casey, *Son of Man: The Introduction and Influence of Daniel 7* (London: SPCK, 1979); B. Lindars, *Jesus, Son of Man* (London: SPCK, 1983).

14. Lane, *Mark*, pp. 98, 120.

15. The threefold Passion prediction, for instance, is sometimes held to be a community development based upon a single authentic saying. Cf. G. Strecker, 'The Passion and Resurrection Predictions in Mark's Gospel', *Int* 22 (1968), pp. 421-42.

to be proverbial;[16] but what of the 'I came' clause? It is more christological in tone, and structurally alien from what precedes.[17] Is it an
authorial accretion? How, then, should it appear on the lips of Jesus?
Again, much of Jesus' speech in 8.14-21 is now felt to be a redactional
haggadah built around the leaven saying in 8.15. Even in the days prior
to the rise of redaction criticism, the Markan imprint on this passage was
keenly felt.[18]

Even the parables which, more than any other of Jesus' words, are
reckoned to be authentic, do not escape unscathed. The parable of the
Sower (4.3-9), for instance, may be genuine enough, but whose is the
interpretation (4.14-20)?[19]

Of course, the less we can establish as being authentic *logia Jesu*, the
less are our chances of being able to determine a distinctive point of
view of Jesus. In the last analysis, however, it matters very little precisely
because Jesus' point of view is not distinctive; it is the self-same point of
view that is shared by the narrator and the implied author. That is why
Jesus' language defies isolation from its context to any extensive degree.

c. *Spatio-Temporal Point of View*
Uspensky's third category is the *spatio-temporal* plane.[20] The concern
here is with the spatial and temporal position of the various participants
in relation to the story-world. The characters, for instance, are constrained
by it. They live in this world, and although they may reflect on the past
and anticipate the future, they cannot step outside the realm of the

16. Cf. Lane, *Mark*, p. 104, and n. 43.

17. Mk 2.17a is structurally self-contained in the form of the following chiasm:

οὐ χρείαν ἔχουσιν ('No need have...')
    οἱ ἰσχύοντες ('...those who are strong...')
        ἰατροῦ ('...of a physician...')
    ἀλλ' οἱ κακῶς ('...but those who are sick...')
ἔχοντες ('...have...')

This adequately completes the pronouncement story in 2.15-17. Mk 2.17b reads very
much like an accretion dealing with Jesus' christological function, and drawing out
the significance of v.17a for the benefit of Christian readers.

18. Cf. V. Taylor, *The Gospel according to St Mark* (London: Macmillan, 2nd
edn, 1966), pp. 363-64.

19. J. Jeremias, *The Parables of Jesus* (trans. S.H. Hooke; London: SCM Press,
rev. edn, 1963), pp. 77-79, 149-51.

20. Uspensky, *Poetics*, pp. 57-80.

narrative. By contrast, the omniscient narrator seems to enjoy an almost unlimited spatial and temporal freedom. The Markan narrator, for instance, glides effortlessly from one place to another in a manner that would be impossible for the actors in the story.

The paragraph above suggests very briefly how Uspensky's spatio-temporal category might be applied to Mark, but given that the previous chapter was devoted to a consideration of time and space in Mark's Gospel,[21] it is unnecessary to consider the matter further here. We mention it simply for the sake of completeness, and pass on to the next category.

d. *Psychological Point of View*
Uspensky's final category is the psychological point of view,[22] which allows the narrator and his or her audience access to the mind and emotions of the characters. From this perspective, it is possible to gain some insight into what they are thinking or feeling. In Mark, Jesus is the most transparent character in this respect (1.41; 2.8; 3.5; 5.30; 6.6, 34; 8.2, 12, 17; 10.14, 21; 11.12), but the disciples, too, are open to the same kind of treatment (6.49-52; 9.6, 32; 11.21; 14.40), as are the opponents (2.6-7; 8.11; 10.2; 11.18; 12.12, 34) and some of the minor characters (1.34; 5.29; 6.19, 20-26; 8.25; 15.10, 15; 16.8). This is a particularly effective device because it allows the implied author to control the distance between the implied reader and the various points of view by means of particular emotional responses. For instance, we learn that the disciples' response to Jesus' wonder-working and to his person is typi-cally one of fear. Yet, given that Jesus himself tends to commend faith over fear (4.40; 6.50), we are left to wonder whether the disciples' reaction might not be inappropriate. So too, the inner thoughts of the opponents are frequently directed towards Jesus' destruction, and so can only be negative.

By contrast, Jesus always makes the correct emotional response to every situation, as befits one with a totally reliable point of view. The kind of emotions which might normally be regarded as negative—anger, indignation, impatience and so on—are in his case simply positive responses to negative situations. If he is angry (instead of compassionate) in the case of the leper (1.41), it is because of the evil which the disease

21. On time and space in Mark, see Chapter 4 above.
22. Uspensky, *Poetics*, pp. 81-100.

embodies; if he is grieved, it is because of the obstinacy of his opponents (3.5); if he is indignant, it is because of his disciples' utter failure to learn the lesson of humility (10.14).

It should be mentioned that certain conservative scholars would argue that these references to emotional responses are based on factual reporting. Jesus and the other characters might have communicated their feelings through facial expression or verbal report,[23] or perhaps they may have been deduced from the nature of the situation. But in the last analysis it is perhaps better to regard all such references as the fruits of a narrative device for adding a psychological dimension to the account. Their narratival significance supersedes the question as to whether or not the characters actually experienced these emotions on the occasions specified.

2. *Genette: Voice and Mood*

A rather different model for determining point of view in a text is that proposed by Gérard Genette, which takes account of mood and voice. 'Mood' (or atmosphere) '...is the tonality pervading a literary work, whether happy or...terrifying or disastrous.'[24] According to Genette, it consists of two aspects—distance and perspective. 'Voice',

> ...signifies the equivalent in imaginative [i.e. narrative] literature to Aristotle's 'ethos'[25] in a work of persuasive rhetoric, and suggests also the rhetorician's concern with the importance of the physical voice in oration. The term in criticism points to the fact that there is a voice beyond the fictitious voices that speak in a work, and a person behind all the dramatis personae, including even the first-person narrator. We have the sense of a pervasive presence, a determinate intelligence and moral sensibility, which has selected, ordered, rendered, and expressed these literary materials in just this way.[26]

23. It could be pointed out, for example, that Jesus' compassion on the multitudes, recorded by the narrator in Mk 6.34, is confirmed by Jesus himself in the parallel passage, Mk 8.2.

24. Abrams, *Glossary*, p. 11.

25. Aristotle, *Ars Rhetorica* (LCL; trans. J.H. Freese; Cambridge, MA: Harvard University Press; London: Heinemann, 1926) 1.2.3; 9.38; 2.1-18; 21.16; 3.7.1; 16.8-9. By 'ethos' Aristotle means the ethical aura or character expressed by a speaker through rhetoric.

26. Abrams, *Glossary*, p. 136.

This sense of authorial voice, which is present in works of intrusive and unobtrusive narration alike, may be identified with the expression 'implied author' which Wayne Booth uses to indicate that the implied reader of a work of fiction should have the sense not only of a voice actually speaking, but of a total human presence. Genette subdivides voice into three categories: person, narrative level and time of narration. His classification as a whole, therefore, may be shown as follows:

$$
\text{Mood}
\begin{cases}
\text{distance} \\
\\
\text{perspective}
\end{cases}
$$

$$
\text{Voice}
\begin{cases}
\text{person} \\
\text{narrative level} \\
\text{time of narrating}
\end{cases}
$$

Let us examine these five sub-categories systematically.

a. *Distance*

It has been widely established that control of distance (the extent to which one is identified with or polarized from the action or, more pertinently, a particular point of view) is regulated essentially by the relative proportions of 'telling' and 'showing' in a work.[27] 'Telling' signifies the narrative mode (or 'picture' mode, as Lubbock terms it[28]), the narration of a story by a more or less intrusive third-person narrator; 'showing', on the other hand, represents the dramatic mode in which the narrator appears to recede into the background, allowing the story to tell itself, as it were, by means of direct speech and superfluity of pictorial detail. Any good narrative work tends to fashion its effect upon the reader by sensitive and judicious use of these two modes.[29] Climactic points in a novel, for instance, are generally more effective when they are handled dramatically, and contrasted with a largely narrative or scenic context. There are no hard-and-fast rules, obviously, but this can be taken as a general principle.

So much for the means of controlling distance. But what, in fact, does

---

27. P. Lubbock, 'The Craft of Fiction: Picture, Drama and Point of View', in Scholes (ed.), *Approaches to the Novel*, pp. 245-63; Booth, *Rhetoric of Fiction*, pp. 3-16, *passim*; Genette, *Narrative Discourse*, pp. 161-85.

28. Lubbock, 'Craft of Fiction', p. 245.

29. Lubbock, 'Craft of Fiction', p. 251.

distance imply? What manner of concept is it? While the mere fact of telling and showing has been evident since classical times,[30] it is only relatively recently that any systematic attempt has been made to classify distance itself. In his seminal work on the subject, Wayne Booth recognized the complexities involved both in relation to a proper classification of the term, and in respect of the various constituent parties associated, in one way or another, with the narrative.[31] Prior to his work, scholars tended to assume that all 'distance' was, broadly-speaking, aesthetic distance. What Booth did was to ascribe this to a category of its own. Thus, aesthetic distance became an essentially cultural phenomenon, incorporating temporal, spatial and linguistic concerns, and was deemed to be quite independent of other types of distance—moral, intellectual and physical, for example.

As to the rôle of distance in the relationships between the implied author, reader, narrator and characters, Booth conceives of five possibilities:

> The narrator may be more or less distant from the implied author...The narrator may also be more or less distant from the characters in the story he tells...The narrator may be more or less distant from the reader's own norms...The implied author may be more or less distant from the reader...The implied author (carrying the reader with him) may be more or less distant from other characters.[32]

In all these cases, the distance can, of course, be aesthetic, moral, intellectual and so on, and it is possible for several kinds of distance to be operable at once.

We may obtain a clearer idea of this phenomenon by applying it to Mark's Gospel. So complex is this issue that if I were to treat the text systematically, I should need to devote an entire volume to it. All I can do here is draw upon a few pericopae to illustrate the theory.

First, then, does Mark both 'tell' and 'show'? Although the answer to this is affirmative, we have to recognize that he was not attempting to conform to some modern literary theory. It is unlikely, therefore, that he intentionally distributed passages of telling and showing for literary effect. This seems clear when we examine passages known to be of vital

30. Friedman ('Point of View', p. 110), for instance, has shown that the distinction is made in classical authors such as Plato (*Rep.* 3.392-94), Aristotle (*Rhet.* 3.11.2-4) and Quintilian (*Inst.Or.* 4.2.63; 6.2.28-34; 8.3.61-62).

31. Booth, *Rhetoric of Fiction*, pp. 155-59; *idem*, 'Distance', pp. 87-107.

32. Booth, *Rhetoric of Fiction,* pp. 156-58.

importance. On the basis of modern literary technique, we might have expected 8.27-33, which marks the pivot of the Gospel, to be dramatized in such a way as to draw the reader onto the stage, as it were. This, as we have seen, could have been achieved by use of direct speech and extraneous detail; but neither is especially prominent here. Mark is capable of telling a story in more colourful detail than is evident at this point (cf. 2.1-12), and he can devote entire chapters to direct speech when he has a mind to, even though the parables (4.2-32) and the apocalypse (13.5-37) do require it. In these instances, the narrator seems to withdraw into the background, leaving the reader with the impression of actually 'being there': he is sitting at the feet of Jesus there by the lakeside, and only the intrusion of the occasional 'and he said' (καὶ ἔλεγεν) gives the game away.

Similarly, Petersen has shown how, in some instances, Mark uses a 'zoom-lens' technique to draw the reader into the action.[33] Thus, in 2.1-12 the narrator (and hence the reader) is at first an external observer as he watches Jesus enter Capernaum. The aorist passive, ἠκούσθη ('...it was *heard* that he was at home'), underlines the initial distance; it is as if someone else, not the narrator, had obtained this information. But then, using his omniscience, he goes into the house, and the reader follows him. The crowd is jostling around the door, but narrator and reader have a ringside seat. Vivid description, particularly at 2.2-4, increases the impression of actually being present. Then, during Jesus' confrontation with the scribes, the reader is taken even further into the narrator's confidence, for he is even able to discern what the scribes are thinking (2.6-7), and the only others capable of doing that are the narrator himself and Jesus (2.8).

Similar instances of this technique can be found in 8.14-21; 9.33-37; 11.27-33; 14.32-42, all but the last of which are characterized by a διαλογίζομαι clause in which Jesus perceives what others are trying to hide from him.

By contrast, 8.27-33 uses a narrator-intrusive technique which at first sight would appear to increase the distance between the reader and the dramatic action. The secrecy motif in 8.30 reverts to third-person narration, even though Jesus has just been allowed a first-person voice (8.27, 29). Similarly, the first passion prediction which follows (8.31) is

---

33. Petersen, '"Point of View"', pp. 99-100.

cast in the third person, even though the later ones (9.31; 10.33-34) are in direct speech, and the clause, καὶ παρρησίᾳ τὸν λόγον ἐλάλει ('And he said this plainly', 8.32a) is clearly an authorial aside which draws attention to the reported Passion prediction.

Undeniably, the narrator keeps a high profile in this section, thereby keeping the reader at bay; but this control of distance is exerted for a good reason, for it enables the narrator to draw the reader close at two crucial points where, by using the historic present here and nowhere else in the section, he lets the reader in on the action. The first of these is at 8.29b, where Peter *says* (λέγει) to Jesus, 'You are the Christ.' This, the turning-point of the entire Gospel, recalls 1.1, and is obviously meant to be the doctrinal (or, following Booth, we might say the intellectual) point of view shared by implied author, reader, narrator and Jesus alike.

The second instance is at 8.33: Jesus turns to Peter and *says* (λέγει), 'Away from me, Satan! For you do not think the things of God, but the things of men.' Here, the doctrinal (perhaps Booth's moral) point of view is again to the fore. The reader is invited to witness this statement directly, without narrational mediation, precisely because it challenges him to appreciate the distinction between the only two points of view possible in Mark: the correct one, represented by 'the things of God'; and the incorrect one, represented by 'the things of men'.

The foregoing discussion shows that there is no firm law of relationship between point of view and distance—not in Mark, at any rate. Keeping the reader at a distance from the characters does not necessarily imply that he or she is to divorce him or herself from their point of view. We have just seen that, in 8.27-33, distance is carefully controlled precisely because the implied author wants his audience to grasp the one reliable point of view which the Gospel offers.

We can learn something, too, about Mark's treatment of *types* of distance. When we examine a passage such as 2.1-12, we find that the reader is invited into the action temporally, spatially and culturally. He is made to feel that he or she is participating in a place and time other than his or her own, and though his or her world may be very different from the story-world, it somehow does not seem strange that people should climb onto a roof and break through with such apparent ease. The distance in question here is purely aesthetic distance which, according to Booth, should be reserved for describing 'the degree to which the reader or spectator is asked to forget the artificiality of the work and "lose himself" in it'.[34]

But in the same pericope there is also a matter of moral distance. As in 8.27-33, a judicious use of the historic present highlights the issue. In 2.6-7, the scribes cast doubt on Jesus' authority to forgive sins, in response to which Jesus *says* (λέγει), 'Why do you reason these things in your hearts?' The question shows that Jesus' point of view is opposed to that of the scribes. Then, given that 2.10a is an authorial aside, the narrator interposes with the news that Jesus has, indeed, authority to forgive sins. Finally, another historic present introduces a confirmation of that assertion: '—he *says* (λέγει) to the paralytic, "I say to you, arise, take up your pallet, and go to your house" ' (2.11).

It must be noted that the historic present is a very common device in Mark,[35] and to an extent its use may be somewhat arbitrary. Its frequent use in 2.1-5 tends to help shorten the aesthetic distance between reader and characters, but it is also frequently the case that it introduces a reliable comment in direct speech which, occasionally, may be confirmed by an authorial aside.[36]

It is clear enough here, as elsewhere in Mark, that the different varieties of distance can operate quite independently of one another. Thus, while in 2.1-12 the reader is drawn extremely close to the action aesthetically, his moral distance from the actors depends on the character in question. Obviously he is expected to share Jesus' point of view, and therefore must be opposed to that of the scribes.

Since our discussion has now moved on to the distance between narrator, reader and characters, it will be convenient at this point to reconsider the five possibilities of relationship outlined by Booth and see to what extent they apply to Mark's Gospel.

i) 'The narrator may be more or less distant from the implied author.' In Mark there is no moral or intellectual distance between these two, for they share an identical point of view—namely, that Jesus is the Christ, the Son of God. Everything that happens in the story hinges on this, and

34. Booth, 'Distance', p. 97.

35. J.C. Hawkins (*Horae Synopticae* [Oxford: Clarendon Press, 1909], pp. 143-48) lists 151 occurrences.

36. Thus, the instances of λέγει ('he says') in 2.10, 17; 3.4, 33-34; 4.13; 5.36; 7.18; 8.12, 17, 33; 9.35; 10.11, 23-24, 27, 42; 11.22; 14.27, 30, all precede reliable logia or comments by Jesus. The use of the historic present in this manner also extends to the reliable comments of others (cf. 7.28; 8.29; 14.61; 16.6).

nothing that the narrator says deviates from it. He, like the protagonist Jesus, provides totally reliable information. This is in sharp contrast to a large body of modern narrative which depends for its effect on the unreliability of the narrator as opposed to the reliable point of view of the implied author.

ii) 'The narrator may...be more or less distant from the characters...' This is certainly true of Mark. The narrator here betrays the differing degrees of distance between himself and the various characters in the way he describes them. Thus, in a telling third-person comment, we are told that Jesus taught with authority, not as the scribes (1.22). And the narrator fully believes what he says; for he never once passes critical judgment upon what Jesus says or does. His treatment of the opponents, on the other hand, is totally different. In language which is often clearly redactional, we are told that they watch Jesus 'so that they might accuse him' (3.2), 'question in their hearts' (2.6), 'argue with him, seeking...to test him' (8.11; cf. 10.2), try to 'entrap him in his talk' (12.13), and seek to arrest and destroy him (3.6; 11.18; 12.12; 14.1-2). The description of the people's reaction is also revealing: they may not truly understand Jesus, but at least they are open to his words and works. They are overawed by them (1.22, 27; 2.12; 5.20; 7.37; 9.15), they come from miles around to hear Jesus (1.45; 3.7-8), they follow him everywhere (6.33, 55), and they hear him gladly (12.37b). The people (ὄχλος) and the Jewish leaders are played off against each other in the way that the story is told. Thus, in 1.45, news of Jesus spreads, and he becomes so popular that he cannot so much as enter a town. Then he meets the opponents and, in the midst of hostility, Jesus is alone with all but the inner circle of disciples (2.1–3.6). But as soon as he retreats to the Sea of Galilee the multitudes crowd in on him again (3.7-12). Again, we learn that the opponents would like to destroy Jesus, but are prevented from doing so by his popularity with the crowds (11.18; 12.12; 14.2; cf. 11.32). The disciples, too, as we shall see, are not painted in a totally negative light. Thus, by sensitive story-telling, the narrator isolates the opponents, polarizing their point of view, and commending all other characters— even a scribe (12.34)—whenever they accept the point of view espoused by Jesus.

iii) 'The narrator may be more or less distant from the reader's own norms.' In Mark's case, we know that narrator and reader are very close. There is no unreliable commentary which might conceivably throw or confuse the reader; on the contrary, the narrator frequently intervenes with comments calculated to clarify or increase the reader's understanding. Mark 2.10a, for instance, is a narratorial aside which aims to prove to the reader, in the light of 2.1-9, that Jesus really does have the authority which the narrator, in 1.22, has already claimed for him. Similarly, the narrator is keen to emphasize the necessity for Jesus' Passion by adding, after the first Passion prediction, 'And he said this plainly' (8.32a). The imperatival 'let the reader understand' (13.14) sums up this relationship: the narrator wants the reader to share his point of view, and seeks to achieve that end, in part, by maintaining a direct line of communication with him.

iv) 'The implied author may be more or less distant from the reader.' The proximity of the implied author to the reader in the case of Mark's Gospel can be established deductively. It has been shown already that the narrator and the implied author share the same point of view throughout, and that the narrator also shares the reader's norms. This being so, it is evident that the implied author's point of view is identical with that of the reader. Indeed, it should be said that the reader in view here is the *implied* reader, an authorial device over which he has complete control. In the present case, the reader shares the norms of the implied author because the latter has chosen him to do so. This compliance with the authorial point of view represents the ideal which the implied author has determined to produce. Thus, in the words of W.J. Ong's perceptive essay, 'The Writer's Audience Is Always a Fiction'.[37]

v) 'The implied author...may be more or less distant from other characters.' Ultimately, it is the implied author who controls distance in a narrative. The narrator may exercise a certain influence over the reader and the characters, but it is the implied author who dictates what kind of narrator he or she shall be: dramatized or undramatized, first-person or third-person, omniscient or limited, intrusive or unobtrusive, reliable or unreliable (fallible). It is the implied author, too, who creates the characters, decides which shall be good and which bad, which central and which peripheral, and how each shall relate to the others. And, as we have seen, it is the implied author who fashions the implied reader, thereby manipulating him or her to make the desired response. If the omniscient narrator is an Olympian god, it is the implied author who plays Father Zeus.

37. W.J. Ong, 'The Writer's Audience is Always a Fiction', *PMLA* 90 (1975), pp. 9-21.

But before we can proceed to examine the means by which the implied author exercises his authority over the narrative world of Mark, we have to face a difficulty: authorial freedom is all very well in a work of fiction, but Mark's Gospel is not such a work, even though it may embody some creative elements. The consensus is that it was fashioned from the oral tradition of the early church, and that the final editor or redactor was responsible for arranging the disparate pericopae into a continuous story based, perhaps, on a kerygmatic outline. This would mean that the redactor did not actually write the independent stories, but merely adapted them for his own purposes. It would also indicate that his creativity was limited both by the traditions at his disposal, and by the early church's reverence for them (that is, he was not permitted to change them wholesale). In short, it might be questioned whether the implied author of Mark's Gospel could have had the kind of creative freedom enjoyed by the implied author in a work of fiction. Various responses have been made to this objection:

1. Culpepper urges that we should guard against confusing actual with implied authors.[38] If Mark used certain written complexes in the composition of his Gospel, as some scholars believe he did,[39] it follows that a multiplicity of real authors has been at work in the making of Mark; but this does not eliminate the presence of the implied author in the final form of the work, nor does it have any bearing upon his point of view beyond the fact that these earlier hands supplied the final author with the materials through which to express it.

2. On the basis of evidence advanced by Scholes and Kellogg,[40] it may be argued that, far from eroding the author's freedom and authority, the availability of existing traditions actually enhanced it. An author's authority in the ancient world rested, usually, on one of three sources: the eyewitness account (written from a markedly detached point of view); historical evidence, yielding accurate results (in the case of historical writing); and established tradition. Mark's authority is certainly founded, to some

38. Culpepper, *Anatomy of the Fourth Gospel*, pp. 15-16.
39. So, *inter alia* A.T. Cadoux, *The Sources of the Second Gospel* (London: James Clarke, 1935); Knox, *Mark*; Kuhn, *Ältere Sammlungen*; Pesch, *Markusevangelium*, I, pp. 63-68.
40. Scholes and Kellogg, *Nature of Narrative*, pp. 242-48.

extent, upon community tradition but, unlike Luke (cf. Lk. 1.1-4), he does not labour the fact; rather, he stresses the authority of his protagonist, so that the justification for the evangelist's authorial venture emanates from the story itself. Unlike other ancient authors, Mark has no need to commend his work to his audience: it commends itself. Thus, the implied author is accorded his narratival freedom from within, in the very act of creating his story.

3.   Petersen's response to the problem of whether Mark can be regarded as a coherent narrative or simply a collection of stories, each with an independent narrator, is to demonstrate the consistency of points of view throughout the Gospel.[41] If the stories were but pearls on a string, each pericope would embody its own points of view, irrespective of whether or not they conflicted with those of other stories in the collection. But, using Uspensky's model, Petersen shows that the points of view in Mark are consistent throughout the narrative. In case we are left in any doubt about this conclusion, there is the corroborating evidence, supplied many years ago by C.H. Dodd,[42] of a Markan framework, a basic sequential outline borrowed from the early kerygma. While the theory as it stands has come in for criticism,[43] it does serve to indicate that the seams and summary passages, where so much of Mark's redactional language is to be found, can be read in sequence as a narrative, no matter how rudimentary.

So, then, given that Mark's Gospel may be read as a coherent narrative irrespective of its underlying sources, by what means does the implied author exercise his control over it? First of all, he uses his omniscience. Of course, we have spoken of the omniscience of the intrusive narrator, but in the case of Mark the narrator is a device serving the implied author's purposes: his point of view is identical with that of the implied author. In regard to point of view and distance, this omniscience

---

41. Petersen, '"Point of View"', pp. 102-105.

42. C.H. Dodd, 'The Framework of the Gospel Narrative', *ExpTim* 43 (1930–31), pp. 396-400.

43. D.E. Nineham, 'The Order of Events in St Mark's Gospel—An Examination of Dr Dodd's Hypothesis', in D.E. Nineham (ed.), *Studies in the Gospels: Essays in Memory of R.H. Lightfoot* (Oxford: Basil Blackwell, 1955), pp. 223-39.

is put to effective use not only in the third-person narration, but also in asides, inside views and direct speech, as a means of evaluating right and wrong points of view.

1.   Although it is not always easy to establish when the author is making a comment to his readers, the more obvious 'asides'[44] tend to serve the purpose of evaluating the various points of view of the characters. We have already referred to 2.10a, 28, both of which suggest to the reader that Jesus has real authority to take the action or say the things he does. Similarly, the comment, 'And he said this plainly' (8.32a), underlines the necessity (δεῖ, 8.31) of Jesus' Passion, and shows that the implied author shares Jesus' point of view.

On the other hand, authorial asides sometimes demonstrate a disapproval of the opponents' point of view. In 3.30, immediately after Jesus' pronouncement on the eternal sin (3.28-29), Mark adds, '—for they had said, "He has an unclean spirit"', thereby explaining the reason for Jesus' damning remark. Given that the implied author shares the correct point of view, espoused by Jesus, it is clear that the opponents' point of view, reflected in the aside of 3.30, is deemed to be wrong. Again, in 11.32, the comment that the opponents were afraid of the people draws out the fact that while Jesus and the people shared a common view, namely that John the Baptist was a (true) prophet, the Jewish leaders held the erroneous view that he was not (11.31). And the aside in 7.19c, 'Thus he declared all foods clean', serves to contrast the correct view with the incorrect one of the opponents who clearly did *not* regard all foods as clean (7.1-5).[45]

2.   Mark's Gospel is replete with inside views.[46] While these tend to be provided by the omniscient intrusive narrator, we must remember that the implied author is in overall control, and in this case has chosen to create the narrator's point of view in the image of his own. Like the asides, the inside views often

44. Fowler, *Loaves and Fishes,* pp. 160-620.

45. Other 'asides' take the form of explanatory comments in regard to foreign customs (7.2, 3-4; 9.43; 12.18, 42; 14.12; 15.16, 42) and translations of Aramaic expressions (3.17; 5.41; 7.11, 34; 10.46; 14.36; 15.22, 34).

46. See the list compiled by Fowler, *Loaves and Fishes,* p. 166.

help to regulate the distance between the implied author and his implied readers on the one hand, and the two essential points of view, as expressed through the characters, on the other. Thus it is that by means of this device we first learn that Jesus has true authority, unlike the scribes who merely claim to possess it (1.22). We are told of Jesus' emotions which, as we have seen, are always an appropriate response to the situation in question. Similarly, the expression of fear (in the sense of awe), wonder and amazement, or astonishment, by those who witness his marvellous works and teaching (1.22, 27; 2.12; 4.41; 5.15, 20, 33, 42; 6.2, 49, 52; 7.37; 9.6, 15, 32; 10.24, 26, 32; 12.17; 15.5, 44; 16.8) is perfectly proper to the occasion.

By contrast, inside views are also used by the implied author to distance his readers from the erroneous points of view evident in the opponents and, sometimes, the disciples. We discover that the scribes secretly accuse Jesus of blasphemy (2.6-7), and the success of the healing of the paralytic, as well as the rhetoric of Jesus' perceptive reaction, convinces us that this is an erroneous view. Then the leaders want to 'accuse' (κατηγορέω) him of healing on the Sabbath (3.2), and Jesus is 'aggrieved at their hardness of heart' (συνλυπούμενος ἐπὶ τῇ πωρώσει τῆς καρδίας αὐτῶν, 3.5). Later, they maliciously seek to 'test' (πειράζω) him (8.11; 10.2) or catch him out (ἀγρεύω, 12.13), and their attempts to bring Jesus down are thwarted by their fear of the people (11.18, 32a; 12.12; 14.1) with whom Jesus remains popular.

Once again, it is frequently the inside view which highlights the misunderstanding of the disciples, Jesus must upbraid them for their lack of faith (4.40); in the midst of the lake 'their hearts were hardened' (which brackets them with the opponents in 3.5), 'for they did not understand about the loaves' (6.52). Mark 8.16-21 is an extended inside view which develops the same theme: the barrage of rhetorical questions there betrays Jesus' exasperation over their failure to perceive the correct point of view. Again, it is only our inside knowledge of the disciples' secret discussion on greatness that makes possible Jesus' important corrective response (9.33-37).

3.   Finally, the implied author uses direct speech as an effective device for controlling the reader's distance from the various

points of view. At certain points, notably chapters 4 and 13, he maximizes the dramatic effect of such speech by allowing the protagonist a virtually unimpeded freedom to speak, while the narrator and implied author recede into the background. Here, the *logia Jesu* are intended to exert a direct impact upon the reader. The reader already knows that whatever Jesus says is bound to be reliable; all he or she must do is to give ear to what is expressed.

There is an immediacy and directness about direct speech which is not possible through third-person narration, and the author occasionally takes advantage of it to speak thus to his readers. The second-person plural pronoun (ὑμᾶς) in 9.41 ('...whoever gives *you* to drink...'), for instance, is no doubt deliberately ambiguous, addressing both the characters in the story-world, and the post-resurrection community. A yet more distinguished example of this device is the apocalyptic discourse (13.5-37), throughout which the series of second-person plurals (13.5, 7, 9, 11, 13, 14, 21, 23, 28, 29, 30, 33, 35, 37) is addressed not only to the four disciples on the Mount of Olives, but to the Markan community as well. Indeed, the narrator's one and only interposition ('let the reader understand', 13.14b) is designed to stress this very point, and the final verse ('And what I say to you, I say to all', 13.37) confirms it.[47] The effect of this is to create the illusion in the implied reader that the word of the implied author is really coming to him or her direct from the protagonist. The Jesus of the story-world is directly addressing the reader's present (although the reader, too, is drawn into the story); it is forgotten that he is actually a reflector of the implied author's point of view.

Direct speech comes into its own in the controversy stories (2.1–3.6; 3.22-30; 7.1-23; 8.11-12; 10.2-9; 11.27-33; 12.13-40) and the section on discipleship (8.27–10.52), where contrasts between the negative views of the opponents/disciples and the positive views of Jesus are far more graphically drawn than would have been the case had the dialogue been simply reported in the third person.

47. This technique of extending a message aimed first at a limited group to 'all' (πᾶς) is repeated in Mk 7.14: 'Hear me, all of you, and understand'.

Quite apart from the various techniques which the author uses in the actual text, it should be recognized that he is also a redactor who is at liberty to select his material. The reader is allowed to know only as much as the author chooses to reveal. We know, of course, that in Mark's case the author takes the reader into his confidence, and the latter feels privileged to share in his omniscience, thereby enjoying a considerable advantage over most of the characters who know much less. But, to some extent, this sense of security is false: the reader is manipulated by the implied author into knowing only what he wants him to understand. Jesus is seen to be a reliable character only because the author selects his material accordingly. The Jesus of the story-world never dithers, is never mistaken,[48] always does the right thing, no matter what the circumstances: but that is the only kind of Jesus the author wishes to present to his readers.

The same is true of the opponents. The picture painted of them is almost wholly negative, which would never have been the case in real life. The early rabbinic writings, indeed, present a totally different point of view. But the author allows his readers to see only what he wants them to see. He distances them from the opponents by means of his negative presentation, thereby aligning them, by contrast, with the correct point of view represented by Jesus.

b. *Perspective*

We have considered in some detail the manner in which Mark presents various points of view and handles distance. It is hoped that we can now deal with the remainder of Genette's categories more summarily.

Perspective concerns the vantage point from which a story is told. An omniscient narrator may decide to *tell* the narrative, making comments *about* the characters, or may choose to 'focalize' it through one (or more) of them. In this latter case, the story is told through the eyes of a specific character or group. Such focalization can be internal (when the narrator allows open access to inside views) or external (when the narrator does not).[49]

---

48. Studies on the humanity of Jesus have sometimes alleged that he was mistaken—mistaken in believing that the consummation of the Kingdom was imminent, for instance. But this really has no effect on Jesus as a literary character. It matters not for the Markan story-world whether or not the historical flesh-and-blood Jesus was omniscient.

49. Genette, *Narrative Discourse*, pp. 185-94.

Dewey has applied Genette's category to the Markan text and demonstrated that most of it is non-focalized—that is to say, 'presented directly by an omniscient and omnipresent narrator'.[50] Nevertheless, a small body of focalized narrative is evident. Occasionally, we see events through the eyes of Jesus—his baptism (1.9-11), his call of the first disciples (1.16-20; 2.14), or his observation of the poor widow at the Temple treasury (12.41-44), for instance. Here, the focalization tends to be external: there are no insights into what Jesus is thinking or feeling; the reader is simply invited to see what Jesus sees from his perspective; it is as if the reader is emerging from the Jordan with Jesus, or walking along the beach with him and encountering the first disciples just as he does.

Other events are internally focalized. In Gethsemane (14.33-42), for instance, everything is seen from Jesus' perspective; the reader moves to and fro with him as he shuttles between the three disciples and his prayer-spot; but this time the reader learns of Jesus' mental state (14.33), and is able to listen to his prayer (14.36), even though none of the other characters are close by. So, too, with the disciples at the transfiguration (9.2-8). On this occasion they are the focalizers: everything happens through their eyes. But again, the reader is allowed access to their inner feelings: '…they were exceedingly afraid' (9.6).

A regular, though not indispensable feature of these focalized narratives is the use of verbs of seeing. Jesus 'saw' (εἶδεν) Simon and Andrew (1.16), James and John (1.19), and Levi (2.14); he 'saw' the heavens opened at his baptism (1.10); he 'watched' (ἐθεώρει) people placing money in the Temple treasury (12.41); so, too, there 'appeared' (ὤφθη) to the disciples (αὐτοῖς) Elijah and Moses (9.4), and afterwards, when they 'looked round' (περιβλεψάμενοι), they 'saw' (εἶδον) no-one but Jesus.

It is perhaps not without significance that a fair proportion of focalization is given over to events of particular moment—Jesus' baptism (1.9-11), the call of the first disciples (1.16-20), the transfiguration (9.2-8), the agony in Gethsemane (14.33-42) and, not least, the empty tomb episode (16.1-8) which is seen through the eyes of the women.

---

50. J. Dewey, 'Point of View and the Disciples in Mark', *SBL Seminar Papers* (1982), pp. 97-106 (101-102).

c. *Person*

Genette's first sub-category under 'voice' is 'person'. This simply refers to the matter of who is speaking. There is hardly need for comment here except to reaffirm that the Markan narrative is presented by an omniscient third-person intrusive narrator—one who never assumes the guise of a character within his own tale, but remains outside it, looking down from his Olympian throne, though not, like the gods of old, in an impassive, detached manner. As we are about to discover, however, small sections of the narrative are taken up by characters in the story-world—notably Jesus—and presented by them.

d. *Narrative Level*

Extended narratives are rarely presented at the same level throughout. A third-person narrator may deliver the bulk of the story, but parts of it may be mediated through others. Thus, while an omniscient narrator (controlled by the implied author) may relate the account at the first level, a character in the first-level narrative may tell a second-level story and, in more complex cases, a second-level narrator may tell a third-level story. Theoretically this could go on *ad infinitum*, but in practice it is, of course, limited by the work's finite length.

Corresponding to narrator level is audience level. A third-person narrator at the first level speaks to a first-level audience—that implied by the implied author; but a second-level narrator speaks to a second-level audience, one which lies in the story-world.

How does this apply to Mark's Gospel? Most of the narrative, as we have seen, is presented by a third-person first-level narrator whose first-level audience is the implied reader. It should be noted here that the situation in Mark diverges somewhat from that in the typical novel in that the evangelist begins with a known factor—his community. In producing his Gospel he is influenced by the needs of flesh-and-blood Christians, so the nature of the correspondence between implied author and implied reader tends to be dictated by the relationship between the real author and his known addressees. Modern novelists, on the other hand, often write with only the vaguest idea of their audience. They may have in mind a specific market, but they cannot know their readers as intimately as Mark probably knew his. Thus, the novelist is freer than Mark was to create an ideal audience—one which is calculated to respond to the narrative in exactly the manner intended by the implied author.

A few significant passages in Mark operate at the second level of discourse. In 3.23-29; 4.3-9, 11-32; 7.6-23; 8.34–9.1; 9.39-50; 12.1-11; 13.5-37, for instance, Jesus is the second-level narrator, and the audience is the one specified—'them'—presumably the crowd (3.23); 'a very large crowd' (4.1); 'those who were about him with the twelve' (4.10); 'the Pharisees and the scribes' (7.5); 'the people' (7.14); 'the disciples' (7.17); 'the crowd with his disciples' (8.34); John (and the other disciples?) (9.38); 'them' (chief priests–scribes–elders—cf. 11.27) (12.1); Peter, James, John and Andrew (13.3). In these cases, the implied reader is not being addressed directly, but is 'listening in', as it were, on the second-level discourse. Yet the omniscient narrator is free to use the second-person narratee to draw the reader into direct relationship with the second-level narrator, as in Mark 4 and 13, for instance. This device is particularly effective for commending the 'correct' ideology (that is, the things of God), for we know that in Mark the points of view of the implied author, the omniscient narrator and the protagonist (the one and only second-level narrator in the Gospel) are identical.

The fact that second-level narration in Mark is deemed to be reliable is confirmed by the fact that the implied reader is twice called to understand it—first with regard to Jesus' teaching on purity (7.14), then the 'abomination of desolation' (13.14). Similarly, when the second-level narrator calls the disciples to be vigilant in respect of the eschaton (13.37), he is extending his exhortation to 'all' (πᾶσιν).[51]

e. *Time of Narrating*
We have already discussed in some detail the question of narrative time. Suffice it now to draw attention, as Genette does,[52] to the important distinction between the time of the story-world, and the time at which the story is told. For Mark, this means the distinction between the period of Jesus' earthly activity, ending with his crucifixion in about AD 29, and the time of the Gospel's composition, possibly around AD 69. The intervening period of some forty years creates certain complexities. At the first level of narration, most of the events are told in retrospect because the author stands posterior to the earthly life of Jesus; but those of the apocalyptic discourse remain in the future: the story is told from a

51. Dewey ('Point of View', pp. 97-106) uses Genette's methodology to demonstrate that the implied reader of Mark would identify with both Jesus (sharing his values) and the disciples (sharing their situation).

52. Genette, *Narrative Discourse*, pp. 215-22.

post-resurrection, pre-apocalyptic perspective. For the second-level narrator and narratees, however, some of the events which the omniscient author describes as past still lie in the future: the Passion predictions are a prime example. Moreover, at this second level the narration is occasionally simultaneous with the events in question. Jesus' dispute with the scribes and Pharisees in 7.6-23 is told as it unfolds, as is the teaching in 9.39-50. This tactic draws the implied reader into the immediacy of the situation. The third-person omniscient narrator, from his post-resurrection vantage point, is unable to achieve this in the same manner, but his use of the historic present has a similar effect, lifting the reader out of his own time into the time frame of the story-world.

3. *Summary*

In this chapter we have examined two models for understanding point of view—those devised by Uspensky and Genette. Uspensky classifies point of view according to four levels—ideological, phraseological, spatio-temporal and psychological. The first of these is concerned with the moral or evaluative judgments made by the implied author, the narrator or the various characters. These judgments can, and often do conflict, but in Mark's Gospel the position is simple: implied author/narrator and protagonist all share the same point of view. The belief that Jesus is Son of God is confirmed by what Jesus himself says and does.

The phraseological point of view denotes the manner in which point of view can be conveyed by language, while the ideological point of view may be expressed in terms of the characteristic language used by the implied author, narrator or characters. The problem for the Gospel narrative, of course, is that it is very difficult to ascertain exactly who is saying what. Words are placed on the lips of Jesus which may not be his at all, but those of the author, or the Christian community. But perhaps in the last analysis this really does not matter since, at the literary level, the characters frequently provide the mouthpiece for the implied author.

The spatio-temporal plane is concerned with the way in which time and space affect the point of view of the various participants in the narrative. The point of view of the story characters, for instance, is necessarily determined by the parameters of the story itself, whereas the implied author or the omniscient narrator are able to view events in a more holistic manner. Thus, the Markan narrator can move effortlessly through the time and space of the narrative, as has been shown by the examples presented during the course of the chapter.

The last of Uspensky's levels is the psychological, which allows the reader some insight into the thoughts and emotions of the characters. Just as in some Shakespearean soliloquy the audience is made privy to the true thoughts of a character as opposed to the viewpoint he expresses in open dialogue, so in Mark's Gospel the reader is admitted into the hearts and minds of characters like the scribes (2.6-7) and the disciples (6.49-52; 9.6, 32), as well as the thoughts of Jesus himself (1.41; 2.8; 3.5; 5.30; 6.6, 34; 8.2, 12, 17).

Genette's model is based on a classification of point of view into two categories—mood and voice, of which the first is subdivided into distance and perspective, and the second into person, narrative level and time of narrating. Distance is the technique whereby one 'person' in a narrative (implied author, implied reader, narrator, characters) is more or less polarized from the others. A key factor in controlling distance is the telling–showing axis. If a narrator tells a story and obtrudes in it, he or she is more likely to create a distance between reader and characters than if the material is presented dramatically. Skilfully handled, this technique can be used to enable the reader to identify with the particular point of view the author wants. Mark both tells (as in most of the prologue, 1.1-13) and shows (as in chapters 4 and 13).

Perspective concerns the vantage point from which a story is told. A narrative can be related by an omniscient narrator, or focalized through one of the characters. Most of Mark's Gospel is narrated from the perspective of the narrator himself, but a few passages are focalized through the eyes of Jesus (1.9-11; 12.41-44) or the disciples (9.2-8).

'Person' simply relates to the question of who is speaking. In Mark's Gospel it is generally the third-person intrusive narrator who tells the tale from an omniscient vantage point outside the narrative, but there are a few passages which are given over to one of the story-world characters (namely Jesus) and presented by him. This leads on to the question of narrative levels. A third-person narrator may tell the story at the surface or first level, but character–narrators within the story itself will operate at a second level, as Jesus does in Mk 4.3-9, 11-20; 12.1-11.

The final category suggested by Genette is 'time of narrating', which draws attention to the distinction between the time of the story-world and the time at which the story is narrated, which, in Mark's case, includes a gap of some forty years. At the first level of narration in Mark, all the events except the Parousia are told in retrospect; but for the second-level narrator and narratees, far more of the story-world events lie in the future. Thus it is that Jesus, the story-world prophet, is prevailed over by Mark's omniscient narrator.

Chapter 6

IRONY IN MARK'S GOSPEL

Since the pioneering studies of H. Clavier, E.M. Good and J. Jónsson,[1] there has been a burgeoning interest in irony as applied to the Bible. During the course of its long history, however, the nature of irony has changed considerably, so that what was meant by that term in Classical times is very different from its meaning today. For one thing, the classification of irony has grown over the past couple of centuries, so naturally, many kinds of modern irony were unknown in the Classical period. Yet it is often precisely the current understanding of irony of which the literary critics make use when they apply themselves to the biblical text.[2] We need to tread carefully here. Modern insights can be extremely useful in that they tend to urge upon us a well-considered, systematic treatment of the text; we are deterred from approaching the topic in an over-generalized or haphazard fashion. On the other hand, these contemporary insights, valuable though they may be, must not be allowed to violate the ancient understanding of irony if they are to be of any real use in studying New Testament irony.

It will be my purpose in the present chapter to acknowledge the development of irony in ancient and modern times, and to establish a suitable definition and classification of the term to enable adequate discussion of the use of irony in Mark's Gospel. I shall then consider the Markan text in order to determine how and to what extent irony is used to enhance its message.

---

1. H. Clavier, 'La méthode ironique dans l'enseignement de Jésus', *ETR* 4 (1929), pp. 224-41, 323-44; *idem*, 'L'ironie dans l'enseignement de Jésus', *NovT* 1 (1956), pp. 3-20; E.M. Good, *Irony in the Old Testament* (London: SPCK, 1965); J. Jónsson, *Humour and Irony in the New Testament* (Leiden: Brill, 1985).

2. Among the works most frequently referred to are D.C. Muecke, *The Compass of Irony* (London: Methuen, 1969) and W.C. Booth, *A Rhetoric of Irony* (Chicago: University of Chicago Press, 1974).

1. *Irony in the Classical Period*

No-one can be sure how irony originated. Presumably the ironic situation was possible from the dawn of humanity. What is clear is that ironic possibilities were being exploited by playwrights and historians alike long before the word 'irony' (εἰρωνεία) came to serve as a rhetorical figure.[3] In the comic drama of Aristophanes, for instance, the ironic character (εἴρων) is set against the boaster (ἀλαζών) who endeavoured to vaunt his qualities.[4] The whole point of this kind of drama was to develop a contest between the εἴρων who deliberately tried to underplay his qualities or pretend he was other than he really was, and the boastful ἀλαζών, and the enjoyment of the audience lay in the downfall of the latter; the ἀλαζών was exposed for what he really was, leaving the εἴρων to triumph. Tragic irony, on the other hand, involves the truly great person's demise by means of his or her own *hubris*, which is the tragic counterpart of comic εἰρωνεία.

I must pass over the long and colourful history of irony in Greek literature in the centuries prior to the composition of Mark's Gospel. This development has, in any case, been traced in some detail by others, and I have cited the most relevant works in this regard. The essential point to note is that, in time, the ironist (εἴρων) and the boaster (ἀλαζών) came to be seen as two sides of the same coin. Thus, Aristotle is able to assert,

> Sometimes...mock humility [εἰρωνεία] seems to be really boastfulness [ἀλαζονεία], like the dress of the Spartans.[5]

---

3.   The two definitive studies of irony in its classical context are J.A.K. Thomson, *Irony: An Historical Introduction* (London: Allen & Unwin, 1926); G.G. Sedgewick, *Of Irony, Especially in Drama* (Toronto: University of Toronto Press, 1935). See also L. Bergson, 'Eiron und Eironeia', *Hermes* 99 (1971), pp. 409-22; Z. Pavlovskis, 'Aristotle, Horace and the Ironic Man', *Classical Philology* 63 (1968), pp. 22-41; G. Markantonatos, 'On the Origin and Meanings of the Word Εἰρωνεία', *Rivista di filologia e di istruzione classica* 103 (1975), pp. 16-21; O. Ribbeck, 'Über den Begriff des εἴρων', *Rheinische Museum* 31 (1876), pp. 381-400. W. Büchner, 'Über den Begriff der Eirōneia', *Hermes* 76 (1941), pp. 339-58.

4.   This is seen very clearly in Aristophanes, *The Clouds*, 1.449, where the term εἴρων is used to describe the ironic character, and is set in sharp distinction to the ἀλαζών. The ironic point can hardly be missed, either, that in this play the supreme ironist, Socrates, is presented as the ἀλαζών.

5.   Aristotle, *Nichomachean Ethics*, 4.7.14, 16. The dress of the Spartans, though

This tendency to identify the two extremes was carried right down to the time of Mark, as can be seen from a comment made by the rhetorician Philodemus (first century BC):

> The ironic man is, for the most part, a kind of pretender.[6]

The customary suspicion of, or distaste for irony also persisted, to some extent,[7] but by the first century BC a more positive appraisal was beginning to take hold, especially among the rhetoricians for whom it had become a figure of speech. It is true that Cicero could still regard it as a kind of game or pastime more than a useful literary device,[8] but now irony was being conceived more seriously too. During the following century Quintilian established it as a genuinely rhetorical figure, recognizing not only various kinds of irony, but different methods of communicating it:

> ...that class of allegory in which the meaning is contrary to that suggested by the words, involves an element of irony, or, as our rhetoricians call it, *illusio*. This is made evident to the understanding either by the delivery, the character of the speaker or the nature of the subject. For if any one of these three is out of keeping with the words, it at once becomes clear that the intention of the speaker is other than what he actually says... I have found some who speak of irony as dissimilation but, in view of the fact that this latter name does not cover the whole range of this figure, I shall follow my general rule and rest content with the Greek term.[9]

The fact that, at this stage of its development, irony could be classified into several different types is evident from a perusal of the Greek rhetoricians represented in Spengel. Among the words used are: στεῖσμος (a form of joke); μυκτερίσμος (sneer); σαρκάσμος (sarcasm); χλευασμός (derision); διασυρμός (disparagement); ἐπικερτόμησις (mockery); κατάγελως (raillery); εἰκασμός (guess); χαριεντισμός (wittiness); and ἀντιμετάθεσις (a kind of irony).[10]

---

simple, was regarded by Aristotle as a mark of affectation.

6. From Philodemus, *Peri kakiōn*, cited in Pavlovskis, 'Aristotle', p. 26.

7. Aristotle, *Rhet.* 2.2.5; Theophrastus, *Characters*, 1.3-5. There is what appears to be a post-Theophrastian accretion to this chapter which states, in starkly *non-ironical* terms, the attitude one should take to the ironist: 'Such be the speeches, tricks and retractions to which dissemblers resort. These disingenuous and designing characters are to be shunned like serpents' (1.7).

8. Cicero, *On Oratory*, 2.269-70.

9. Quintilian, *Inst.Or.* 8.6.54; 9.2.44.

10. L. Spengel (ed.), *Rhetores Graeci* (3 vols.; Leipzig: Teuberni, 1853), 3.235.

Our brief survey of irony in Classical literature leads to the conclusion that what began as a rather sordid, underhand device for ridiculing or taking advantage of people had, by the first century AD, gained a measure of respectability as a rhetorical figure which, used under the right circumstances, could drive home a point with considerable force. And Mark, as we shall see, certainly uses it to stunning effect. First, though, we need to see how irony has developed more recently.

2. *Irony in more Recent Times*

a. *Classifications*

With the burgeoning of European literature in the past few centuries, irony has inevitably become a far more complex affair than was the case in Classical times. As a result, the problem of classification has become notoriously difficult. There cannot, indeed, be any single, broad classification, but only a number of more specific classifications at various levels. At one level we must distinguish between spoken (or verbal) and situational irony; at another level between overt and covert irony; and at yet another between general and specific irony. Then there is the vexed question of who the ironist is, and his or her mode of operation. And who is the victim? How much of the irony is the audience or reader permitted to see? Might the audience/reader perceive an irony which even the ironist did not intend? All these are intriguing questions which naturally cannot be properly addressed here. Nevertheless, in order to define what I mean when speaking of irony in Mark, it will be necessary to say something, however brief or inadequate, about classification.

One of the few books to have been devoted wholly to a consideration of classification of irony is that by D.C. Muecke.[11] According to this author, all irony must be double-layered ('saying one thing, but meaning another'), must involve some kind of opposition between the two levels of meaning (a contrast between reality and appearance), and must contain some element of unawareness (there is normally an ironic victim).[12] Muecke elsewhere stresses that all irony must take account of four factors: (i) the field of observation in which the irony is noticed; (ii) the degree of conflict between appearance and reality; (iii) the identity of

11. Muecke, *Compass*; *idem, Irony and the Ironic* (The Critical Idiom, 13; London: Methuen, 1970).
12. Muecke, *Compass*, pp. 19-20.

the players—victim, audience and author; (iv) the emotional impact which the irony creates.

Hard on the heels of Muecke came W.C. Booth whose work takes account of, but significantly modifies that of the former.[13] Taken together, these authors allow us to establish a number of important antitheses or distinctions:

i) *General/specific irony*. Specific irony involves, in Muecke's words, 'single victims or victimizations, single exposures of aberrancy in a world otherwise moving on the right track', while general irony is 'life itself or any general aspect of life seen as fundamentally and inescapably an ironic state of affairs... We are all victims'.[14]

ii) *Verbal/situational irony*. Students of irony are not in total agreement on how these should be defined, but Muecke's pronouncement probably represents the consensus:

> Verbal irony implies an ironist, someone consciously and intentionally employing a technique. Situational irony does not imply an ironist but merely a 'condition of affairs' or 'outcome of events' which...is seen and felt to be ironic.[15]

Verbal irony, then, is a term usually applied to spoken irony, where an ironist in full view is spelling out the irony of a particular occurrence, and it can take many different forms: praise in order to blame; blame in order to praise; pretended agreement with a victim; pretended error or doubt, and so on.

Situational irony, too, can come in many guises—dramatic irony, irony of events, irony of self-betrayal and irony of characterization. We shall return briefly to some of these types later on.[16]

iii) *Stable/unstable irony*. Stable irony, according to the definition advanced by Wayne Booth,[17] is that on which author and reader are agreed, while unstable irony suggests that there is no fixed meaning, and

13. Booth, *Rhetoric of Irony*.

14. Muecke, *Compass*, pp. 119-20.

15. Muecke, *Compass*, p. 42.

16. It should be noted that the distinction between verbal and situational irony is seldom absolute; the two frequently operate together, and verbal irony is often more than *purely* verbal.

17. Booth, *Rhetoric of Irony*, pp. 5-6.

that different readers may offer conflicting interpretations of a passage. Occasionally, the author will lead the reader on to what appears to be a stable platform, only to snatch away the planks and send him or her plunging into further, deeper ironies.

Irony which is genuinely stable demands from the reader, (i) a judgment that the surface meaning of a passage is not the intended meaning, and (ii) a decision about the author's knowledge, beliefs and values which enables the reader to arrive at a new understanding of the passage. The latter requirement may be fulfilled not only by means of a close examination of the body of a work, but also by reference to its title or—if there is one—its epigraph or prologue.

Stable/unstable irony can fall into a number of sub-categories:

1. Intended/unintended irony. As we have seen, stable irony, in order to be truly stable, must be intended by the author. In cases where a reader perceives an irony which the author has failed to anticipate, this stability flips over into instability. Sometimes a change in circumstances turns what was intended as a serious statement into an ironic one.

2. Covert/overt irony. Covert irony is that which is hidden behind a façade of reality. The reader is invited to play the ironic game, and not simply told that irony is present. Overt irony, on the other hand, is disclosed by the author (or ironist) him or herself, as if saying, 'Isn't situation X ironic?' While the latter kind makes life easy for the reader, it is covert irony which tends to have the more impact, because it forces the reader into a quest of discovery in which the irony becomes the pot of gold at the end of the rainbow.

3. Local/infinite irony. According to Booth, local irony is that of a specific or punctiliar occurrence, as if, for instance, we were to say, 'Isn't it ironic that the lifeboat crew had to be rescued from the sea?' This type is also known as 'fixed' or 'finite' irony. Infinite irony, on the other hand, deals in general assertions or comments on universals. The adage, 'The bigger they are, the harder they fall', well illustrates this.[18]

At this point it should be noted that views concerning the relationship between local and infinite irony can differ

---

18. Booth, *Rhetoric of Irony*, p. 236.

appreciably. P.D. Duke,[19] for instance, distinguishes between
local irony (which he seems to understand in the same sense as
Booth) and 'extended' irony, which here appears to be substi-
tuted for 'infinite' irony. Again, E.M. Good distinguishes
between local (he calls it 'punctual') irony on the one hand,
and episodic and thematic irony (the latter denoting a collection
of episodes all pointing to a single ironic theme or motif) on the
other.[20] Duke's 'extended' irony appears to be of a different
order from the 'infinite' irony of Booth. Duke's term could
simply refer to a particular ironic situation which is spread over
a full section of text, so that the whole must be considered for
full effect; but Booth's infinite irony refers, as we have seen, to
general or universal ironic assertions which, however, can be—
and usually are—applied to specific or punctiliar situations
which Duke wants to confine to local irony.

Even if the meaning of the terminology remains a little uncertain, it is
clear enough that the different categories outlined above can be used in
concert with one another. Thus, as Booth has shown, a particular irony
might be stable–covert–local, or stable–overt–infinite, or unstable–
covert–infinite, and so on. Booth's explanatory diagram reveals eight
possibilities in all.[21]

b. *The Ironist and the Victim*
If we make good use of both Muecke and Booth, we can say some
important things about the relationship between the ironist and the
victim. As applied to the biblical text, these have been clearly classified
by Duke,[22] and it will be convenient to use his sub-headings here:

i) *Reliability.* In modern fiction, the implied author of a work may be
deliberately presented as unreliable, and this can apply to irony as much
as to anything else. Sometimes it is difficult for the reader to discern
whether or not the author is being ironical at all—and if so, in what
sense. The line between irony and non-irony can be so fine as to be
virtually imperceptible to all but the well-trained eye. Happily, in Classical

    19. P.D. Duke, *Irony in the Fourth Gospel* (Atlanta: John Knox, 1985).
    20. Good, *Irony in the Old Testament*, pp. 81-82.
    21. Booth, *Rhetoric of Irony*, p. 235.
    22. Duke, *Irony in the Fourth Gospel*, pp. 29-42.

literature generally—and certainly in the Gospel narratives—the implied author or narrator is reliable. If he or she wants to be ironic, he or she ensures that the audience is in no doubt about it; there is no danger, as is the case in some modern fiction, of the audience or reader becoming the ironic victim. Classical irony is always stable, and the reader can always be assured of standing shoulder to shoulder with the author on firm ground.

ii) *Voice*. Generally-speaking, the authorial voice tends to be concealed behind the action of the narrative or the speech of the characters. It is not normally good policy for the author to tell the reader where the irony lies, though there are certain techniques for making it evident. According to Muecke, there are four 'modes' of irony:[23]

1. Impersonal irony, when we hear the ironist without really being aware of him or her as a person.
2. Self-disparaging irony, in which the ironist's real opinion is in contradistinction to that of his or her persona. He or she may put him or herself in the guise of an ignorant or credulous person, as Socrates did supremely well, and as Jesus does on the road to Emmaus (Lk. 24.18-19).
3. Ingénu irony, where the ironist withdraws behind another character—perhaps an innocent person who is used as a mouthpiece for conveying an ironic truth. Duke mentions the biblical story of David and Bathsheba (2 Sam. 11), where Uriah serves as the unwitting ironic mouthpiece, as a good example of this kind.
4. Dramatized irony, where the author withdraws entirely, leaving the audience to work out the irony of particular situations. This, '…is no more…than the presentation in drama or fiction of such ironic situations or events as we may find in life'.[24]

iii) *Detachment*. The ironist and the audience need to be removed far enough from the ironic situation and its victims in order to be able to appreciate the whole, but not so far removed that they feel no sympathy with what is taking place. If no affinity with the ironic victim is felt, the irony cannot have its full impact.

23. Muecke, *Compass of Irony*, pp. 61-63.
24. Muecke, *Compass of Irony*, pp. 62-63.

iv) *Clues.* Obviously, an ironic author must present irony in a different manner from an ironist who has visual contact with the audience. He or she cannot literally wink or demonstrate by facial expression or voice inflexion the intended irony. There must instead be textual signals. Booth devotes a long section of his book to this question.[25] Briefly, he classifies the authorial clues to irony as follows:

1. Direct warnings in the author's own voice. There may be an announcement that irony is present or, more likely, some indication in a title or epigraph, or postscript, or in an authorial aside. Booth's caution that these warnings might themselves be ironic in some instances[26] is no doubt relevant to modern literature, but not to the less sophisticated world of ancient texts.

2. Proclamation of known error. A speaker may betray ignorance of what the reader already knows to be true. Although the author can feign any kind of error, Booth cites in particular errors of historical fact and of popular expressions. As a clear example of what is meant, we can do no better than quote Booth on a passage from Mark Twain:

    > 'Animals talk to each other, of course. There can be no question about that; but I suppose there are very few people who can understand them. I never knew but one man who could. I knew he could, however, because he told me so himself.' Mark Twain knew that you would know that he knew that his speaker is talking nonsense here.[27]

3. Conflict of facts within a single work. When facts are presented which are later contradicted by other facts, it is clear that, unless the author has been careless, one set of facts must be intentionally wrong, and may well indicate the presence of irony. This technique, Booth avers, works particularly well in the case of dramatic irony. He notes that soliloquies, like that of Iago in *Othello*, Act 1, Scene 3, often provide stable, reliable information against which the irony of contradictory facts or comments can be gauged.[28]

---

25. Booth, *Rhetoric of Irony*, pp. 53-76.
26. Booth, *Rhetoric of Irony*, p. 55.
27. Booth, *Rhetoric of Irony*, p. 57.
28. Booth, *Rhetoric of Irony*, p. 63.

4.   Clashes of style. 'If a speaker's style departs notably from whatever the reader considers the normal way of saying a thing, or the way normal for this speaker, the reader may suspect irony'.[29] Although we mention this clue for the sake of completeness—it *is* one of those discussed by Booth—it is not likely to be pertinent to ancient literature.

5.   Conflicts of belief. When a speaker makes a statement of belief which is opposed to our own, we are entitled to suspect the presence of irony, particularly if we suspect the author of sharing our view. Booth, in a different context, treats us to a detailed discussion of Swift's *A Modest Proposal* in which the author suggests that many social ills in Ireland could be solved if young children were bred and slaughtered for human consumption;[30] but, of course, this example perfectly illustrates the present point. The reader obviously finds abhorrent the suggestion Swift makes here—but, of course, so does Swift. Very few serious readers have made the mistake of assuming that Swift was in earnest.

v) *Reconstruction.* Finally, the ironic meaning is to be regarded as hovering between two worlds—namely, the old one which the author wants the audience to reject, and the new one which he or she expects it to adopt. The old must be demolished, and from the débris the new must be constructed. Booth contends that this process occurs in four stages:

1.   The reader is bidden to reject the literal meaning of the text.
2.   Alternative explanations are tried. It is possible, of course, that there has been a misunderstanding between author and reader, but it is equally likely that irony is present.
3.   The reader must weigh up the evidence and make a decision. If he or she is satisfied that a particular statement could not have been made in earnest by that author, the chances are that it is ironic.
4.   The choice of a new meaning is made, based upon the reader's conclusions reached in the previous steps.[31]

29. Booth, *Rhetoric of Irony*, p. 67.
30. Booth, *Rhetoric of Irony*, pp. 105-20.
31. Booth, *Rhetoric of Irony*, pp. 33-44.

3. *The Uses of Irony*

Muecke regards irony as having three basic uses.[32] As a verbal device, it may be used by the speaker to underline the author's intended meaning, rather as drabness in a painting may function to accentuate the highlights. It can also operate as a satirical device to attack a particular point of view, or expose ignorance or folly. Finally, as a heuristic device, it may lead the reader to appreciate that things are not as simple as they seem—or, on the contrary, that they are *more* simple than they seem. These functions may operate independently, or in combination.

Duke simplifies the above scheme, preferring to discuss the matter under only two headings: irony as appeal, and irony as weapon.[33] The first of these denotes the positive aspect of irony. The reader shares the author's covert but genuine meaning, and by doing so experiences a sense of achievement, and also a sense of community with others who have perceived the author's meaning.[34] As Booth indicates—during a discussion of Mark 15, appropriately enough—such irony has a far greater impact upon the reader than if the author were simply to make a plain statement of fact instead.[35]

In a more negative sense, irony can be used as a weapon against its victims, although, as Booth again declares, 'Even irony that does imply victims...is often much more clearly directed to more affirmative matters'.[36] This brand of irony, which often takes the form of sarcastic irony or ironic satire, may be made clear to the victim, but more frequently the victim remains blissfully unaware that he or she is the butt of irony at all. Oedipus is a classic example here.

4. *Biblical Irony*

a. *Clavier, Good and Jónsson*
It is not my purpose here to undertake a thorough review of the scholars named above. Nevertheless, since they are the generally-acknowledged pioneers in the study of biblical irony, no work in this field would

---

32. Muecke, *Compass of Irony*, pp. 232-33.
33. Duke, *Irony in the Fourth Gospel*, pp. 36-41.
34. Duke, *Irony in the Fourth Gospel*, p. 39.
35. Booth, *Rhetoric of Irony*, pp. 28-29.
36. Booth, *Rhetoric of Irony*, p. 28.

be complete without a brief word about them.

Clavier's main contribution is a study of irony in the teaching of Jesus,[37] but it should be stressed that he *is* a pioneer, and that consequently later developments have tended to outstrip those early incursions into the seemingly fathomless labyrinths. Certain statements made then can now, with the hindsight of over 35 years of further study, be seen to be inadequate. For instance, Clavier's view that textual irony is difficult to interpret since true ironic effect depends on factors such as tone, gesture and facial expression, can now be seen, in the light of Booth's impressive study, to be untenable. Even his comments on Jesus' use of irony seem to be more concerned with specific aims than with general principles of usage. He declares that Jesus' irony served to disarm resistance (for example, Mk 2.21-22), to invite renewed appeal (for example, Mk 7.24-30) and to parry accusations (for example, Mk 2.1-12).[38] This may be so, but if we are going to be as specific as this, we might as well say that Jesus—and other Gospel characters, too—used irony for scores of other reasons. Yet this would certainly not make for a helpful classification of ironic usage.

E.M. Good defines irony as 'a dramatic exposure, in either comic or tragic form, of pretence, of the incongruity of things as they are, between what they are and what they ought to be, or between what they are and what the object of ironic criticism thinks they are'.[39] While this might pass as a rough working definition, it should be noted that the term 'dramatic' in this context must be understood in the most general terms, and not specifically as dramatic irony which, of course, is but one category among many.

Given that Good's work is devoted solely to a study of irony in the Old Testament it will not be necessary for us to outline it. Suffice it to say that one of the most significant contributions of his work is to demonstrate conclusively that irony is not merely a 'Greek thing', as Thomson asserted,[40] but very much a 'Hebrew thing' too, and, by implication, a feature of cultures world-wide.[41]

Jónsson attempted the gargantuan task of considering both humour

37. Clavier, 'L'ironie', pp. 3-20; *idem*, 'La methode ironique', pp. 224-41, 323-44.

38. Clavier, 'L'ironie', pp. 10-14.

39. Good, *Irony in the Old Testament*, p. 30.

40. Thomson, *Irony*, p. 2.

41. Good, *Irony in the Old Testament*, p. 13.

and irony in the New Testament. While his book contains some valuable insights, and illuminates some instances of irony which have been overlooked by others, it is nonetheless guilty of attempting too much. Jónsson has just too many other irons in the fire to attempt much of a classification of irony; he merely arranges his comments under five headings—rhetorical irony, parables, polemical irony, theological irony and irony of familiarity—and leaves it at that. Yet this classification is a purely subjective one; it takes no account whatsoever of either Classical or modern categories. Booth has suggested that Quintilian was wrong in his classification of irony;[42] nevertheless it was a classification, no matter how rudimentary, and Jónsson seems blissfully unaware of the fact that distinctions between ironic types were being attempted, on a literary-critical basis, even as the New Testament was being written.

b. *Culpepper, Duke and O'Day*

With this triumvirate we reach the mid-eighties,[43] the era after Muecke and Booth. This is significant, for it means that insights provided by these two critics were now available for scholars of biblical irony—an observation not lost on Duke in his estimation of his predecessors:

> It is unfortunate that none of these [earlier] studies reflects much critical understanding of what irony is and is not. Definitions tend to be loose or faulty; the goal often seems to be to soften some hard saying by imagining Jesus with a grin.[44]

Valid criticism, perhaps; but does having Muecke and Booth at hand improve matters? Some recent critics would say not. J.E. Botha has observed that the above three scholars not only all deal with Johannine irony, but also reach remarkably similar definitions, classifications and conclusions.[45] All conceive of irony as two opposing layers of meaning, or a contrast between appearance and reality, and all note that the concept of ignorance or unawareness is a significant factor in the making of irony. It is also generally agreed that Johannine irony is stable, covert, fixed and finite, and that the presence of this irony serves to create or

---

42. Booth, *Rhetoric of Irony*, p. 68; cf. Quintilian, *Inst. Or.* 9.2.45

43. Culpepper, *Anatomy of the Fourth Gospel*; Duke, *Irony in the Fourth Gospel*; G.R. O'Day, *Revelation in the Fourth Gospel: Narrative Mode and Theological Claim* (Philadelphia: Fortress Press, 1986).

44. Duke, *Irony in the Fourth Gospel*, p. 170 n. 25.

45. J.E. Botha, 'The Case of Johannine Irony Re-Opened', *Neotestamentica* 25 (1991), pp. 209-32.

confirm the sense of community; those who perceive the author's true meaning are, as it were, part of his circle.

Why do these students of Johannine irony enjoy such a large measure of agreement? Botha suggests that it is because all three have relied on the same sources for their theoretical foundation (i.e. Muecke and Booth), and that since the latest of these was written nearly twenty years ago, it is high time to press on to new developments.[46]

There can be no objection to Botha's call to keep on the move. However, the mere fact that a book is twenty years old does not invalidate it. The insights afforded by Muecke and Booth are as valuable now as they were to literary-critics in the seventies. There is just a suggestion in Botha's remarks that the passing years has made them obsolete, and this is by no means the case. Nevertheless, Botha believes these studies of Culpepper, Duke and O'Day to be problematic for other reasons too.

1. The theoretical principles on which the discussion of the Johannine text is based are not sufficiently applied to the specific examples under consideration.

2. There is generally not sufficient attempt to distinguish between the various levels of communication—between the level of the characters in the story-world, and that of the implied author and implied reader, for instance. It is conceivable that irony might apply to one level and not to another.

3. It seems likely that Culpepper and Duke, especially, have 'discovered' just far too many examples of irony in John. Many instances have been virtually plucked out of the air, and are certainly not based on the theoretical principles established at the outset. Approaching irony in this way undermines its very nature; that is to say, irony is supposed to be used judiciously so that it is conspicuous in its context; seeing irony in almost every other verse naturally renders it ineffective.

4. Following Booth, some biblical ironists (for example, Duke) have identified 'clues' which could betray the presence of irony; but some of these, it is contended, might just as readily indicate the presence of other phenomena instead. For instance, repetition *could* point to an irony in the text, but it might just as well be there purely for emphasis.[47]

46. Botha, 'Johannine Irony', p. 213.
47. Botha, 'Johannine Irony', pp. 222-23.

Of these criticisms, perhaps 3. is the most potent. It is difficult to imagine that John would have intended all the ironies supposedly identified by Culpepper and Duke, and if he did not, then there is something wrong with the claim that Johannine irony is always stable. Perhaps there is room for a little more caution than has been shown hitherto. The other criticisms, too, are valid to an extent. Certainly, the theoretical principles should be applied to the discussion of irony in the text as far as possible, though this might not always be very practicable if, as in the case of Culpepper,[48] the author's comments on irony extend to just part of one chapter of a book devoted to narrative criticism as a whole.

c. *Botha and Camery-Hoggatt: Two Fresh Approaches*

Having taken Culpepper, Duke and O'Day to task for their over-reliance on Muecke and Booth, Botha sets forth his own approach. It is founded on speech-act theory which was developed by J.L. Austin and J.R. Searle in the 1960s–70s, and has more recently been applied to biblical studies.[49] Basic to the theory is the view that speech is not so much a syntactical device as a sequence of acts: namely, the locutionary act which is concerned with the production of recognizable or intelligible utterance; the illocutionary act in which the utterance is viewed in terms of its meaning or intention (greeting, ordering, warning, requesting and so on); and the perlocutionary act which is viewed in terms of its effect on the addressee. The context of these acts is of great importance. For instance, to say, 'Well done', may be a compliment if taken at face value, but an irony if it is intended as a sarcasm (praising in order to blame).

According to speech-act theory, any utterance should abide by certain maxims. There is, for example, the general co-operation principle, 'Make your conversational contribution such as is required…by the accepted purpose or direction of the verbal exchange in which you are involved'. Subsumed under this principle are several other maxims—the Quantity Maxim ('Be neither more nor less informative at any stage in the conversation than is necessary'); the Quality Maxim ('Do not say anything which is not true, or for which evidence is lacking'); the Relevance Maxim ('Be relevant'); the Maxim of Manner ('Be perspicuous; be brief; be orderly'); the Politeness Maxim ('Be as courteous as possible'); the

48. Culpepper, *Anatomy of the Fourth Gospel*, pp. 165-80.

49. In recent times, an issue of the experimental journal, *Semeia* (vol. 41, 1988) has been devoted to the application of speech-act theory to biblical studies.

Morality Maxim ('Do not reveal information that *should* not be disclosed'). Of course, it is permissible for the speaker to violate any of these maxims in order to produce a particular effect. It should be noted, too, that there is a considerable difference between orality and textuality, and different speech-act rules have to be drawn up for each.

According to Botha, irony operates within this system by 'covert negation' of some of the speech-act maxims.[50] It could be argued, for instance, that the element of repetition, which Duke (following Booth) regards as a possible indicator of irony, could indeed serve this purpose if it appears to violate the Maxim of Quantity (saying too much). The essential difference between ironic and non-ironic speech-acts is that whereas the latter usually contain but one proposition, the former contain two conflicting ones.

Now, this theory of Botha is all very well, but it does little, in my view, to advance the study of biblical irony beyond the work of those he criticizes. I fail to see what insights are afforded by speech-act theory which have not already been provided in the earlier studies based on Muecke and Booth. Apart from this general criticism, it seems that there are also certain *specific* drawbacks to Botha's theory:

1. It is extremely theoretical. For all his criticism of Duke and Culpepper, Botha never applies the speech-act theory to specific examples from the Johannine text; so we never see the theory put into practice—the very weakness for which Botha castigates his predecessors.
2. Botha claims that some passages, which cannot be regarded as ironical in the traditional sense, may be so in a new sense suggested by speech-act theory.[51] But surely this assertion undermines his criticism of Culpepper and Duke that overusing irony serves only to blunt its effect.

Another recent study of biblical irony, this time in Mark, is that by Jerry Camery-Hoggatt.[52] Although it is valuable in its own right, its title, *Irony in Mark's Gospel*, is rather misleading. Like Botha's article, this is an interdisciplinary study, making use not only of narrative criticism, but

50. Botha, 'Johannine Irony', p. 227, quoting D. Amante, 'The Theory of Ironic Speech Acts', *Poetics Today* 2 (1981), p. 77.

51. Botha, 'Johannine Irony', p. 230.

52. J. Camery-Hoggatt, *Irony in Mark's Gospel: Text and Subtext* (SNTSMS, 72; Cambridge: Cambridge University Press, 1992).

also of sociology of knowledge. Irony, however, seems predisposed to take equal place with other disciplines at the round-table of interdisciplinary study.

In his introductory comments on method, Camery-Hoggatt makes the valid point that it is of little value simply to have recourse to the literature on modern irony and to expect it to be adequate for informing a discussion on Markan irony, which is of a quite different order; though he does appear to ignore his own advice later on in the book.

Perhaps Camery-Hoggatt's most important contribution is to develop systematically what others have suggested in more arbitrary fashion— that one cannot properly think about irony without also having some concept of community; hence, the sociological aspect of the book. The dissonance of narrative, we are told, is an essential dynamic for drawing up social conventions to which initiates must adhere if they are to be accepted into the group. Irony, with its dissonant levels, is an important means of establishing the requisite linguistic tensions. The competing perspectives of the two ironic levels create crises of loyalty which force the reader/hearer to a decision. It is not simply that he or she is required to choose the 'right' way of telling; by making this choice and aligning himself or herself with the group to which this particular perspective belongs, he or she is also 'retelling his own story', thereby moving into a new social world.

Nearly half the book is devoted to a systematic reading of Mark's Gospel in which Camery-Hoggatt endeavours to apply his theoretical principles to the text in order to identify and elucidate the ironies it contains. Strangely, however, the textual commentary seems quite remote from all the hypothesis-building of the preceding chapters. One gains the distinct impression, in fact, that it could well have been written without recourse to the author's socio-literary theory. This is not to say that his ironic reading of Mark is not useful in its own right, only that it does not seem very well grounded in the theoretical soil.

5. *Irony in Mark's Gospel*

a. *Terminology and Classification*

Because the problem of irony is a difficult one it has been necessary to spend time discussing the theoretical and terminological issues, and establishing the current state of studies in biblical irony. It is time now, however, to decide how best to approach Markan irony, using the discoveries we have made so far as a foundation. The following considerations may be of relevance:

1. The survey above suggests that the irony in Mark's Gospel is likely to be invariably stable and unsophisticated rather than unduly subtle and complex. The chances are that the evangelist followed the conventions of his day, and nothing in Classical literature suggests that irony then was anything other than a simple, direct interaction between levels of appearance and reality which theauthor sought to share with readers. Conventionally, the reader/hearer was never an ironic victim; he or she always went hand in hand with the author, fully cognisant of the ignorance or unawareness of key characters in the story-world. If there are ironic victims in Mark's Gospel, it is in the narrative itself that we shall find them.

2. The most recent developments in the study of Gospel irony— those associated with Botha and Camery-Hoggatt—are not, in the last analysis, particularly helpful for understanding Markan irony. Certainly, they do not appear to offer any significant advance on those slightly earlier studies which took Muecke and Booth as their point of departure. This is not to say, of course, that they are of no use at all. Camery-Hoggatt's understanding of Markan irony as a community-building device is especially valuable, though it does raise an awkward question: namely, whether it was possible for some readers to miss the point of the irony after all, thereby remaining outside the orbit of the genuine community. If such a possibility did exist, it would naturally present a challenge to my stated opinion that all Markan irony would have been wholly stable.

3. In my view, the classification of irony offered by Booth, which simplifies the slightly earlier one of Muecke, still holds good as an aid to classifying biblical irony, despite the objections raised by Botha. After all, categories such as 'stable', 'local', 'finite', and so on—not to mention 'verbal'/'situational'—can apply just as well to ancient as to modern literature. Obviously, we should not expect to find examples covering the entire range of Booth's classification in the Markan text, but some categories are inevitably represented there, as we shall see.

4. Of the bewildering varieties of irony discussed by Muecke, many apply only to comparatively modern literature: 'Catch 22

Irony' and 'Romantic Irony' are obvious examples.[53] Others,
of course, are relevant. Clues to the kinds of irony we should
expect to find in Mark's Gospel may be provided by the genre
of the work itself. I have previously called attention to its
dramatic structure and character, and especially to its tragic
tendencies, so we should not be surprised to discover dramatic
(particularly tragic) irony there. This, indeed, is more significant
than any other kind, though there *are* others—sarcastic irony,
for instance.

Now that the theoretical foundation stones are in place, we must pass
on to consider some instances of irony in the Markan text.

b. *A Rapid Survey of Irony in Mark 1–13*
i) *The Rôle of Mark 1.1.* As both Booth and Duke have indicated, the
presence of irony may occasionally be indicated by means of a work's
title or epigraph. Mark 1.1 is generally accepted as Mark's own title for
his Gospel: 'The beginning of the gospel of Jesus Christ, the Son of
God.' Much hinges on whether 'Son of God' is part of the original text;
the manuscripts are broadly divided. Nevertheless, it is a title which
Mark uses judiciously (cf. 3.11; 15.39), and it is attested here by some
important manuscripts. If it does belong to the original, it is clear that it
is a statement made by the reliable author: that Jesus is the Son of God
is a fact which Mark wants his readers to accept at face value. Thus, any
statement which conflicts with this elsewhere must be viewed as unreliable, and the possibility of *ironic* unreliability is not to be dismissed.
Depending on how we interpret the term 'Son of God', there is a
possible instance of this in Mk 10.18. Speaking to the rich man, Jesus
appears to distance himself from God: 'Why do you call me good? No-
one is good but God alone.' Yet if the title 'Son of God' has divine
connotations, and the reader understands the Markan title as conveying
reliable information, he or she can hardly accept Jesus' statement in
10.18 at face value. Might it not, therefore, be intended as an ironic
statement made in order to reinforce the recognition of Jesus' true
identity?

ii) *Verbal/Situational Irony.* There are many instances of both verbal
and situational irony in Mark, and in some cases the two have to be seen

53. Muecke, *Irony and the Ironic*, pp. 12-13.

in conjunction. Situational irony, because it is dramatic, is of particular importance in this gospel, and can be detected at both local and extended levels. Verbal irony, it will be noted, may be inherent in the statement itself (it is inescapably ironic), or it may prove ironic under certain conditions. Thus, the statement, 'The bigger they are, the harder they fall', is inherently ironic, whereas to say 'Well done' may be meant seriously or ironically, depending on the situation. Both these kinds are evident in Mark. Let us now, then, turn to some examples:

1. *Mark 2.17*. Jesus' pronouncements (to use that term form-critically) are often ironic. In the present case, Jesus compares himself to a physician, but one who has come to deal with sin rather than physical illness (though he does that too, of course). He remarks, rather sarcastically, that those who are well have no need of a physician, only those who are sick. The irony of this saying, as noted below, would not be lost on the scribes to whom Jesus was speaking.

2. *Mark 6.4*. Having returned to his home town of Nazareth, Jesus tells his detractors, 'A prophet is not without honour except in his own country, and among his own kin, and in his own house.' The source of this may be a popular proverb. The irony is established in the first part of the statement, and is not strengthened by the addition of the last two phrases. Mark himself may have appended these in order to apply the general proverb to the specific rejection of Jesus at Nazareth. Indeed, we find that they are missing from the Lukan parallel (Lk. 4.24), suggesting, perhaps, that they do not belong to the original. The irony, though general to the proverb, is made to apply specifically to this episode.

3. *Mark 7.9*. Jesus 'congratulates' the scribes and Pharisees for allowing their own laws (the tradition of the elders) to take precedence over God's law. They can be in no doubt as to what Jesus means, and so cannot fail to perceive the irony in the words. Sarcastic irony like this must, of course, be verbal irony, because it depends for its effect on the necessity of the ironic victim being aware of the sarcasm, and thus of the fact that he or she *is* the ironic victim.

4. *Mark 7.15*. Sayings of reversal, again, depend for their impact on the expectation that the hearer, rather than falling an unwitting victim to them, will spot the deliberate upsetting of

values which accrues from them. Here, the usual expectation is that food which passes into someone's stomach could conceivably contaminate them, certainly in a ritual sense, according to the religious authorities. Ironically, however, people can be so engrossed in maintaining ritual purity that they fail to appreciate the power of that which defiles from within—evil thoughts. By juxtaposing the expected with the unexpected, then reversing their importance so that it is the unexpected which is of primary concern, Jesus is able to drive home his point, using the irony of the reversal.

5.   *Mark 12.14*. Here we have the mock-flattery of the Pharisees and Herodians: 'Teacher, we know that you are true, and care for no man; for you do not regard the position of men, but truly teach the way of God.' Obviously, this is empty flattery: the reader knows full well what the opponents *really* think. But the reader also knows that, unbeknown to them, their words are in fact an accurate assessment of Jesus, who really is true, and really does teach the way of God. Here, then, we have a verbal irony that recoils upon itself: those who seek to put the ironic noose around Jesus' neck are themselves hanged in it.

So much, then, for verbal irony, of which there are many other examples. Now let us mention a few instances of situational irony, that is to say irony made by what happens rather than by what is said.

1.   One of the most obvious examples of situational irony in the Gospel is that Jesus is acclaimed as the Son of God not by the religious leaders who might have been expected to recognize him as such, but by demons (1.24; 3.11; 5.7) and Gentiles (15.39). The religious authorities had come face to face with the Son of God and rejected him, while those whom they consciously despised—the Gentiles and the demon-possessed—were aware of Jesus' true sonship.

2.   In Mk 1.38 we are told of Jesus' intention to move on to other villages to deliver the gospel there, 'for that is why I came out'. But when he does so, and cleanses a leper along the way (1.40-45) he finds that because of the leper's disobedience in spreading the word, he can no longer enter a town openly (1.45), which is quite the opposite of his original intention.

3. In Mk 3.16 we are informed that Jesus conferred the nickname Peter ('Rocky') upon Simon. The verbal declaration is not, of course, ironic in itself, but it becomes ironic when set against the story of Peter's life with Jesus. The name Peter would lead us to expect a man who is prepared to stand firm in adversity, but his record shows us just how wrong that expectation turns out to be. In particular, he boasts that he really will live up to his name by remaining loyal to Jesus come what may (14.29-31), and then only a short while later is found denying that he ever knew Jesus (14.66-72). 'Rocky' indeed!

    As if by deliberate contrast, Mark tells us that when he commissions his disciples, Jesus nicknames two others—the brothers James and John, whom he calls Boanerges, 'sons of thunder'. The fact that they live up to their name so exactly (cf. 9.38; 10.35-40) stresses even more clearly the irony behind the singular inappropriateness of Simon's new name.

    This example of irony demonstrates how, very often, it is not simply a question of verbal or situational irony alone, but a subtle combination of the two.

4. In Mk 10.46-52 Jesus heals blind Bartimaeus, who then follows him along the way. The irony of this situation is that though blind, Bartimaeus does in fact see what the physically-sighted disciples of Jesus have never fully seen—that Jesus is the messiah (Bartimaeus acclaims him as Son of David, which is a messianic title). Thus, because Bartimaeus has metaphorical sight, he becomes a *true* disciple of the kind that the physically-sighted disciples, who *ought* to have seen, but were metaphorically blind, have been struggling to become throughout the Gospel. This use of blindness versus sight to create an ironic situation was nothing new by Mark's time; it had been used to great effect by Sophocles in his *Oedipus Rex*, where Teiresias, the blind seer, sees clearly what the sighted king cannot. And, of course, the dramatic apex of that play is the inversion where Oedipus at last gains metaphorical sight, and loses his physical vision.

5. Mark's juxtaposition of the scribes' condemnation (12.38-40) with the story of the poor widow (12.41-44) is another good example of situational irony. One of the misdeeds of which the scribes stand accused by Jesus is 'devouring widows' houses'. There is some question about what this means exactly, but it is

contended by some that it could denote a practice whereby the scribes, as trained lawyers, were appointed to manage the estates of women whose husbands had died, and charged extortionate fees for doing so.[54] Whatever the precise details of the matter, it is clear that the scribes were taking full advantage of these women.

Hard on the heels of this objection comes the story of the poor widow who contributes her entire living—two small coins—to the Temple treasury. The irony is that it is one of the very people of the kind whom the scribes have been exploiting who serves to demonstrate to Mark's readers what true worship is all about. Giving their all to God is precisely what the scribes should have been doing; instead, they stand to be shown their duty by one of the very people they were using as a means of not paying due honour to God.

iii) *Local/Infinite (Extended) Irony.* As we have seen, while most scholars are agreed on what local irony is, there is some difference of opinion about the meaning of infinite irony: is it an irony dealing in general assertions as Booth defines it, or is it irony which extends temporally and spatially beyond what would be expected of local irony? Perhaps it will be as well, for the sake of clarity, to treat these as two separate types, and to see if we can find instances of each one in Mark.

Instances of local irony in this Gospel are too numerous to admit of discussion here (cf., for example, 2.7, 17, 19, 27; 3.22; 4.41; 5.30-31; 6.4, 37; 7.9; 8.11-12, 15, 29; 11.10; 12.10, 14; 14.65; 15.16-19, 31, 33-34, 39), nor is it necessary to treat each case independently. Local irony is simply that which takes place at a particular point in time, and can be fully appreciated as such. To take just one example, the scribes in 3.22 accuse Jesus of casting out demons by Beelzebul, the prince of demons. It would be ironic, of course, if Satan were to be found driving out his own minions. The irony is complete within the limits of the event, and no other texts need to be drawn upon in order to understand it. It is local irony, pure and simple.

What of infinite irony, understood according to Booth's definition? Occurrences of this in Mark are much less common. One can be found in 3.31-35, where Jesus contends that his real family consists of all who

---

54. J.D.M. Derrett, '"Eating up the Houses of Widows": Jesus' Comment on Lawyers', *NovT* 14 (1972), pp. 1-9 (7).

do God's will. The hub of the irony is in the inversion of insiders and outsiders. Those who do not believe in him (and hence fail to do God's will) are cast out, even if, like Jesus' generic family, they might expect to be insiders; but those who, by worldly standards, could be regarded as outsiders have the opportunity to be on the inside. The infinite aspect of this situation is that Jesus' invitation is limitless; it is open to all, and for all time. Moreover, the irony of disappointed expectancy extends to the indefinite future. The victims in the text are the members of Jesus' generic family who unexpectedly find themselves on the outside. Their modern counterparts are surely those who believe themselves to be ritual and doctrinal insiders, but are outsiders in their ethical devotion.

Another example of infinite irony is 6.4: 'A prophet is not without honour except in his own country'. Jesus (or Mark) is here applying what was probably a common proverb of his day to his own situation at Nazareth, as we have seen; but again the irony has a general application. Jesus' experience here is the experience of 'prophets' in general down the ages.

Several passages in Mark constitute examples of infinite irony in the sense meant by Duke—that is, episodic or thematic irony. We have already noted a few in passing—the fact that it is the demons and Gentiles who most readily acknowledge Jesus as Son of God, for instance; and the fact that, despite his nickname, Peter turns out to be anything but 'rocky'. The point is, of course, that the full implication of these ironies becomes evident only when large sections of the Gospel—or even the entire Gospel—are taken into account.

The inside/outside antithesis is another example of extended irony. We have already noted that 3.31-35 is ironic in its own right: it is ironic that those who might have been expected to be insiders (Jesus' earthly family) actually end up on the outside. In 8.18, this same irony is repeated, except that here it is the disciples who are the victims. The full force of the irony, however, is not evident unless 4.11-12 is taken into account. In this latter passage we are told that the parables are meant to conceal the mystery of God's kingdom from the outsiders, that 'seeing they may see, and not perceive; and hearing they may hear, and not understand' (cited from Isa. 6.9). We can ignore, for the present purpose, the difficulties of interpretation which this passage raises,[55] and

---

55. For a recent discussion of views on Mk 4.11-12, see Gundry, *Mark*, pp. 195-204.

simply note that 8.18 takes up the 'outsider' theme once more. The disciples are with Jesus in a boat, and they have failed to understand Jesus' saying about the leaven of the Pharisees and of Herod (8.15); their own minds are fixed on the provision of physical bread (8.16). Then Jesus cries, in a state of exasperation, 'Why do you discuss the fact that you have no bread? Do you not yet perceive or understand? Are your hearts hardened? Having eyes do you not see, and having ears do you not hear?' (8.17b-18a). Those final words are deliberately reminiscent of the citation from Isaiah in Mk 4.12 (although the question in 8.18 is actually taken from Jer. 5.21), the implication being that like the 'outsiders' in 4.11-12, the disciples, too, fail to 'see' and 'hear'. Moreover, like the Pharisees and Herodians in 3.5-6, whose position as outsiders is not in doubt, the disciples' hearts have been hardened (Mark uses the same Greek verb, or derivative thereof, in both cases), a fact confirmed in 6.52 where, as here, they fail to 'understand about the loaves'. Thus, like Jesus' earthly family, the disciples, who should have been ideologically closer to Jesus than anyone else, find themselves, ironically, on the outside. As a matter of fact, none of the chief actors in Mark's narrative can claim to be consistently on the inside; that privilege is reserved for the reader, who alone is privy to all the author's ironies.[56]

The story about Bartimaeus (10.46-52), which we have already discussed, is another instance of extended irony, for it has to be seen in connection with the attitude and behaviour of the Twelve. We note that, in 1.16-20, Jesus calls (καλέω) and they follow (ἀκολουθέω). Again, when he commissions them (3.13) and sends them out on their mission (6.7), he calls them to him (προσκαλέω). They turn out to be a good deal less than perfect, however, and frequently misunderstand and fail him. But in 10.46-52, Jesus 'calls' Bartimaeus, and he 'follows' (the Greek words are those used in 1.16-20 of the immediate circle of disciples). Bartimaeus, however, unlike the Twelve, recognizes Jesus for who he really is (Son of David). And so, ironically, it takes an apparently insignificant blind beggar, one who was despised by the 'respectable' people, to demonstrate what true discipleship is all about.

iv) *Stable/Unstable Irony*. Stable irony, as we have noted, is irony upon which author and reader are agreed: it is what is intended, fixed and

---

56. See S.H. Smith, '"Inside" and "Outside" in Mark's Gospel', *ExpTim* 102 (1991), pp. 363-67.

finite. Unstable irony, on the other hand, entails that the ironic meaning is unfixed, and that different readers may offer different or conflicting interpretations of a passage. The tension between stable and unstable irony must take account of certain sub-factors, including the intended/unintended, and covert/overt antitheses.

1. *Intended/Unintended Irony*. Classical irony, so far as we can tell, always set out to be intentional: it was devised by the author and intended to be understood by the reader. But even then, there must have been a potential for unstable irony. That which was intended by the author must frequently have been missed by individual readers, while readers then, as now, may well have picked up an irony not consciously intended by the author. In that sense, unstable irony was unavoidable.

The irony in Mark's Gospel is intentional, and hence stable. We should not be tempted to endow the author with the necessary literary subtlety for consciously creating an unstable situation. The ruse whereby a modern author might lead readers onto a deceptively stable platform only for its actual instability to lead into further, deeper ironies would have been unknown to Mark and his contemporaries. Nevertheless, it would certainly have been possible for stable irony to flip over into unstable irony on an accidental or unintentional basis. Some of the irony which modern scholars unearth in Mark today might not have been intended by the evangelist at all; and, conversely, can we be confident that we have discovered all the irony it is possible to discover in this Gospel?

How, then, can we distinguish between intended and unintended irony in Mark? The best way is to look for signs or signals implanted in the text by the author. When we find these we can be relatively confident that intentional irony is present. We have seen that such signs may well be present in the form of clashes of point-of-view, belief or doctrine, conflicts of fact, or direct authorial warnings. I have alluded incidentally to some of these in earlier comments. We saw in 10.18 that Jesus is careful to draw back from identifying himself with God, but Mark has already told us what he thinks in his opening comment—that Jesus is the Son of God (1.1). Now *if* that is supposed to mean that Jesus is felt to be in some sense divine, the incongruity between 1.1 and 10.18 must be explained in one of two ways: either Mark is reporting the words of the historical Jesus *verbatim*, even though they appear not to coincide with his own belief; or he is aware that by having Jesus seemingly distance himself from identity with God, he is creating an irony which will confirm Jesus' divinity a good deal more forcefully than if Jesus had simply affirmed his identity quite openly.

In Mk 12.13-14 we can perhaps detect another kind of sign. There Mark re-introduces us to the Pharisees and Herodians who approach Jesus with flatteries: '...we know that you are true...[and] truly teach the way of God'. If they mean it, they cannot be ironic, so how do we know that they are insincere? The authorial comment in 12.13 tells us: they were out to entrap Jesus in his talk. Armed with this information, provided by Mark himself, even the dullest reader cannot fail to spot the irony.

Another *possible* example of this is in 2.7, but here we are dependent upon the origin of the word βλασφημεῖ. If, as may just be possible, Mark inserted the word himself, he could be using it to underscore the irony of the scribes' words. Jesus has just forgiven someone's sins. The scribes say, 'Why does this man speak thus?...Who can forgive sins but God alone?' Most of Mark's readers would have spotted the irony immediately, but of course it only works if we can be sure that the authorities were denouncing Jesus' claims. If their question had been genuine it would not necessarily have been ironic at all, and as this is the first controversy story in the Gospel, any reader without prior knowledge of the Gospel story would as yet be unsure about the scribes' attitude to Jesus. So, by inserting that one word, βλασφημεῖ, 'It is blasphemy', Mark stresses the antagonistic, and hence the ironic, nature of the scribes' comment. It is clear, then, that while they rightly conclude that God alone can forgive sins, they fail to see that the one to whom they are raising objections is the very one who has divine authority as God's own Son. The authorial nature of the word βλασφημεῖ here can perhaps be seen in the fact that the very charge with which the whole series of controversy stories begins is precisely that with which the long quest to condemn Jesus is concluded—blasphemy (cf. 14.61-62).

Mark may also alert us to the presence of irony by means of repetition. For instance, we can understand the irony of Jesus' inner circle being relegated to the outside in 8.18 mainly because the language used there is a virtual repetition of that used in 4.12 where the blind and deaf are specifically *said* to be outsiders. Without this repetition, it might not have been very clear that the disciples were being classified as outsiders. Again, the irony of a blind beggar who turns out to be a truer disciple than Jesus' more intimate circle of disciples is reinforced by the repetition of the words 'call' and 'follow' (1.18, 20; 10.49, 52) which serve to draw the two cases into sharp contrast (although it should be noted that in the case of 'call', the Greek word is different in each case—καλέω in 1.20, as opposed to φωνέω in 10.49).

A further indication of intended irony is the conflict of doctrine or belief. Thus, we are alerted to the possibility of irony in 3.22 because the scribes suggest that Jesus exorcises by Beelzebul, the prince of demons. We know that this cannot be true because Mark has shared with us the secret of Jesus' identity (1.1; 3.11). The ultimate irony here is that even the demons themselves know more than the scribes. The latter attribute Jesus' exorcisms to the devil. Jesus himself spells out the irony of that situation: how could Satan survive if he cast out his own demons? (3.23-26). But the greater irony is that the very demonic beings with whom Jesus is supposed to be possessed, according to the scribes, actually know what the scribes themselves should have understood—that Jesus is the Son of God, and works in the power of the Holy Spirit, not in the power of evil spirits (1.24; 3.11).

2. *Covert/Overt Irony*. It is often alleged that irony in the Gospels is covert rather than overt. The reader must play the ironic game and discover the irony for him or herself, using whatever clues the author chooses to provide. It has been well said that the thrill of discovery makes this a more powerful device than overt irony. This may be so. Nevertheless, the Gospels are not entirely free from the latter.

Because covert irony is so common in Mark, it would be a fruitless exercise to engage in a complete survey. It will be sufficient to note one simple example. In 6.45-51 the disciples are toiling on the lake in the middle of the night, when they see Jesus coming across the water. They cry out in fear, for they think they have seen a ghost; but Jesus reassures them with the words, 'Take heart, it is I; have no fear' (6.50). The disciples are astounded because they do not understand about the loaves (6.52), but at least Jesus has announced who he is—at two levels. At one level, the disciples understand what he is saying: 'It is I, Jesus' (that is, not a ghost as you first thought, but your familiar teacher and companion). At a deeper level, however, Jesus is announcing who he *really* is, and it is *that* which the disciples fail to understand. The Greek ἐγώ εἰμι means, literally, 'I am'—the very name by which God announces himself at the burning bush (Exod. 3.14). The story in Mark 6.45-51 is shot through with divine activity. Jesus not only proves that he has control over the waters, just as God does in the Old Testament (for example, Gen. 1.2; Exod. 14.21-32; Pss. 77.19; 107.28-29), but he even identifies himself before the disciples using God's name (as he does again in 14.62 where the High Priest accuses him of blasphemy). All this is lost on the disciples, but not on the attentive reader. Given that Mark's audience knew its Septuagintal onions, the irony in Mk 6.50, covert though it is, would have been detected without too much difficulty.

There are some instances in Mark, however, where the evangelist or his characters spell out the irony of a saying or situation; it is, in other words, overt irony. The irony in 5.30-31 works in this way. The woman with the haemorrhage makes her way through a large crowd thronging around Jesus and touches his garment. The reader is furnished with the inside information that Jesus perceived the power go out of him, so that when he says, 'Who touched my garments?' the reader knows precisely what he means. The disciples, of course, are the ironic victims: 'You see the crowd pressing around you, and yet you say, "Who touched me?"' But the irony for the reader is transparent because he or she has been given the relevant information: the reader knows the situation is ironic because the author has, in effect, told him or her so.

The proverb, 'A prophet is not without honour except in his own country' (6.4), is another example of overt irony, as is the sarcasm, 'You have a fine way of rejecting the commandment of God in order to keep your tradition', in 7.9. In both these cases the irony should be obvious to any reader. Sayings of reversal such as '…whoever would be great among you must be your servant, and whoever would be first among you must be slave of all' (10.43-44), also come under this category. It is clear to anyone that, according to worldly standards, what Jesus says here just does not apply, so the truth of the saying must be at a deeper level.

As a final example of overt irony in Mark, we can mention 2.19. People ask why Jesus' disciples, unlike those of the Pharisees and John, are not fasting. Jesus replies, 'Can the wedding guests fast while the bridegroom is with them?' (that is, would not *that* be ironic?). The irony is already obvious, surely, but just in case anyone should be in any doubt as to the answer, Jesus (or Mark) supplies it (thereby weakening the irony, it seems to me): 'As long as they have the bridegroom with them, they cannot fast.'

v) *Types of Irony in Mark's Gospel.* The impressive list of ironic types given by Muecke is based on his reading of modern literature. A good many items on that list do not apply to ancient literature at all. Nevertheless, some of them are to be found in Mark's Gospel, particularly dramatic, tragic and sarcastic irony, so a brief consideration of these will be in order.

1. *Dramatic Irony.* Dramatic irony, as its name suggests, is typical of, but by no means confined to drama. Obviously, it is rife in the Greek dramatists, and Thirlwall equated it with what he termed 'Sophoclean irony',[57] but it is older than Sophocles, and is certainly not confined to the tragic situation. It arises when the audience (or reader) shares with the author a knowledge of a situation of which one or more of the characters in the story-world is ignorant. This superior knowledge may be conveyed to the reader by the author in authorial asides, a prologue, or through the mouth of a reliable character; or the knowledge could already be assumed as part of the reader's experience. Mark, in fact, uses a combination of all these devices. In the prologue of the Gospel (1.1-13), we are told not only who Mark himself thinks Jesus is, but who John the Baptist thinks he is as well (1.7-8); and we keep on being reminded of Mark's opinion in authorial asides like 2.10 ('But that you may know that the Son of man has authority on earth to forgive sins...'). But this is not all. Mark can also assume a foreknowledge of the Jesus story on the part of his readers since, of course, they are Christians living in the post-resurrection era; so their very acquaintance with the story is necessarily going to give them an advantage over the characters who are confined by the spatio-temporal limits of the narrative world.

Of the many instances of dramatic irony in Mark, the following five are offered for discussion:

First, Mk 2.7. Jesus has just forgiven the sins of the paralytic. The scribes mutter indignantly, 'Why does this man speak thus? It is blasphemy. Who can forgive sins but God alone?' In saying this, they believe themselves to be condemning Jesus' claims—they are the claims of an imposter and blasphemer; but in fact the opponents are unwittingly confirming for the reader precisely who Jesus is. It is as if they are saying sarcastically, 'Who does this fellow think he is? God?' And, of course, for Mark and his readers that is exactly the right answer. If only the scribes knew what they were saying! How can the reader be so confident of the irony? For one thing, the divinity of Jesus would have

---

57. C. Thirlwall, 'On the Irony of Sophocles', *The Philological Museum*, II (Cambridge: Deightons, 1833).

been fundamental to their faith. And for another, Mark confirms them in this belief: Jesus is the Son of God (1.1), the one who can even take upon himself the very essence of God in the divine name, ἐγώ εἰμι—'I am' (6.50; 14.62).

Secondly, Mk 4.41. The disciples' exclamation after Jesus had calmed the storm is another clear example of dramatic irony. 'Who then is this, that even wind and sea obey him?' By performing such a stupendous miracle, Jesus has just demonstrated who he is. His power over the sea is precisely what we expect of God in the Old Testament (Pss. 77.19; 107.28-29, for example); yet the disciples fail to grasp Jesus' identity, even when he is demonstrating it before their very eyes. Of course, the reader can enjoy the irony. The reader has a distinct advantage over those first disciples which not only gives him or her a feeling of superiority over them, but a sense of knowing Christ in a way that, at the time, even his closest followers did not.

Thirdly, Mk 6.37. Jesus has spent the day teaching a large crowd. As evening draws in, the disciples, as frequently in Mark, begin to think of physical needs: how might everyone be fed? Jesus answers, 'You give them something to eat.' Already we know enough of the disciples to anticipate what they might say, and enough of Jesus to expect an unusual response. The disciples, of course, remain entirely on the surface level of understanding: 'Shall we go and buy two hundred denarii worth of bread, and give it to them to eat?' Jesus ignores the question; he knows what answer the eye of faith would have given. Jesus, surely, is sufficient for every need. It is a message which had yet to dawn on the disciples, but which would have been evident to the average reader in Mark's community.

The 'bread' irony is, in fact, sustained throughout these central chapters of Mark. In 7.24-30, Jesus suggests that his 'bread' is for Jews only. Does he mean it? Certainly, this does not sound like the Jesus we have so far been led to expect. The Syrophoenician woman resolves the issue: surely he has bread sufficient for both the children (Jews) and the dogs (Gentiles). The woman's faith has been tried in the fire of irony, and has come through. Of course Jesus' bread is sufficient.

Next comes a second feeding miracle (8.1-10). We notice that on this occasion, Jesus does not wait for the disciples to broach the question about how to feed so many people. He has just tested a Gentile woman, and she passed the test with flying colours. Can the disciples match that? He prompts them with the comment, 'I have compassion on the crowd, because they have been with me now three days, and have nothing to eat; and if I send them away hungry to their homes, they will faint on the way; and some of them have come a long way' (8.2-3). The answer to the problem ought not to have been too difficult for the disciples; after all, in 6.35-44 Jesus had demonstrated it! In the event, their reply is little more than tautologous: 'How can one feed these men with bread here in the desert?' (8.4). Well, is not that precisely what Jesus had been asking them? The disciples have manifestly failed the test.

The final episode in the series occurs at 8.14-21. Jesus and his disciples are in a boat crossing the lake. Jesus warns them against the yeast of the Pharisees and of Herod, by which he means their influence or, if we follow the interpretation given in Lk. 12.1, their teaching; but all it brings to the minds of the disciples is that they have no bread (8.16) or, if we allow for the slight inconsistency, only one loaf (8.14). Jesus chides them. Have they learned nothing from the two feeding miracles? The disciples are as dull as ever. The reader's mind, however, dwells on verse 14: they did have one loaf with them in the boat. The message which the disciples had failed to grasp throughout these episodes was consistent enough: Jesus is sufficient for every need.

Fourthly, Mk 8.11-12. In this passage the Pharisees ask Jesus for a sign from heaven 'to test him'. The word 'heaven' here is really a circumlocution for God, as it is also in 11.30: the opponents really want to know how he can demonstrate that he comes from God; what messianic credentials does he have? The irony is, of course, that the previous two or three chapters have been packed with spectacular miracles—stilling a storm (4.35-41), curing someone with a legion of demons (5.1-20), raising Jairus' daughter (5.21-24, 35-43), healing a woman with a haemorrhage (5.25-34), feeding five thousand people (6.35-44), and then another four thousand (8.1-10), walking on the water (6.45-51), and exorcising the Syrophoenician woman's daughter (7.24-30). And still the Pharisees ask for a sign of Jesus' messiahship! The irony is not especially weakened by the suggestion that they were looking for a special, predetermined sign such as we find in the later rabbinic literature.[58] The point is that such stupendous miracles should have alerted them to who Jesus really was.

Fifthly, Mk 11.10. The acclamation of the crowd as Jesus enters

58. See the evidence collected in L. Ginzberg, *The Legends of the Jews*, IV (4 vols.; Philadelphia: Jewish Publication Society of America, 1938), p. 234.

Jerusalem is ironic in that their words, though totally befitting the coming of the messiah, are uttered in ignorance. Subsequent events confirm for us that the crowd's understanding of messiahship does not conform to Jesus' view so that, while the words are apt, the expectation which underlies them is wrong.

Numerous scholars have noted that this acclamation is drawn in part from Ps. 118.26, a psalm that would have been sung at festival time in any case,[59] and some have gone so far as to suggest that the words were directed at pilgrims in general and were not uttered specifically in recognition of Jesus' messiahship. Even if we were to accept this as a feasible historical reconstruction of the event, the irony would still be there, if not to an even greater extent; for then we should have the prospect of a crowd perhaps totally ignorant of Jesus' messiahship, nevertheless unwittingly acclaiming him as messiah.

2. *Tragic Irony.* According to Sedgewick, tragic irony is used as a device for dramatic emphasis.[60] It points up the significance of a situation, brings the conflict of dramatic forces into sharp focus, and heightens the sense of pity and terror which the audience feels for the tragic victim. This sense of pity in Mark does not so much arise out of local irony as out of the general tragic situation. Moreover, we feel pity for Jesus not because he is an ironic victim, like Oedipus, but because, as the one character who sees everything clearly, he falls victim to those who are blind to the reality of the situation. The very one whom God has sent to save his people is rejected by them because they fail to realize who it is in their midst. The tragic heroes of Greek drama are pitied because, while they act in good faith, they also act in ignorance, and their own *hubris* leads to their downfall. Jesus is to be pitied even more, if anything, because he has no *hubris* to speak of, unless it is his single-minded determination to see his mission through, despite the hostile forces which are conspiring to crush him, and which he knows will do so at the last. This sense of tragic irony reaches a climax in the Passion narrative (Mk 14–15) which we shall be discussing separately.

3. *Sarcastic Irony.* Sarcastic irony, as the name implies, is meant to make its point by means of some sarcasm aimed at the ironic victim. Usually, this victim is meant to be aware rather than ignorant of the irony. In Mark's Gospel, sarcastic irony is of the praise-in-order-to-blame

---

59. Nineham, *Saint Mark*, p. 296; Lane, *Mark*, p. 397; Hooker, *Gospel according to St Mark*, p. 259; Gundry, *Mark*, p. 630, among others.

60. Sedgewick, *Of Irony*, p. 63.

variety. Thus, in 2.17 Jesus says, 'Those who are well have no need of a physician, but those who are sick'. Doubtless Jesus' audience of scribes knew what was intended. There was no point in Jesus endeavouring to heal their sin-sickness, since they considered themselves righteous, and set apart from 'real' sinners—the ones who *recognized* their guilt. This much is evident from the irony in 2.17a. The additional comment, 'I came not to call the righteous, but sinners', does not add anything to the sense, and after 2.17a seems to state the obvious. It could well be an ecclesiastical accretion.

Another instance of mock-praise is 7.9: 'You have a fine way of rejecting the commandment of God, in order to keep your tradition.' Jesus, of course, is objecting to the fact that the Pharisees and scribes have disregarded one of the Ten Commandments, 'Honour your father and your mother', in order to keep the man-made Korban rule. He could, of course, have chided them with words like, 'You should not allow your oral laws to overrule the Ten Commandments'; but how much more incisive is the objection when clothed with the irony of mock-praise.

It is not only Jesus who uses this device. Sometimes it is used in ignorance against him. In 15.18, for instance, the soldiers mockingly hail Jesus as King of the Jews. But just as sarcastic irony can be a potent weapon against its victims, so it can be more potent still in the hands of the victims themselves. Thus, here, the soldiers think that Jesus is the victim, when the reader knows the truth of the situation. There is nothing more devastating for the *real* victims than to use an irony of mockery which will be turned against them.

c. *Irony in Mark 14–15*
As the climax of Mark's Gospel is reached, the irony becomes so rich and interwoven that it is well worth considering the main examples in the form of a brief, ironic commentary on the final two chapters (excluding 16.1-8).

i) *Mark 14.10-11*. These verses, which tell how Judas offered to betray Jesus to the chief priests, are not ironic in themselves. There is, however, a contextual irony. We have seen that throughout the Gospel the Jewish authorities have been seeking to condemn Jesus. The closer to Passion week we come, the more intense become their efforts. Yet all the weight of their combined endeavours fails to meet with success until, by 14.1, the chief-priests are at their wits' end regarding what they can do to secure Jesus' arrest. It is at just that moment that Judas appears on the scene to offer his services, and from then on events proceed apace. How ironic, then, that after Jesus has thwarted all attempts by the authorities to condemn him, his downfall is brought about by a fifth columnist— one of those closest to him.

ii) *Mark 14.29-31*. We have already mentioned this passage above, so little more need be said. Simon boasts that he will live up to his nick-name, Peter (the Rock), and will *never* deny Jesus. Of course, Jesus' prediction in 14.27 proves right: not only does Peter deny Jesus (14.66-72) but, along with James and John, he cannot even stay awake and keep watch in the Garden of Gethsemane (14.37). Peter's behaviour, then, ironically, is a direct negation of his nickname.

iii) *Mark 14.65*. The use of sarcastic irony in this verse is specially powerful. We may note that when Jesus makes use of this device (2.17; 7.9) his opponents are put to shame, whereas when the opponents use it, they only succeed in ensnaring themselves, in the eyes of the reader. Such is the case here. The mockers cover up Jesus' face, spit on him, abuse him and urge him to 'prophesy'. The call to do so is intended as sarcastic irony, of course; but the deeper irony is that Jesus has already prophesied—he has prophesied the mockery he is suffering at that very moment (10.34). Some would go further and suggest that it was foretold by one of the truly great Old Testament prophets, Isaiah (Isa. 53). In addition, as Camery-Hoggatt has noticed, the mockers' command to Jesus to prophesy also takes place at the same time as Peter is fulfilling Jesus' prophecy that he would deny him.[61] Of all this, the opponents are blissfully ignorant: they are ironic victims with a vengeance.

iv) *Mark 14.66-72*. We return briefly to the denials of Peter to note a further insight of Camery-Hoggatt.[62] He observes that the Jewish trial of Jesus (14.55-65) is intercalated into the Peter episode (14.53-54, 66-72) precisely because the two stories run parallel to each other: they are, in fact, *both* trials. Just as the false witnesses accuse Jesus of something he

---

61. Camery-Hoggatt, *Irony in Mark's Gospel*, p. 174.
62. Camery-Hoggatt, *Irony in Mark's Gospel*, pp. 171-72.

did *not* say,[63] so the maid and the bystanders accuse Peter of being something he is—a follower of Jesus. But while Peter denies their accusation, Jesus admits to the final charge made at his trial—that of being the messiah (14.61-62). The ironical climax of this episode, as Camery-Hoggatt points out, is Peter's claim in 14.71, 'I do not know this man of whom you speak.' Those are truer words than Peter can know, for indeed he does *not* know Jesus—a fact which Mark has made obvious to the reader throughout his Gospel.

v) *Mark 15.1-15*. The trial before Pilate is deliberately structured to parallel the trial before the High Priest. Again, Jesus is accused of 'many things' (15.3; cp. 14.56), and again he maintains his silence (15.3; 14.61), so that the judge in each case questions this policy (15.4; 14.60)—in identical words (οὐκ ἀποκρίνη οὐδέν). In both cases, too, the judge directly questions Jesus about his identity (15.2; 14.61). It is highly likely, then, that Mark intends the reader to compare these two trials, and when the reader does so, he or she finds an intentional inconsistency which turns out to unveil an irony. It is easy to spot that the nature of the charge changes from one trial to the next. In the first, Jesus is accused of blasphemy, whereas in the second he is charged with being King of the Jews. The change is expedient: a charge of blasphemy would not have impressed a pragmatic Roman procurator, whereas one of treason would certainly have struck a chord. But how ironic that, having accused Jesus of blasphemy because he failed to live up to being the kind of messiah the Jews expected—a nationalist messiah—the chief-priests were now prepared to condemn him before Pilate as precisely

63. We should beware, however, of an apparent discrepancy between Mark and John here. Mark seems to indicate that the saying about Jesus' destruction of the Temple was being falsely attributed to him (Mk 14.57-58), whereas John does ascribe a very similar utterance to Jesus (Jn 2.19), but argues that the Jews misunderstood it. It is significant that in John, Jesus does not himself threaten to destroy the Temple, but says only that if it were destroyed, he could raise it up—and then, says John, he has in mind his own body, not the Temple building (Jn 2.21). Reading between the lines, it could well be that Jesus did say something about the Temple, perhaps along the lines of the pronouncement in Jn 2.19, and that Jesus' opponents took it out of context and exaggerated it.

On the use of intercalation in Markan irony, see G. van Oyen, 'Intercalation and Irony in the Gospel of Mark', in F. van Segbroech, *et al.* (eds.), *The Four Gospels 1992* (Festschrift Frans Neirynck; BETL, 100: Leuven: Leuven University Press, 1992), pp. 949-74.

that kind of political figure. To my knowledge, Lane was the first to point this out,[64] though it has been noted by others since.

vi) *Mark 15.16-20*. Again, we have an instance of sarcastic irony, and once more it works at two levels. The soldiers, in hailing Jesus as King of the Jews (15.18),[65] are obviously being overtly ironic, but the reader knows that they are the real victims because, for the Markan community, Jesus is indeed King of the Jews. E.M. Good would no doubt wish to question this assessment. Sarcasm, he says, is too heavy-handed to be called irony, which 'uses a lighter tone, and will therefore have a more ambiguous effect'.[66] It is true that the soldiers' sarcasm in 15.16-20 is obvious, but it is irony for all that if, by 'irony', we have in mind the broad classical definition of 'saying one thing and meaning another'.[67] However that may be, the significant point is that the sarcastic irony (or sarcasm) which operates at one level serves to make the irony operating at the second level much more potent. The truth that Jesus really is King of the Jews strikes home all the harder because the soldiers, in mockery, *say* he is.

vii) *Mark 15.29-39*. When Jesus is nailed to the cross, irony is heaped on irony to form a rich tapestry. The nearer Jesus gets to the cross, it seems, the more ironical the narrative becomes. Let us try to unpick the strands:
    1. *Mark 15.29*. As Jesus hangs on the cross, the passers-by taunt him with the accusation made by the witnesses at his trial before the High Priest (14.58)—that he had claimed he would destroy the Temple and build another in three days. Here we have the same pattern of dramatic irony that we so frequently find elsewhere in the Passion narrative. The mockers use sarcastic irony, but are not fully cognisant of what they are saying, for, as Mark's readers are aware, Jesus does indeed fulfil the terms of the charge. The 'three days' provides the clue to interpreting it, and John, in his Gospel (Jn 2.21), spells it out: the Temple he raises up is that of his body. But, of course, the mockers are aware only of the surface meaning of the statement. It is interesting that in John's Gospel,

64. Lane, *Mark*, pp. 550-51.
65. On Mk 15.18, see Booth, *Rhetoric of Irony*, pp. 28-29, 91-92.
66. Good, *Irony in the Old Testament*, p. 26.
67. Quintilian, *Inst.Or.* 6.2.15.

too, it provides the occasion for irony.[68]

2. *Mark 15.31*. The mockery is sustained, providing Mark with the opportunity to indulge himself in the irony it affords. 'He saved others; he cannot save himself', the chief priests cry. In saying this, they fall victim to irony on two counts. First, their own attempt to be ironic backfires because, for the reader, Jesus genuinely *did* save others. The second part of the saying is a direct statement of belief: there is no attempt on the part of the opponents to be ironic here; nevertheless, they still turn out to be in error. 'He cannot save himself.' Yes, perhaps there is some truth in that, but the chief priests and scribes fail to realize the greater truth that Jesus is saved—or vindicated—by God himself; and to that fact, the empty tomb bears testimony.

3. *Mark 15.32*. 'Let the Christ, the King of Israel, come down now from the cross, that we may see and believe.' Like the Pharisees in 8.11-12, the chief priests here want visible proof that Jesus is the messiah, so the irony of the earlier passage is repeated here: if the chief priests had only had the eyes to see (that is, the eyes of faith), they would have seen God at work throughout Jesus' ministry. There is irony, too, in that these opponents, normally so hard to please or convince, would have been satisfied in seeing Jesus descend unaided from the cross, for the fact that he has to be taken down from it as a dead body turns out to be in preparation for an even greater spectacle—his resurrection from the dead. In demanding the lesser miracle, the chief priests are unconsciously trivializing God's power. They do not, of course, even expect Jesus to step down from the cross. When he is taken down dead, they feel that their own sarcastic irony has been vindicated, but in fact it is Jesus who is vindicated—and his opponents are confounded—when, on the third day, he is raised from the dead.

4. *Mark 15.34-36*. Jesus' cry of dereliction, 'My God, my God, why hast thou forsaken me?' has some delicate ironical touches. At one level it seems that the one who claimed identity with God in 14.62 now feels abandoned by him. But, at the very moment when God would seem to have deserted him, the bystanders unknowingly give expression to the

---

68. The irony in Jn 2.19-21 arises from the fact that the Jews take Jesus to be referring to the Temple building rather than metaphorically to himself. The reference to 'three days' should, of course, alert the reader to the fact that Jesus *is* speaking metaphorically, but just in case this fact is not grasped, John provides the additional information that Jesus is speaking about the Temple of his body. This is an irony as stable as the author can make it.

possibility of his messianic identity, for they misinterpret Jesus' Aramaic to mean that he is summoning Elijah, the very prophet who, according to popular tradition, was to herald the arrival of the messiah. 'Let us see whether Elijah will come to take him down', declare the bystanders. But the impression we receive is that they are engaging in idle superstition; they do not really *expect* anything to happen. Yet the reader of Mark's Gospel knows that Jesus has been closely associated with Elijah throughout. He has been mistaken for him (6.15; 8.28); he has spoken with him (9.4); and John the Baptist has been identified with him (9.12-13) in order to show that Jesus is indeed the one who should come after, the messiah. The bystanders, of course, are oblivious to all this.

There is, however, one further layer of irony to be considered. It has been commonly recognized that the cry of dereliction (15.34) is in fact a quotation from Ps. 22.1, and this opens up the possibility of there being a hint of unstable irony here even though, as we have said, unstable irony was most uncommon in the ancient world. Let us see, though, how the situation works out. The reader clearly has an advantage over the characters in the story. The latter misunderstand what Jesus is saying, whereas the reader can see the irony of a man who claims identity with God (or at least accepts identity as God's messiah) in 14.62, but then feels abandoned by him in 15.34. The reader must feel at this stage that he or she has been led onto a stable platform. But has he or she? There may be a further irony for the more perceptive reader which will serve to reverse the previous one. Those who were familiar with the whole of Psalm 22 (and that would probably have included most of the Markan church) would have been aware that although it is essentially a psalm of lament, and begins as such, it concludes on a note of confidence, affirming God's power (Ps. 22.22-31). So, in uttering the first words of the psalm, Jesus may have simultaneously had in mind its affirmative ending. The final irony, then, could be that at the very moment when it seemed that God's own Son had been abandoned by his Father, he was in the act of extolling his name and affirming his omnipotence. To arrive at this ultimate understanding, the reader must have the insight and the courage to step from the platform of what appears to be stable irony, into the unstable waters of a yet deeper irony.

5. *Mark 15.39*. Although, in translation, the centurion at the cross is reported as saying, 'Truly, this man was *the* Son of God', there is no article in the original Greek. At the narrative level, therefore, the centurion could be taken to mean, 'Truly, this man was innocent', as the

commentators have frequently observed.[69] In that case, the centurion himself is an innocent ironic victim, since he is unaware of the deeper truth of his words. For the reader, however, their full impact is evident. It is precisely at the moment of Jesus' death that a human character (as opposed to a demon) announces what the author has declared from the outset, that this man is none other than the Son of God. And, again ironically, it is not announced by the religious leaders, who might have been expected to declare it, but by one of those whom they despised—a Gentile.

vii) *Mark 15.42-43.* Significantly, after the climax of the Gospel has been reached, and the narrative tension slackens off, the web of ironies begins to dissolve. In the aftermath of the cross, only the odd independent irony remains. Perhaps we can see one in the reference to the Day of Preparation (15.42). Preparation for what? Well, at one level, preparation for the Sabbath. But running alongside this is another idea. Jesus' body is taken down from the cross, wrapped in linen, and laid in a tomb. We might see in this the first stages of preparation for Jesus' burial, a job which the women intend to complete after the Sabbath. So, the Day of Preparation for the Sabbath is at the same time a day of preparation for something else. What the characters of the story-world do not realize, however, is that their preparations will turn out not to be for Jesus' burial at all, but for his resurrection. They are attending to a body which they think is destined for decomposition, but which in fact is destined for new life.

Finally, we can note that the person who receives Jesus' body from the cross is not a member of his family or one of his disciples, but a 'respected member of the council', Joseph of Arimathea (15.43-45). Earlier, the chief priests and scribes had challenged Jesus to come down from the cross (15.32), so it is ironic that the person who takes him down from there after his death should be one of their own number, a member of the very council (the Sanhedrin) which had condemned him.

6. *Summary*

The first section of this chapter dealt with the history of irony both in the Classical period, and in more recent times. We saw that irony, as

---

69. The various interpretations of the centurion's declaration in Mk 15.39 are conveniently discussed in Gundry, *Mark*, pp. 973-75.

presented dramatically in the interplay between the εἴρων and the ἀλαζών, was in regular use long before it became a rhetorical figure of speech. Mark, himself no mean dramatist, must have been aware of this development, for he uses irony supremely well in his Gospel.

In the following section I undertook a brief survey of studies in biblical irony. Clavier, Good and Jónsson represent the first generation of biblical 'ironists', and can rightly be regarded as pioneers. As with all pioneers, of course, they were responsible for laying the foundation on which later scholars have built, but they did not manage to develop a solid methodology by which to proceed, so that, in consequence, some of their conclusions were rather nebulous.

The second generation of biblical 'ironists' includes Culpepper, Duke and O'Day. Their work is more methodologically sound, and they tend to draw similar conclusions, perhaps because they are all dependent upon the work of the literary-critics Muecke and Booth. Some later scholars have regarded this dependency as a weakness, but mutual reliance upon works written 25 years ago does not of itself invalidate the conclusions reached.

The most recent studies of biblical irony, those of Botha and Camery-Hoggatt, are more interdisciplinary in character than the earlier studies. Botha makes use of the speech-act theory developed by Austin and Searle in the late 1960s and early 1970s, but, while his approach is innovative, it is doubtful that it takes us any further along the road in understanding biblical irony than the studies made by his predecessors. In Camery-Hoggatt's contribution, the study of irony tends to get lost in a maze of interdisciplinary issues: sociology of knowledge and narrative-criticism are discussed as disciplines in their own right, and not simply as factors in the ironic puzzle. However, Camery-Hoggatt's keen awareness of the concept of community as an indispensable factor in any full discussion of irony is certainly useful.

The final section of the chapter deals with irony in Mark's Gospel. I argued, by way of introduction, that the irony of Mark's day would have been stable and unsophisticated, and that most of the categories enumerated and discussed by Muecke would be irrelevant to the evangelist's work. However, some categories, particularly dramatic and sarcastic irony, are as applicable to ancient as to modern literature, and it is hardly surprising that they feature in the Gospel.

In the final survey of ironic passages in Mark, we discovered a rich tapestry of examples of various types which operate at various levels—

verbal and situational, local and extended, stable and unstable. Although a good deal has already been written on Markan irony, the ironic vein runs deep into the literary infrastructure of his Gospel, and is far from having been exhausted.

CONCLUSION

Markan scholarship has come a long way since those primitive critical endeavours of the eighteenth century. The next two hundred years of traditional literary-criticism produced, in successive, but overlapping phases, source-, form- and redaction-criticism; but always the underlying assumption was that the texts under scrutiny were essentially about historical events. Today's modern brands of literary-criticism, and narrative-criticism in particular, have rather set aside the issue of historicity. In dealing with implied authors and readers, and their creation of or inter-action with the story-world, we have in view a narrative dimension of reality which does not, or need not, impinge upon the historical question at all; the Markan narrative can just as easily be understood without it. Indeed, the prospect of historical truths are inimical to the work of some narrative critics:

> It is one matter that the gospel narrative claims to be true; it is quite another matter whether it actually is true. Can it, for example, withstand historical criticism that mercilessly adopts the task of assessing its credibility as a source of actual historical events? The answer here is clear: it cannot. From an historical viewpoint that remains true to itself, the gospel narrative as it directly appears, i.e. as a single coherent assertion, is of no value as a source for the events it recounts.[1]

It is true enough that the narrative-critic need not, and perhaps should not concern himself with the Jesus of history when he or she seeks to apply narrative-critical canons to the Gospel material; but equally, narrative-criticism does not *preclude* the historical; it can perfectly well operate alongside it. History is simply a separate issue which can be considered in its own right independently of the Gospel as pure story, and that is the policy I have sought to adopt in the present work. It is of no concern to me here to discover whether Jesus actually walked on water, or healed blind Bartimaeus; but that is not to say it is of no

---

1. O. Davidsen, *The Narrative Jesus: A Semiotic Reading of Mark's Gospel* (Aarhus: Aarhus University Press, 1993), p. 365.

concern at all; to millions of believers it clearly is, and to challenge the historicity of such events seems unwarranted unless good reasons to do so are forthcoming. The sceptical approach of Ole Davidsen, the author of the quote above, appears to be challenged by that scholar himself when he admits that an historical source should be accepted as credible unless it is, (i) contradicted by other sources in which the historian has greater confidence, and, (ii) contradicted by his understanding of reality. Claims to the historicity of the Markan narrative remain unaffected by criterion (i), since we do not have other accounts contemporary with it (other than the Gospel parallels) for the purposes of comparison. Criterion (ii) must be unpacked before it can become applicable. The Gospel narratives neednot contradict the modern historian's understanding of reality, and if historians disagree over this issue, how do we determine who is right? Yet, on Davidsen's view, this is precisely what we must do if we are to make an objective judgment as to whether or not the Markan narrative is historically credible. Given the criteria supplied, we must surely accept the fundamental historicity of Mark's account until it can be proven otherwise.

But if, as I suggested above, the question of historicity is peripheral to the concerns of narrative-criticism, of what permanent value is this discipline? Why study Mark's Gospel in the manner of a literary classic? The basic answer must surely be the one given for *any* literary classic—a Shakespeare play, or a Hardy novel, for example: it opens up for us new worlds of truth. It enables us to discover fresh realms of being, and there to be baptized into new depths of faith hitherto unexplored. And unlike the objective historical quest, the reader's voyage into the story-world is a personal pilgrimage towards his or her own spiritual identity—a quest for what it means to be human, and how the divine breaks in upon one's experience of the mundane. By engaging with the narrative characters, and their activities as mapped out by the implied author, the reader—or more precisely the reader's second, implied, self—is able to discover anew the significance of the mythical Christ for his or her own life of faith and personal destiny. As into the Pauline waters of baptism (Rom. 6.3-4), the reader immerses his or her old, mundane self into the story-world of Mark, and re-emerges as the new, dynamic person of the Spirit, for whom the title Son of God is no longer an anachronistic or exhausted christological claim buried by history, but a living acclamation at the heart of the new life of faith. Mark's is an existential text that draws its reader to the foot of the cross and impels him or her to decision. In engaging with it one must choose, and is chosen by it, and the result is the shaping of one's eternal destiny, no less. In this book I have sought, by way of survey and comment, to outline the mechanics of this process, suggesting how implied author and implied reader interact to produce a living, dynamic text which ever and again renews and reinterprets itself in the heart and mind of the believer. If I have been even partially successful in that quest, my labours will not have been in vain.

BIBLIOGRAPHY

1. *Primary Sources*

Aeschylus, *Prometheus Bound and Other Plays* (trans. P. Vellacott; Harmondsworth: Penguin, 1961).

Aristophanes, *The Clouds* (LCL; trans. B.B. Rogers; Cambridge, MA: Harvard University Press; London: Heinemann, 1924).

Aristotle, *Nichomachean Ethics* (LCL; trans. H. Rackham; Cambridge, MA: Harvard University Press; London: Heinemann, 1926)

—*Ars Rhetorica* (LCL; trans. J.H. Freese; Cambridge, MA: Harvard University Press, 1982; London: Heinemann, 1926).

—*Poetics* (LCL; trans. W. Hamilton Fyfe; Cambridge, MA: Harvard University Press; London: Heinemann, 1927).

Cicero, *De Oratore* (LCL; 2 vols.; trans. E.W. Sutton and H. Rackham; Cambridge, MA: Harvard University Press; London: Heinemann, 1939–54).

[Cicero], *Rhetorica ad Herennium* (LCL; trans. H. Caplan; Cambridge, MA: Harvard University Press; London: Heinemann, 1954)

Euripides, *The Bacchae and Other Plays* (trans. P. Vellacott; Harmondsworth: Penguin, 1954).

Eusebius, *The Ecclesiastical History* (LCL; 2 vols.; trans. K. Lake, J.E.L. Oulton and H.J. Lawlor; Cambridge, MA: Harvard University Press; London: Heinemann, 1926–32).

Quintilian, *Institutio Oratoria* (LCL; 4 vols.; trans. H.E. Butler; Cambridge, MA: Harvard University Press; London: Heinemann, 1920–22).

Plato, *The Republic* (LCL; 2 vols.; trans. P. Shorey; Cambridge, MA: Harvard University Press; London: Heinemann, 1930–35).

Seneca, *Four Tragedies and Octavia* (trans. E.F. Watling; Harmondsworth: Penguin, 1966).

Seneca, *Three Tragedies* (trans. F. Ahl; Ithaca, NY: Cornell University Press, 1986).

Sophocles, *The Three Theban Plays* (trans. R. Fagles; Harmondsworth: Penguin, 1984).

Theophrastus, *Characters* (LCL; trans. J.M. Edmonds; Cambridge, MA: Harvard University Press; London: Heinemann, 1929).

2. *Secondary Literature*

Abrams, M.H., *A Glossary of Literary Terms* (New York: Holt, Rinehart & Winston, 5th edn, 1988).

Achtemeier, P.J., 'Toward the Isolation of Pre-Markan Miracle Catenae', *JBL* 89 (1970), pp. 265-91.

—'The Origin and Function of the Pre-Markan Miracle Catenae', *JBL* 91 (1972), pp. 198-221.

Albertz, M., *Die synoptischen Streitgespräche* (Berlin: Trowitzsch & Sohn, 1921).

Amante, D., 'The Theory of Ironic Speech Acts', *Poetics Today* 2 (1981), pp. 77-96.

Anderson, H., *The Gospel of Mark* (London: Oliphants, 1976).

Bacon, B.W., 'Pharisees and Herodians in Mark', *JBL* 39 (1920), pp. 102-12.

—*Studies in Matthew* (London: Constable, 1930).

Beach, C., *The Gospel of Mark: Its Making and Meaning* (New York: Harper & Row, 1959).

Beavis, M.-A., 'The Trial Before the Sanhedrin (Mark 14:53-65): Reader-Response and Greco-Roman Readers', *CBQ* 49 (1987), pp. 581-96.

Bennett, W.J., 'The Herodians of Mark's Gospel', *NovT* 17 (1975), pp. 9-14.

Bergson, L., 'Eiron und Eironeia', *Hermes* 99 (1971), pp. 409-22.

Best, E., *The Temptation and the Passion: The Markan Soteriology* (SNTSMS, 2; Cambridge: Cambridge University Press, 1965).

—'The Role of the Disciples in Mark', *NTS* 23 (1976–77), pp. 377-401.

—*Following Jesus: Discipleship in the Gospel of Mark* (JSNTSup, 4; Sheffield: JSOT Press, 1981).

Bickerman, E., 'Les Hérodiens', *RB* 47 (1938), pp. 184-97.

Bilezikian, G.G., *The Liberated Gospel: A Comparison of the Gospel of Mark and Greek Tragedy* (Grand Rapids: Baker, 1977).

Black, C.C., *The Disciples according to Mark: Markan Redaction in Current Debate* (JSNTSup, 27; Sheffield: JSOT Press, 1989).

—*Mark: Images of an Apostolic Interpreter* (Columbia: University of South Carolina Press, 1994).

Bland, D.S., 'Endangering the Reader's Neck: Background Description in the Novel', in Stevick (ed.), *Theory of the Novel*, pp. 313-31.

Bleich, D., *Readings and Feelings: An Introduction to Subjective Criticism* (Urbana, IL: National Council of Teachers of English, 1975).

—*Subjective Criticism* (Baltimore: The Johns Hopkins University Press, 1978).

Booth, W.C., *The Rhetoric of Fiction* (Chicago: University of Chicago Press, 1961 [Harmondsworth: Penguin, 2nd edn, 1983]).

—'Distance and Point of View: An Essay in Clarification', in Stevick (ed.), *Theory of the Novel*, pp. 87-107.

—*A Rhetoric of Irony* (Chicago: University of Chicago Press, 1974).

Bornkamm, G., G. Barth and H.J. Held, *Tradition and Interpretation in Matthew* (trans. P. Scott; London: SCM Press, 1963).

Botha, J.E., 'The Case of Johannine Irony Re-Opened', *Neotestamentica* 25 (1991), pp. 209-32.

Bower, G.H., 'Experiments on Story Understanding and Recall', *QJEP* 28 (1976), pp. 511-34.

Bruce, F.F., 'The End of the Second Gospel', *EvQ* 17 (1945), pp. 169-81.

Büchner, W., 'Über den Begriff der Eirōneia', *Hermes* 76 (1941), pp. 339-58.

Bultmann, R., *The History of the Synoptic Tradition* (trans. J. Marsh; Oxford: Basil Blackwell, 1963).

Burch, E.W., 'Tragic Action in the Second Gospel: A Study in the Narrative of Mark', *JR* 11 (1931), pp. 346-58.

Cadoux, A.T., *The Sources of the Second Gospel* (London: James Clarke, 1935).

Camery-Hoggatt, J., *Irony in Mark's Gospel: Text and Subtext* (SNTSMS, 72; Cambridge: Cambridge University Press, 1992).

Capel, J.C., and S.D. Moore (eds.), *Mark and Method: New Approaches in Biblical Studies* (Augsburg: Fortress Press, 1992).

Case, S.J. (ed.), *Studies in Early Christianity* (New York: Century, 1928).

Casey, M., *Son of Man: The Introduction and Influence of Daniel 7* (London: SPCK, 1979).

Chatman, S., *Story and Discourse: Narrative Structure in Fiction and Film* (Ithaca, NY: Cornell University Press, 1978).

Clavier, H., 'La méthode ironique dans l'enseignement de Jésus', *ETR* 4 (1929), pp. 224-41, 323-44.

—'L'ironie dans l'enseignement de Jésus', *NovT* 1 (1956), pp. 3-20.

Collins, R.F., *Introduction to the New Testament* (London: SCM Press, 1983).

Conzelmann, H., *The Theology of St Luke* (trans. G. Buswell; London: Faber, 1960).

Cook, M.J., *Mark's Treatment of the Jewish Leaders* (NovTSup, 51; Leiden: Brill, 1978).

Crane, R.S., 'The Concept of Plot', in Scholes (ed.), *Approaches to the Novel*, pp. 233-43.

Crossan, J.D., 'Mark and the Relatives of Jesus', *NovT* 15 (1973), pp. 81-113.

—'Empty Tomb and Absent Lord', in Kelber (ed.), *The Passion in Mark*, pp. 135-52.

Culler, J., *Structuralist Poetics: Structuralism, Linguistics and the Study of Literature* (Ithaca, NY: Cornell University Press, 1975).

Cullmann, O., *Christ and Time: The Primitive Christian Conception of Time and History* (trans. F.V. Filson; Philadelphia: Westminster Press, 1964).

Culpepper, R.A., *Anatomy of the Fourth Gospel* (Philadelphia: Fortress Press, 1983).

Daniel, C., 'Les "Hérodiens" du Nouveau Testament sont-ils des Esséniens?', *RevQ* 6 (1966), pp. 31-53.

Danker, F.W., 'The Demonic Secret in Mark: A Re-examination of the Cry of Dereliction (15:34)', *ZNW* 61 (1970), pp. 48-69.

Daube, D., 'ἐξουσία in Mk 1:22 and 27', *JTS* 39 (1938), pp. 45-59.

—*The New Testament and Rabbinic Judaism* (London: Athlone Press, 1956).

—'Responsibilities of Master and Disciples in the Gospels', *NTS* 19 (1972–73), pp. 1-15.

Davidsen, O., *The Narrative Jesus: A Semiotic Reading of Mark's Gospel* (Aarhus: Aarhus University Press, 1993).

Derrett, J.D.M., '"Eating Up the Houses of Widows": Jesus' Comment on Lawyers', *NovT* 14 (1972), pp. 1-9.

Dewey, J., *Markan Public Debate: Literary Technique, Concentric Structure and Theology in Mark 2:1-3:6* (SBLDS, 48; Chico, CA: Scholars Press, 1980).

—'Point of View and the Disciples in Mark', *SBL Seminar Papers* (1982), pp. 97-106.

—'Oral Methods of Structuring Narrative in Mark', *Int* 43 (1989), pp. 32-44.

—'Mark as Interwoven Tapestry: Forecasts and Echoes for a Listening Audience', *CBQ* 53 (1991), pp. 221-36.

—'The Gospel of Mark as an Oral-Aural Event: Implications for Interpretation', in McKnight and Malbon (eds.), *New Literary Criticism*, pp. 145-63.

Dibelius, M., *From Tradition to Gospel* (trans. B. Lee Woolf; Cambridge: James Clarke, 1935).

Dobschütz, E., von, 'Zur Erzählerkunst der Markus', *ZNW* 27 (1928), pp. 193-98.

Dodd, C.H., 'The Framework of the Gospel Narrative', *ExpTim* 43 (1930–31), pp. 396-400.

Donahue, J.R., *Are You the Christ? The Trial Narrative in the Gospel of Mark* (SBLDS, 10; Missoula, MT: SBL, 1973).

Donove, P.L., *The End of Mark's Story: A Methodological Study* (Leiden: Brill, 1993).

Duke, P.D., *Irony in the Fourth Gospel* (Atlanta: John Knox, 1985).

Easton, B.S., 'A Primitive Tradition in Mark', in Case (ed.), *Studies in Early Christianity*, pp. 85-101

Edwards, J.R., 'Markan Sandwiches: The Significance of Interpolations in the Markan Narrative', *NovT* 31 (1989), pp. 193-216.

Egan, K., 'What Is a Plot?', *NLH* 9 (1977–78), pp. 455-73.

Eliot, T.S., *Collected Poems 1909–62* (London: Faber & Faber, 1963)

Enslin, M.S., 'The Artistry of Mark', *JBL* 66 (1947), pp. 385-99.

Ferguson, J., *A Companion to Greek Tragedy* (Austin: University of Texas Press, 1972).

Fetterley, J., *The Resisting Reader: A Feminist Approach to American Fiction* (Bloomington: Indiana University Press, 1978).

Fish, S., *Self-Consuming Artifacts: The Experience of Seventeenth-Century Literature* (Berkeley: University of California Press, 1972).

Forster, E.M., *Aspects of the Novel* (Harmondsworth: Penguin, 1962)

Fowler, R.M., *Loaves and Fishes: The Function of the Feeding Stories in the Gospel of Mark* (SBLDS, 54; Chico, CA: Scholars Press, 1981).

—*Let the Reader Understand: Reader-Response Criticism and the Gospel of Mark* (Minneapolis: Fortress Press, 1991).

—'Reader-Response Criticism: Figuring Mark's Reader', in Capel and Moore (eds.), *Mark and Method*, pp. 50-83.

Freyne, S., *Galilee, Jesus and the Gospels: Literary Approaches and Historical Investigations* (Philadelphia: Fortress Press, 1988).

Friedman, N., 'Point of View in Fiction: The Development of a Critical Concept', in Stevick (ed.), *Theory of the Novel*, pp. 108-37.

—'Forms of the Plot', in Stevick (ed.), *Theory of the Novel*, pp. 145-66.

Frye, R.M., 'A Literary Perspective for the Criticism of the Gospels', in D.G. Miller and D.Y. Hadidian (eds.), *Jesus and Man's Hope* (Pittsburgh: Pittsburgh Theological Seminary, 1971), pp. 192-221.

Funk, R.W., *The Poetics of Biblical Narrative* (Sonoma, CA: Polebridge Press, 1988).

Genette, G., *Narrative Discourse: An Essay in Method* (trans. J.E. Lewin; Ithaca, NY: Cornell University Press, 1980).

Ginzberg, L., *The Legends of the Jews*, IV (Philadelphia: Jewish Publication Society of America, 1938).

Good, E.M., *Irony in the Old Testament* (London: SPCK, 1965).

Grene, D., and R. Lattimore (eds.), *Greek Tragedies*, II (Chicago: University of Chicago Press, 1960).

Guelich, R.A., *Mark 1–8:26* (WBC, 34A; Dallas: Word Books, 1989).

Gundry, R.H., *Mark: A Commentary on his Apology for the Cross* (Grand Rapids: Eerdmans, 1993).

Hartman, G., 'Literary Criticism and Its Discontents', *Critical Inquiry* 3 (1976), pp. 203-20.

Hawkins, J.C., *Horae Synopticae* (Oxford: Clarendon Press, 1909).

Henaut, B.W., *Oral Tradition and the Gospels: The Problem of Mark 4* (JSNTSup, 82; Sheffield: JSOT Press, 1993).

Hirsch, E.D., *Validity in Interpretation* (New Haven: Yale University Press, 1967).

Hoehner, H.W., *Herod Antipas* (SNTSMS, 17; Cambridge: Cambridge University Press, 1972).

Holland, N., *5 Readers Reading* (New Haven: Yale University Press, 1975).

—'Unity, Identity, Text, Self', *PMLA* 90 (1975), pp. 813-22.

—'The New Paradigm: Subjective or Transactive?', *NLH* 7 (1976), pp. 335-46.

Hooker, M.D., *The Son of Man in Mark* (London: SPCK, 1967).

—*The Message of Mark* (London: Epworth Press, 1983).

—*The Gospel according to St Mark* (London: A. & C. Black, 1991).

Hultgren, A.J., *Jesus and his Adversaries: The Form and Function of the Conflict Stories in the Synoptic Tradition* (Minneapolis: Augsburg, 1979).

Iser, W., 'The Reading Process: A Phenomenological Approach', *NLH* 3 (1972), pp. 279-99.

—*The Implied Reader* (Baltimore: The Johns Hopkins University Press, 1974).

James, H., *The Art of the Novel* (London: Scribner, 1935).

Jauss, H.R., 'Literary History as a Challenge to Literary Theory', *NLH* 2 (1970), pp. 7-37.

Jeremias, J., *The Parables of Jesus* (trans. S.H. Hooke; London: SCM Press, rev. edn, 1963).

Johnson, R.E., 'Recall of Prose as a Function of the Structural Importance of the Linguistic Units', *JVLVB* 9 (1970), pp. 12-20.

Jónsson, J., *Humour and Irony in the New Testament* (Leiden: Brill, 1985).

Joüon, P., 'Les "Hérodiens" de l'évangile', *RSR* 28 (1938), pp. 585-88.

Keck, L.E., 'The Introduction to Mark's Gospel', *NTS* 12 (1965–66), pp. 352-70.

Kelber, W.H., *The Kingdom in Mark* (Philadelphia: Fortress Press, 1974).

—'Mark and the Oral Tradition', *Semeia* 16 (1979), pp. 7-55.

—*The Oral and the Written Gospel: The Hermeneutics of Speaking and Writing in the Synoptic Tradition, Mark, Paul, and Q* (Philadelphia: Fortress Press, 1983).

Kelber, W.H. (ed.), *The Passion in Mark: Studies on Mark 14–16* (Philadelphia: Fortress Press, 1976).

Kennedy, G.A., *New Testament Interpretation through Rhetorical Criticism* (Chapel Hill: University of North Carolina Press, 1984)

Kingsbury, J.D., *Conflict in Mark: Jesus, Authorities, Disciples* (Minneapolis: Fortress Press, 1989).

—'The Religious Authorities in the Gospel of Mark', *NTS* 36 (1990), pp. 42-65.

Klijn, A.F.J., 'Scribes, Pharisees, Highpriests and Elders in the New Testament', *NovT* 3 (1959), pp. 259-67.

Knox, W.L., *The Sources of the Synoptic Gospels.* I. *Mark* (Cambridge: Cambridge University Press, 1953).

Kuhn, H.-W., *Ältere Sammlungen im Markusevangelium* (SUNT, 8; Göttingen: Vandenhoeck & Ruprecht, 1971).

Lambrecht, J., 'The Relatives of Jesus in Mark', *NovT* 16 (1974), pp. 241-58.

Lane, W.L., *The Gospel of Mark* (Grand Rapids: Eerdmans, 1974).

Lang, F.G., 'Kompositionsanalyse des Markusevangeliums', *ZTK* 74 (1977), pp. 1-24.

Lategan, B.C., 'Coming to Grips with the Reader', *Semeia* 48 (1989), pp. 3-17.

Latourelle, R., *Finding Jesus through the Gospels: History and Hermeneutics* (trans. A. Owen; Staten Island, NY: Alba House, 1979).

Lawrence, D.H., *The Collected Poems of D.H. Lawrence* (ed. V. de Sola Pinto and F. Warren Roberts; Harmondsworth: Penguin, 1977).

—*Sons and Lovers* (Harmondsworth: Penguin, 1948).

—*The Rainbow* (Harmondsworth: Penguin, 1981).

Lightfoot, R.H., *Locality and Doctrine in the Gospels* (London: Hodder & Stoughton, 1938).

—*The Gospel Message of Mark* (Oxford: Clarendon Press, 1950).

Lindars, B., *Jesus, Son of Man* (London: SPCK, 1983).

Lohmeyer, E., *Galiläa und Jerusalem* (Göttingen: Vandenhoeck & Ruprecht, 1936).

Lohr, C.H., 'Oral Techniques in the Gospel of Matthew', *CBQ* 23 (1961), pp. 403-35.

Longman, T., III, *Literary Approaches to Biblical Interpretation* (Leicester: Apollos, 1987).

Lord, A.B., *The Singer of Tales* (Harvard Studies in Comparative Literature, 24; Cambridge, MA: Harvard University Press, 1960).

—'Homer as Oral Poet', *HSCP* 72 (1967), pp. 1-46.

—'The Gospels as Oral Traditional Literature', in W.O. Walker (ed.), *The Relationships among the Gospels: An Interdisciplinary Dialogue* (San Antonio, TX: Trinity University Press, 1978), pp. 33-91.

Lubbock, P., 'The Craft of Fiction: Picture, Drama and Point of View', in Scholes (ed.), *Approaches to the Novel*, pp. 245-63.

Mailloux, S., 'Reader-Response Criticism?' *Genre* 10 (1977), pp. 413-31.

Maisch, I., *Die Heilung des Gelähmten* (SBS, 52; Stuttgart: KBW, 1971).

Malbon, E.S., 'Galilee and Jerusalem: History and Literature in Marcan Interpretation', *CBQ* 44 (1982), pp. 242-55.

—'Fallible Followers: Women and Men in the Gospel of Mark', *Semeia* 28 (1983), pp. 29-48.

—'The Jesus of Mark and the Sea of Galilee', *JBL* 103 (1984), pp. 363-77.

—'Disciples/Crowds/Whoever: Markan Characters and Readers', *NovT* 28 (1986), pp. 104-30.

—'The Jewish Leaders in the Gospel of Mark: A Literary Study of Marcan Characterization', *JBL* 108 (1989), pp. 259-81.

—*Narrative Space and Mythic Meaning in Mark* (Sheffield: JSOT Press, 1991).

—'Narrative Criticism: How Does the Story Mean?', in Capel and Moore (eds.), *Mark and Method*, pp. 23-49.

—'The Major Importance of the Minor Characters in Mark', in McKnight and Malbon (eds.), *New Literary Criticism*, pp. 58-86.

Malina, B.J., 'Christ and Time: Swiss or Mediterranean?', *CBQ* 51 (1989), pp. 1-31.

Mandler, J.M., and N.S. Johnson, 'Remembrance of Things Parsed: Story Structure and Recall', *CogPs* 9 (1977), pp. 111-51.

Markantonatos, G., 'On the Origin and Meanings of the Word εἰρωνεία', *Rivista di filologia e di istruzione classica* 103 (1975), pp. 16-21.

Marxsen, W., *Mark the Evangelist* (trans. R.A. Harrisville; Nashville: Abingdon Press, 1969).

Matera, F.J., 'The Plot of Matthew's Gospel', *CBQ* 49 (1987), pp. 233-53.

McKnight, E.V., *The Bible and the Reader: An Introduction to Literary Criticism* (Philadelphia: Fortress Press, 1985).

McKnight, E.V., and E.S. Malbon (eds.), *The New Literary Criticism and the New Testament* (Valley Forge, PA: Trinity Press International, 1994).

Mendilow, A.A., 'The Position of the Present in Fiction', in Stevick (ed.), *Theory of the Novel*, pp. 255-80.

Meyer, B.F., 'What Is Recalled after Hearing a Passage?', *JEdPs* 65 (1973), pp. 109-17.

—'What Is Remembered from Prose: A Function of Passage Structure', in R.O. Freedle (ed.), *Discourse Production and Comprehension* (Norwood, NJ: Ablex, 1977), pp. 307-36.

Moore, S.D., *Literary Criticism and the Gospels: The Theoretical Challenge* (New Haven: Yale University Press, 1989).

Muecke, D.C., *The Compass of Irony* (London: Methuen, 1969).

—*Irony and the Ironic* (The Critical Idiom, 13; London: Methuen, 1970).

Nineham, D.E., 'The Order of Events in St Mark's Gospel—An Examination of Dr Dodd's Hypothesis', in D.E. Nineham (ed.), *Studies in the Gospels: Essays in Memory of R.H. Lightfoot* (Oxford: Basil Blackwell, 1955), pp. 223-39.

—*Saint Mark* (Harmondsworth: Penguin, 1963).

Notopoulos, J.A., 'Parataxis in Homer: A New Approach to Homeric Literary Criticism', *TAPA* 80 (1949), pp. 1-23.

—'Continuity and Interconnexion in Homeric Oral Composition', *TAPA* 82 (1951), pp. 81-101.

O'Day, G.R., *Revelation in the Fourth Gospel: Narrative Mode and Theological Claim* (Philadelphia: Fortress Press, 1986).

Ong, W.J., 'The Writer's Audience Is Always a Fiction', *PMLA* 90 (1975), pp. 9-21.

—*Orality and Literacy: The Technologizing of the Word* (London: Methuen, 1982).

—'Text as Interpretation: Mark and After', *Semeia* 39 (1987), pp. 7-26.

Parry, M., 'Studies in the Epic Technique of Oral Verse-Making: I. Homer and Homeric Style', *HSCP* 41 (1930), pp. 73-147.

—'Studies in the Epic Technique of Oral Verse-Making: II. The Homeric Language as the Language of Oral Poetry', *HSCP* 43 (1932), pp. 1-50.

Pavlovskis, Z., 'Aristotle, Horace and the Ironic Man', *Classical Philology* 63 (1968), pp. 22-41.

Peabody, D., *Mark as Composer* (Macon, GA: Mercer University Press, 1987).

Perrin, N., *Rediscovering the Teaching of Jesus* (London: SCM Press, 1967).

—'The Evangelist as Author: Reflections on Method in the Study and Interpretation of the Synoptic Gospels and Acts', *BR* 17 (1972), pp. 5-18.

Pesch, R., *Das Markusevangelium* (2 vols.; Freiburg: Herder, 1976–77).

Petersen, N.R., *Literary Criticism for New Testament Critics* (Philadelphia: Fortress Press, 1978).

—' "Point of View" in Mark's Narrative', *Semeia* 12 (1978), pp. 97-121.

—'The Reader in the Gospel', *Neotestamentica* 18 (1984), pp. 38-51.

Poulet, G., 'Phenomenology of Reading', *NLH* 1 (1969), pp. 53-68.

Powell, M.A., *What is Narrative Criticism? A New Approach to the Bible* (London: SPCK, 1993).

Quesnell, Q., *The Mind of Mark: Interpretation and Method through the Exegesis of Mark 6:52* (Analecta Biblica, 38; Rome: Pontifical Biblical Institute, 1969).

Resseguie, J.L., 'Reader-Response Criticism and the Synoptic Gospels', *JAAR* 52 (1984), pp. 307-24.

Rhoads, D., 'Narrative Criticism and the Gospel of Mark', *JAAR* 50 (1982), pp. 411-34.

Rhoads, D., and D. Michie, *Mark as Story: An Introduction to the Narrative of a Gospel* (Philadelphia: Fortress Press, 1982).

Ribbeck, O., 'Über den Begriff des εἰρών', *Rheinische Museum* 31 (1876), pp. 381-400.

Ricoeur, P., 'Narrative Time', *Critical Inquiry* 7 (1980–81), pp. 169-90.

—*Time and Narrative* (3 vols.; Chicago: University of Chicago Press, 1986–88).

Rimmon-Kenan, S., *Narrative Fiction: Contemporary Poetics* (London: Methuen, 1983).

Robinson, J.M., *The Problem of History in Mark* (SBT, 21; London: SCM Press, 1957).

Rowley, H.H., 'The Herodians in the Gospels', *JTS* 41 (1940), pp. 14-27.

Sanders, E.P., and M. Davies, *Studying the Synoptic Gospels* (Philadelphia: Trinity International Press, 1989).

Schmidt, K.L., *Der Rahmen der Geschichte Jesu* (Berlin: Trowitzsch & Sohn, 1919).

Scholes, R. (ed.), *Approaches to the Novel* (San Francisco: Chandler, 1961).

Scholes, R., and R. Kellogg, *The Nature of Narrative* (London: Oxford University Press, 1966).

Sedgewick, G.G., *Of Irony, Especially in Drama* (Toronto: University of Toronto Press, 1935).

Shepherd, T., 'The Narrative Function of Markan Intercalation', *NTS* 41 (1995), pp. 522-40.

Smith, S.H., 'The Role of Jesus' Opponents in the Markan Drama', *NTS* 35 (1989), pp. 161-82.

—'"Inside" and "Outside" in Mark's Gospel', *ExpTim* 102 (1991), pp. 363-67.

Spengel, L. (ed.), *Rhetores Graeci* (3 vols.; Leipzig: Teuberni, 1853).

Staley, J.L., *The Print's First Kiss: A Rhetorical Investigation of the Implied Reader in the Fourth Gospel* (SBLDS, 82; Atlanta: Scholars Press, 1986).

Standaert, B., *L'évangile selon Marc: Composition et genre littéraire* (Brugge: Sint Andriesabdij, 1978).

Stevick, P. (ed.), *The Theory of the Novel* (New York: Free Press, 1967).

Stock, A., *Call to Discipleship: A Literary Study of Mark's Gospel* (Wilmington, DE: Michael Glazier, 1982).

Strecker, G., 'The Passion and Resurrection Predictions in Mark's Gospel', *Int* 22 (1968), pp. 421-42.

Suleiman, S.R., and I. Crosman (eds.), *The Reader in the Text: Essays on Audience and Interpretation* (Princeton: Princeton University Press, 1980).

Tannehill, R., 'The Disciples in Mark: The Function of a Narrative Role', *JR* 57 (1977), pp. 386-405.

—'The Gospel of Mark as Narrative Christology', *Semeia* 16 (1979), pp. 57-92.

Tarrant, R.J., *Seneca's Thyestes* (Atlanta: Scholars Press, 1985).

Taylor, V., *The Gospel according to St Mark* (London: Macmillan, 2nd edn, 1966).

Thirlwall, C., 'On the Irony of Sophocles', *The Philological Museum*, II (Cambridge: Deightons, 1833).

Thissen, W., *Erzählung der Befreiung: Eine exegetische Untersuchung zu Mk 2:1-3:6* (FzB, 21; Würzburg: Echter Verlag, 1976).

Thompson, J.A.K., *Irony: An Historical Introduction* (London: Allen & Unwin, 1926).

Thorndyke, P.W., 'Cognitive Structures in Comprehension and Memory of Narrative Discourse', *CogPs* 9 (1977), pp. 77-110.

Tödt, H.E., *The Son of Man in the Synoptic Tradition* (trans. D. Barton; London: SCM Press, 1965).

Tompkins, J. (ed.), *Reader-Response Criticism: From Formalism to Post-Structuralism* (Baltimore: The Johns Hopkins University Press, 1980).

Trocmé, E., *The Formation of the Gospel according to Mark* (trans. P. Gaughan; London: SPCK, 1975).

Uspensky, B., *A Poetics of Composition* (trans. V. Zavarin and S. Wittig; Berkeley: University of California Press, 1973).

Van Oyen, G., 'Intercalation and Irony in the Gospel of Mark', in F. van Segbroeck *et al.* (eds.), *The Four Gospels 1992* (Festschrift Frans Neirynck; BETL, 100; Leuven: Leuven University Press, 1992), pp. 949-74.

Via, D.O., Jr, *Kerygma and Comedy in the New Testament* (Philadelphia: Fortress Press, 1975).

—*The Ethics of Mark's Gospel: In the Middle of Time* (Philadelphia: Fortress Press, 1985).

Vorster, W.S., 'The Reader in the Text: Narrative Material', *Semeia* 48 (1989), pp. 21-39.

Weeden, T.J., *Mark: Traditions in Conflict* (Philadelphia: Fortress Press, 1971).

Wikgren, A., 'ΑΡΧΗ ΤΟΥ ΕΥΑΓΓΕΛΙΟΥ', *JBL* 61 (1942), pp. 16-19.

Williams, J.F., *Other Followers of Jesus: Minor Characters as Major Figures in Mark's Gospel* (JSNTSup, 102; Sheffield: JSOT Press, 1994).

Wood, H.G., 'The Priority of Mark', *ExpTim* 65 (1953–54), pp. 17-19.

INDEXES

INDEX OF REFERENCES

OLD TESTAMENT

NEW TESTAMENT

INDEX OF AUTHORS

THE BIBLICAL SEMINAR